Becoming a Reader

Becoming a Reader,

The Experience of Fiction from Childhood to Adulthood

J. A. APPLEYARD, S.J.
Boston College

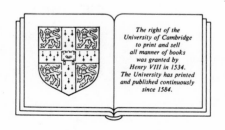

The right of the
University of Cambridge
to print and sell
all manner of books
was granted by
Henry VIII in 1534.
The University has printed
and published continuously
since 1584.

CAMBRIDGE UNIVERSITY PRESS
CAMBRIDGE
NEW YORK   PORT CHESTER   MELBOURNE   SYDNEY

Published by the Press Syndicate of the University of Cambridge
The Pitt Building, Trumpington Street, Cambridge CB2 1RP
40 West 20th Street, New York, NY 10011, USA
10 Stamford Road, Oakleigh, Melbourne 3166, Australia

First published 1990

Printed in the United States of America

Library of Congress Cataloging-in-Publication Data
Appleyard, J. A.
Becoming a reader : the experience of fiction from childhood to
adulthood / by J. A. Appleyard.
   p.   cm.
Includes bibliographical references.
ISBN 0–521–38364–1
1. Reader response criticism. 2. Criticism – Psychological
aspects. 3. Developmental psychology. 4. Reading. 5. Books
and reading. 6. Fiction – Study and teaching. I. Title.
PN98.R38A67 1990
801′95–dc20   90–33314
                                                CIP

British Library Cataloguing in Publication Data
Appleyard, J. A.
Becoming a reader : the experience of fiction from
childhood to adulthood.
1. Fiction. Forms : Novels. Reading. Psychological aspects
I. Title
808.3

ISBN 0–521–38364–1 hardback

For
Stephen, Maureen, Jane, Jennifer, Joe, David, and Billy,
who are among the readers I know best

It is absolutely obtuse to continue to insist on the fictitious and invented nature of the literary, in contrast to the condition of being real and given which the hypothetical real world is supposed to possess. The literary is precisely what is really given us at every moment, what morally conditions our actions, what explains to us scientifically the "truth" of everything around us, everything that creates our identity and a name of our own, the thing that gives form to our amorous transports and our political urgencies.

Fernando Savater, *Childhood Regained*

At root, then, literature rests on a pre-verbal habit of constructing worlds, something visceral, emotional, and personal rather than an act of purely linguistic interpretation.

Norman Holland, *The Brain of Robert Frost*

We humans are the animals who know that we shall die. We know that our lives are shaped like stories, with a beginning, a middle, and an end, and that the end is inevitable. Reading, I am contending, consists, among other things, in recognizing and facing the signs of this pattern, too. We read life as well as books, and the activity of reading is really a matter of working through signs and texts in order to comprehend more fully and powerfully not only whatever may be presented therein but also our own situations, both in their particularity and historicity and in their more durable and inevitable dimensions.

Robert Scholes, *Protocols of Reading*

Contents

Acknowledgments

The roots of this study are probably buried deep in the books that were read to me when I was a child, and my acknowledgments should probably begin there. I remember vividly the books my uncle brought when he came home for visits from Washington and other distant places where in my hazy grasp of things he was one of the central figures fighting the Pacific War. The public library in Malden, Massachusetts, was a storehouse of treasures that were, incredibly, at our disposal – first its local branch, and then as I got older the awesome main building, which much later I discovered truly deserved the distinction it had in our eyes because it is one of Henry Richardson's loveliest achievements. In my family, with the friends I had, not being much interested in sports, with the nuns insisting on rather traditional measures of school success, and with only radio programs and weekly movies to distract us, it was easy to become a reader.

More immediately, the idea for this book grew out of the discussions of the Brownbaggers Lunch Group, colleagues at Boston College with whom I first began talking about how our students changed as they developed. Also influential at the beginning of this project were Arthur Dewey, who introduced me to the work of William Perry, and John D. Golenski, who gave me much sensible advice about psychology and psychologists. Mary McNally arranged for me to meet the very helpful staff of the public library in Watertown, Massachusetts, where I owe special thanks to Charlotte Murray and Jane Eastman. I am also grateful to Mary and Eileen McNally for their serene hospitality at different times while this book was being written. Kathleen Skinner and her colleagues at Somerville High School in Massachusetts allowed me to disrupt their days more than once while I was gathering material that appears in these pages. My own students patiently endured the elaboration of these ideas in several different courses and contributed their own wisdom to the outcome.

At key stages in its evolution, this work was supported by research funds made available to Boston College from the Mellon Foundation and by a semester's leave provided by the Jesuit Community at B.C. Several students and graduate assistants helped with research: Cheryl Beshke, John Borden, Michael Maddelena, Roger Munter, Sara Pike, and Sue Roberts. I am also grateful to friends and B.C. colleagues for assistance of various kinds: Ronald Anderson, S.J., Mel Brannen, A. M. Folkard, the late Weston M. Jenks, Gerry Keough, Fred Lawrence, John J. Neuhauser, William J. Richardson, S.J., and especially the staff of the O'Neill Library.

Several friends read the manuscript and gave me useful criticisms of it from their own experience of teaching literature to high school and college students: Dayton Haskin, Alice Husson R.S.C.J., Eileen Sullivan Shakespear, Paul Shakespear, Andrew Von Hendy, and my brother Richard Appleyard. I am especially indebted to Mary Brabeck and Ellen Winner for encouragement and practical advice when I most needed it.

Finally, this book certainly would not be the kind of book it is if it were not for the insights of Joseph F. X. Flanagan, S.J., with whom I have been carrying on a twenty-year debate about these ideas.

Introduction: Mapping the Terrain

John Kelleher, who taught Irish literature at Harvard for many years, reports the sequence of experiences he had as a reader of James Joyce's novel *A Portrait of the Artist as a Young Man*:

> I remember that when I first encountered Stephen Daedalus I was twenty and I wondered how Joyce could have known so much about me. . . . Perhaps about the third reading it dawned on me that Stephen was, after all, a bit of a prig; and to that extent I no longer identified myself with him. (How could I?) Quite a while later I perceived that Joyce knew that Stephen was a prig; that, indeed, he looked on Stephen with quite an ironic eye. So then I understood. At least I did until I had to observe that the author's glance was not one of unmixed irony. There was compassion in it too, as well as a sort of tender, humorous pride. (1958, 83)

Kelleher presents these responses as successive discoveries about Joyce's novel. We might equally well interpret them as changes in Kelleher himself as a reader. Changes over time – not just in the content of one's response to a story, but in the kind of response itself – require an account of how one develops as a reader. That is the subject of this book.

This topic became interesting to me a few years ago, when I discovered that most of the college students I was teaching used literature for purposes that my classroom canons of interpretation (not to mention the even stricter theories of contemporary critics) had obliged me to disavow. I wanted them to think about how books and poems were structured and how they worked, what values they implied, how they reflected or criticized the culture in which they were produced. The students seemed to want to discover messages about the meaning of their lives, to find interesting characters they could identify with in their fantasies, or to use the ideas of the author to bolster their own beliefs and prejudices. This discrepancy began to puzzle me more and more.

It is a truism of the teacher of literature, of course, that there are many

1

useful critical approaches to a text, but the problem seemed to be that many of my students' responses were uncritical or at best precritical. Nonetheless, they were spontaneous and, even worse, they bore a discomforting resemblance to uses that I myself make of literature in off-duty moments – lying in bed at night with a detective story or interrogating my own experiences alongside those of an Updike character. Further, I had the occasional feeling that if the students' responses were uncritical, my classroom agenda was too critical. Is it possible, I wondered, that there are common ways of reading that a teacher of literature has to disapprove of because his or her theory excludes them as inferior and inadequate? Or could a comprehensive theory be formulated that will allow them some standing as legitimate responses to literature?

I began keeping track of the comments students made in class and in papers that revealed clues about why they responded the way they did to what they read. I asked them to write histories of their reading. I interviewed some sixty or so people who ranged from thirteen to eighty-two years old – high school students from a largely working-class suburb of Boston, middle-class students from the university where I teach, adults from varying backgrounds – about what they read, why they liked or disliked it, and how they changed as readers as they got older. And, of course, I tried to find answers from literary critics, philosophers, and psychologists.

The puzzle became less mysterious as I discovered that it was possible to set the question of how readers respond to literature within the framework of how they develop psychologically and how the culture teaches them to read. I began to see that whatever their individual differences of personality and background, there is a somewhat regular sequence of attitudes readers go through as they mature that affects how they experience stories. The child, for instance, who at age three scarcely distinguishes the world of fantasy play from the world of actual experience, has discovered by age ten or eleven that identifying with the heroes and heroines of adventure tales is a satisfying and instructive alternative to the demands of the pragmatic world. This same reader is likely at seventeen, however, to have become a rather critical seeker of the truth about the world in the stories he or she reads, then at twenty may be further transformed into the English major who can if necessary talk about structure and point of view and tone and the problematic nature of interpretation. In middle age, though, this reader may discover that the keenest pleasure of reading now lies less in understanding how books work than in seeing the ironies of one's own experience mordantly reflected in the predicaments of fictional characters.

Each response (I have by no means exhausted the possibilities) seems to require the development of a set of attitudes toward a story that is qualitatively different from the previous response. If the sequence could be worked out and described, I thought, it would be possible to account for the predominance of certain ways of reading stories at different ages as we develop as readers, and for the puzzling fact that we sometimes seem to regress to earlier ways of reading.

This book, therefore, is about reading and how people become readers. It focuses on the transaction that occurs between reader and text, and particularly on the changes in the reader that shape that transaction. Many factors form the sensibility of a particular reader – individual traits, personal history, educational background, the values of the social group in which one grows up, the cultural moment – but underlying these concrete circumstances there seems to be a set of capacities and expectations that develops according to a fairly orderly pattern and influences the way one reads as one grows from childhood to adulthood. At least that is the hypothesis of this book, that this pattern exists and can be described and to some extent explained and that understanding how it works will help us make sense out of our experience as readers and provide a useful framework for thinking about how we teach literature.

Though I began this study focusing on high school and college students, I discovered that I had to move backward to childhood to make sense of the changes that older readers undergo. The first two chapters, therefore, lay an indispensable groundwork for what follows, because the roots of our responses to what we read lie deep in our first experiences of books and of the imagined world. These chapters deal with younger children and school-age children, with their characteristic responses to what they read, and with studies of cognitive and social development that suggest ways of understanding these responses and ways of thinking about the literary-theoretical issues that these kinds of response raise. The last three chapters carry the analysis forward to adolescents, college-age students, and adults, but with one difference. There is considerable data in psychological and educational studies that is at least of indirect use to someone trying to understand young children's responses to reading; there is much less evidence in print to suggest how older students and adults read fiction. The interviews I have done myself have focused on these older readers to fill in this gap. The resulting information pretends to no quantitative reliability; its value is that it illustrates some hypotheses that have been made about how we respond to stories and suggests others. If these hypotheses are persuasive, it will be because they confirm the reader's own experience as teacher or as reader.

This sketchy outline of intentions needs filling in. Any book joins an ongoing discussion. The discussion I am interested in, of course, is about how we read. But much of that discussion concerns general competence and performance in decoding written or printed text, skills most of us associate with schooling. That is not the area this book deals with, though some of that material has been extremely suggestive, especially the description Jeanne Chall has given of the process children go through in learning to understand written language and Margaret Meek's discussion of the emergence of literacy at each age of the young child's development.[1] Nor, except to draw attention to the general thrust of their work, do I take any special account of those, such as Meek, Marie Clay, Kenneth Goodman, and Frank Smith, who challenge the conventional view that reading is a specialized perceptual skill that has to be taught systematically to children when they are ready to learn it at about age 5 or 6, and argue instead that achieving "literacy" in both reading and writing is a social process that is part of the child's active search for meaning in the environment and that is well advanced long before they go to school.[2] My focus here is rather on how we read fictional stories. Of course, to read a fictional work by oneself presupposes the general ability to read, but the fact is that we are told stories and have very likely been read to long before we can manage to read by ourselves, so that our primary attitudes toward fiction are formed well before we acquire the skill of decoding or constructing meaning out of printed or written language. Nor is it a matter of reading skill only, but of our childhood attitudes toward the whole world of fantasy and imagination. In several ways, then, the realm of fiction is prior to and more extensive than the territory that the ability to read, important as it is, opens up to us.

Of course the domain of fiction includes poetry and drama, but they are beyond the scope of this book. Although the argument I make here about stories probably offers useful analogies for thinking about these other fictional forms (and indeed about how we write), they are not analogies I intend to pursue here. Again, though the elements of poetry and drama may have certain kinds of primacy in our psychic and cultural history (Northrop Frye, for one, has argued this in *The Educated Imagination* and elsewhere), stories (whether in books, on television, or in films or the theater) form our central literary experience, the one most likely to remain a part of our lives from childhood to old age.

READER-ORIENTED THEORY

To focus on fiction and how we read it is to locate this book in the territory only a short while ago marked out as "reader-oriented" critical theory.[3] In a sense this theory and the criticism associated with it have an ancient pedigree in the pragmatic conception of rhetoric as the study of how to produce effects in an audience. This view – summarized in the verbs "instruct," "entertain," or simply "move" – was, as M. H.

Abrams points out, the principal aesthetic attitude of the West from the time of Horace through the eighteenth century, when it began to be supplanted by the Romantics' attention to the psychology of the artist and to the work of literature as an expression of the creative imagination (Abrams 1953, 15–21). But this classical conception of rhetoric had less to do with actual readers than with texts and textual strategies for affecting readers, and it encompassed all kinds of discourse, not just fiction. The more recent interest in audience shifts attention in various ways directly onto the reader of fictive texts: onto the process of interaction with a text, the responses of actual readers, and the historical and social conditions in which reading occurs.

I. A. Richards's *Practical Criticism: A Study in Literary Judgment* (1929) was one of the first signposts in this new territory. His intention was to give the study of literature in the university a new empirical basis drawn explicitly from psychology. His detailed examination of students' written responses to sample poems enabled him to catalogue and describe the mental processes readers used in reading and misreading texts and, of course, to demonstrate that the antidote to careless reading was careful analysis of the minutest details of the text. More than fifty years later his book is still in print, testifying to its exemplary impact. Two somewhat different groups of theorists took up his ideas and adapted them to their purposes.

One group was educationists in teacher-training faculties in Britain and the United States, who were trying to understand how to teach children to read. Much of their work was necessarily concerned with general reading competence and performance, but out of it also came important studies of the process of reading imaginative literature by theorists such as Louise Rosenblatt in the United States (who as early as 1938 offered a description of the transaction between reader and text that anticipated in many ways what Wolfgang Iser and others would propose in the 1970s) and James Britton in England. This vein of interest in reader-oriented theory has continued in numerous studies by researchers in education faculties and by psychologists of child development on learning processes and pedagogical techniques.[4]

The other group for whom Richards's work was important was the poets and literary theorists in U.S. and British universities who in the 1930s and 1940s came to be known collectively as the New Critics. In their determination to disengage the study of literature from philology and history and the biographies of writers on the one hand and from impressionistic interpretation on the other, they found in Richards's work strong support for their program of focusing students' attention on the empirical analysis of the text. It was not an accident that the poetry of their chosen mentors – Eliot, Pound, Yeats, Stevens, and Williams, for example – lent itself to and indeed often required the kind of close scrutiny these critics championed.

Reading, in the sense of careful analysis of features of the text that were thought of as objective – semantic meaning, connotation, implication, syntax, formal features of verse structure, verbal tropes, metaphor, and so forth – flourished under the New Criticism. Actual readers, though, became something of a problem; their responses, as Richards had discovered, tended to interfere with the proper reading of the text. Indeed as New Critical attitudes became the academic mainstream in the 1940s and 1950s, at least in this country if less so in England or elsewhere, the doctrine of the text's autonomy became such an absolute that the notion that a reader's responses to a poem or story might be pertinent to understanding it was labeled a "fallacy" in an influential essay by Wimsatt and Beardsley (1954).

A price was paid for focusing so rigorously on text and excluding everything that functions as context. Such a point of view allowed little to be said about the unconscious processes at work in writing and reading literature, about the social and political conditions under which texts are written and read, about the status of literature as language or as one of a number of cultural sign-systems, about the historicity of meaning and interpretation. In the 1920s and 1930s these issues became increasingly central in the work of influential philosophers, linguists, anthropologists, psychologists, and political and social scientists. A common note in their approaches, Susan Suleiman points out, was to shift the focus of inquiry from the observed – the text, psyche, society, or language in question – to the interaction between observed and observer (Suleiman and Crosman 1980, 4). Thus, when questions were posed from outside literature for which a formalist critical theory was inadequate, and critics began to pay attention to the context in which texts exist, the reader of literature was in the foreground of many of these inquiries. By mapping briefly the reader-oriented theories that have resulted, I hope to locate the ground occupied by this book.

Contemporary reader-oriented theories all have to deal with the same three ingredients of the reading equation – reader, text, and the interaction between the two – but they often emphasize one part of this equation over the others. For example, some theories that invoke the notion of a reader are oriented more to *texts* than to actual readers. Here belong the various discussions of the hypothetical reader who is discovered to be implied or encoded or inscribed in a specific text and who therefore functions as a central clue to how the text is meant to be or can be read.[5] Closely related are structuralist approaches that analyze the codes and semiotic systems that determine how a text functions or that govern its readability for an audience.[6] One might also locate here poststructuralist or deconstructionist notions of the gaps and indeterminacies in a text that subvert both the author's intention and the reader's impulse to see it as a unified whole and that entail that every reading is always radically subjective, historically conditioned, and endlessly revisable.[7]

Most contemporary theories of reading, however, focus more explicitly on the *process of interaction* between reader and text, a view pioneered by Rosenblatt. An influential example is Iser's phenomenological description of how meaning and significance originate in the encounter of reader with text. For Iser, a text is a system of response-inviting structures, organized by reference to a repertory of social systems and literary traditions (that author and reader share) and by means of specific narrative strategies and techniques (that, of course, must be accessible to the reader). But its meaning is only potential until it is actualized by a reader. In dynamic involvement with the text, the reader continually focuses and refocuses expectations and memories, building more consistent and meaningful connections as the interacting structures of the text are traversed from beginning to end. Thus, both the constitutive role of the text and the active participation of a reader in producing the meaning are preserved in this kind of theory of the reading process. Recently Holland has proposed a more elaborate model based on cognitive science and brain physiology that pictures this interaction of reader, text, and world in terms of a hierarchy of feedback loops.[8]

There is scarcely a contemporary philosophical or literary perspective that cannot be enlisted in the discussion of how the reader engages a text and what the result is. In particular, all the theories of interpretation that can be sheltered under the term *hermeneutics* could be located on this part of the map, both the kind that views meaning as a textual reality that can ultimately be elucidated by one or another interpretive strategy and the kind that demonstrates the regression of meaning into cultural codes and systems of discourse and hence its fundamental undecidability.[9]

The reader being talked about in these theories is still a shadowy entity, however, either an idealized good reader or simply a label for the abstract agent who occupies one end of the reader-text equation. To fill out this picture of reader-oriented theories, we have to look at those that make claims directly about *the reader*. Some of these deal with actual readers, either individuals or identifiable reading publics, historical or contemporary. An example of the former is Norman Holland's extension of his earlier psychoanalytic theory of reading to studies of how individual students' readings of sample stories and poems were influenced by their unique personality structures.[10] Of the latter there are sociological critics and literary historians who describe particular reading publics, the conditions that formed them, the value-systems implied by how they read, and their influence on the production of literature.[11] There are also rather generalized and abstract notions of the reader, like the concept that occurs in the works of critics who deal with the problem of subjective-versus-objective interpretation by postulating the regulative influence of *interpretive communities*, groups of readers constituted by particular experiences and values (for example, a specific cultural community, a classroom, or the literary profession), who in a sense validate and legitimize particular interpretations of texts by a process of negotiation and synthesis among their members.[12]

All these theories of reading fill in a blank space in the map of literary relationships previously devoted almost wholly to author and text. Each of them says something useful about the reader's role, and even the ones whose central insights are stated in absolute terms and carried to extreme ideological positions seem to have their core of truth. It is salutary, for example, to be reminded (by structuralists and semioticians) that language and literary structures are sign-systems embodying cultural values that transcend particular uses of those sign-systems, or (by rhetorical critics) that texts are always shaped by assumptions about the audiences to whom they are addressed, or (by sociological and hermeneutical theorists) that responding to textual structures is always a historically situated act, and (by the phenomenologists) a complex one psychologically, or (by deconstructionists) that our critical assumptions may dispose us to find more unity in texts than they have, or (by psychoanalytic critics) that the sources of our most deeply felt responses to what we read may be hidden most of all from ourselves.

But even a shrewd eclecticism that wants to fill out literary theory with the insights of linguistics, psychology, social science, and philosophical hermeneutics will find something incomplete in this picture of the reader. Because, apart from the psychoanalytically oriented critics who talk about actual people and those critics who describe groups of readers historically and sociologically, the reader in these theories is still no more than a generic construct, a hypothetical experiencer of the text, or a name for the place where the reading event occurs. This sketchy notion of a reader does not help us understand the question we started with, namely, Why do we respond differently to what we read as we mature and become more experienced and skilled as readers? To do so we need to fill in this picture of the reader by finding more differentiated ways of picturing how readers do in fact read. We need, I suggest, to think not of one act of reading, but of several distinct kinds of response that change significantly from our first childhood experiences of stories to those of ripe old age. We need a developmental view of reading.

Given the wide interest in theories of development over the past fifty years or so, particularly theories of the development of the cognitive and affective capacities that might be thought to underlie the experience of literature, it is surprising that literary critics have not tried to describe reading from this point of view. Child psychologists and educational researchers do so to some extent, but even in these areas the only attempt to offer a coherent description of a reader's development across a span of time is Arthur N. Applebee's ground-breaking work *The Child's Concept of Story*, which studies the pattern of children's responses from ages 2 to 17 in terms of Jean Piaget's stages.[13] Reading specialists have taken Piagetian approaches to their subject (for example, Jeanne Chall and Margaret Meek) and specialists in children's literature have occasionally organized analyses of the books children read or of particular genres among these books from this point of view,[14] but no one has addressed the psychological development that readers undergo across the whole life span from a literary point of view. This neglect is not easy to understand. It can hardly be due merely to indifference or resistance to psychology; more likely it is a consequence of the hegemony of text-oriented criticism in past decades and therefore the general lack of any attention to the role of the reader until quite recently.

READING AND PSYCHOLOGICAL DEVELOPMENT

Granted then that it would be useful to have an account of how readers change as they mature, how can we construct such an account? Which theories of development offer us help? I shall summarize here the argument that weaves its way through the main chapters of this book.

I assume as a starting point an interactional or transactional view of reading such as might be assembled from the works of Iser, Rosenblatt, and Holland. Around some imaginary seminar table these theorists could probably carry on a long discussion about the precise differences among them, but I find a useful convergence in the main lines of their ideas. From this point of view the act of reading is primarily an encounter between a particular reader and a particular text in a particular time and place, an encounter that brings into existence the story, poem, or work in question. The story is not the same as the text on the page, nor is it simply the reader's uniquely personal response to the text. Rather the story is an event that has roots both in the text and in the personality and history that the reader brings to the reading. The text is a system of response-inviting structures that the author has organized by reference to a repertoire of social and literary codes shared by author and reader. But it does not simply cause or limit the reader's response, nor does the reader passively digest the text. Rather, reader and text interact in a feedback loop. The reader brings expectations derived from a literary and life experience to bear on the text, and the text feeds back these expectations or it does not. The reader filters this feedback through characteristic defenses, imbues them with fantasies, and transforms the event into an experience of moral, intellectual, social, and aesthetic coherence (Iser 1978; Rosenblatt 1978; Holland 1985, 1988).

If we try to understand how this model works in young children's experience of stories, we discover that some of the characteristic features of their responses – the magical, imagistic, concrete, and intermittent way they participate in a tale – can be fairly well explained by a theory of cognitive development such as Jean Piaget's.[15] In his view, to know is to construct meaning out of our interaction with the world of experience, using the cognitive structures at our disposal. From infancy onward, these structures develop and change as our experience grows and our physiological capacities unfold. We acquire new cognitive schemas, combine simpler ones into larger and more adequate ones for dealing with our experience, and internalize this knowledge in increasingly abstract forms.

Piaget's distinctive contribution to the epistemology of development was to divide this progress into stages – periods of equilibrium in the learning process when thinking is characterized by stable structures that are qualitatively different from those of the stages that precede and follow it – and to argue that these stages unfold according to an innate groundplan, that they are therefore universal in human beings, and that they are irreversible, because each one fundamentally transforms the accomplishment of the previous one.

It is tempting to try to explain the pattern of development that readers undergo by recourse to this concept of structurally distinct cognitive developmental stages that unfold according to an innate blueprint. Piaget's schema has, after all, been an influential model for thinking about human growth and learning in a variety of areas (it underlies the work of Lawrence Kohlberg on the stages of moral reasoning, for example, and of James Fowler on faith development). It is not without its problems as a model for reading development, however. The very concept of distinct cognitive stages is under revision among developmental psychologists generally,[16] but even if this were not the case it provides too narrow a framework for thinking about reading. Though cognitive development may be a necessary mechanism for significant change in the way we read as we mature, there are other kinds of development; in addition, cultural influences, as well as the social functions of reading and, especially, the kind of education we get, would also seem to be crucial ingredients of any adequate account of how we respond to stories.

Another limitation of Piaget's theory as a basis for an account of reading is that in his view the kind of thinking that develops is increasingly logical and scientific. This emphasis obliges him to regard the fantasy life of children as a muddle out of which more adequate and orderly ways of thinking will emerge, a severe handicap for any theory that wants to give a positive account of the imaginative power that stories have over us as children. For the affective dimensions of reading we have to look elsewhere.

Psychoanalytic theory would seem to provide a useful complement, because it focuses so much on feeling and on the determinative influence of childhood experience on later development. Sigmund Freud's account of how fantasy gives expression to unconscious desires and fears does help us to understand something of the power of certain kinds of thematic imagery in childhood reading. Bruno Bettelheim, in particular, exploits this theory in an elaborate analysis of the appeal of fairy tales for young children. But Freud's theory has its own limitations for our purposes: its dependence on a particular view of infantile sexuality and the conflict-filled picture of childhood it derives from its clinical orientation. Carl Jung's more controversial but positive view of the role of the unconscious in affective development and his notion of an unconscious that is more than personal – a kind of well of the inherited experience of the race that the images of art embody – suggest something further about why reading matters so much to us on the level of feeling as well as knowing.

But some aspects of reading require a still more inclusive version of development that takes into account the interpersonal and social construction of our values and attitudes. Erik Erikson's map of the life cycle blends Piaget's genetic epistemology with the affective themes Freud describes, but it places them in a broader framework of stages defined by the issues that emerging physiological and psychic capacities and changing social relationships set as the agenda specific to each period of development. Thus, one's *identity*, the distinctive way an individual perceives the self and relates to the world, is reorganized as one confronts and weathers the critical issues proper to each stage of growth and learns through social interaction the distinctive roles that the culture makes available to the developing individual. For Erikson, unlike Piaget, development does not move inevitably in a straight line and by a series of irreversible jumps. The issues of each stage are resolved more or less successfully, the balance among them becomes the foundation on which the next stage builds, but the unresolved issues may have to be renegotiated later. The process may fail to go forward or growth may be differential – advanced in some areas of one's life, slowed down in others. The identity achieved at each stage, then, is a provisional set of abilities and vulnerabilities, a distinctive way of perceiving the self and of relating to the world.

The inclusiveness and flexibility of Erikson's view of development suits a discussion of reading, because maturity in reading does not occur independently of other kinds of development. It involves cognitive structures, affective issues, interpersonal relationships, and particular social roles that the dominant culture proffers to the developing reader. Moreover reading is a skill that not everyone masters and a habit (reading fiction at least) that not everyone continues as a teenager or an adult, even when they have read much as children. Readers can fail to develop, too.

So far, we have been concentrating on the psychodynamics of the individual who is the subject of the growth process, though Erikson's viewpoint does enlarge the evidence for what contributes to that growth so as to include social relationships and cultural roles. But especially in an area like reading, which involves the assimilation of and accommodation to not only the content of a whole cultural tradition but also its specific ways of organizing and interpreting experience, what is communal in the process is at least as significant as what is individual. To comprehend fully the pattern of changes in the reader's sensibility, therefore, we need to refocus our attention explicitly on the social context in which the reader's experience develops. The complete argument about what constitutes the reader's development requires us to consider the extent to which the reader's experience is in part socially constructed, an artifact both of the history of literary invention and of the particular cultural experience that prepares the reader to read.

The latter claim, that particular kinds of cultural experiences have a significant influence in forming the reader's sensibility, is the subject of much current investigation. Some of the studies focus on the determinative effects of factors such as social class, economic level, race, and ethnocentric bias on the responses of particular groups of readers.[17] Of these, gender has been the most frequently cited cultural factor in claiming a distinctive development for different groups of readers. Studies that suggest that the patterns of male and female psychological development are substantially different[18] have led feminist literary critics to propose that there are important differences in how men and women read stories.[19] Some argue that gender difference leads to fundamentally different ways of reading fiction, others that it is at least a significant determinant of empirically observable differences arising out of the socialized learning of sex roles in the family, from peers, at school, and of course through the representation of gender differences in books and other media. All these studies suggest that we are likely to learn much more than we now know about how social influences affect the way readers experience stories, but as yet they have scarcely filled in the outlines of an argument and they are far from agreement among themselves.

Another group of culturally oriented studies has investigated the broader notion of ideological factors operative in the reading experience. Ideology may be conceived as part of the content of a story, representing therefore directly or indirectly the values of the author or of the author's culture;[20] or it may be more deeply embedded in the formal structures of setting, character, and plot;[21] or it may reside in the learned expectations readers bring to the task of interpreting narrative conventions.[22] These approaches make it clear that a crucial task at some point in the reader's development will be to learn to understand and critique the ideological implications of the way one reads.

Ideology spills over into the realm of all the value-laden attitudes through which we organize our experience. Where do these come from? Clearly any answer will be inadequate that does not include the interaction of our developing egos with the cultural institutions, language codes, social rituals, customs, and especially the whole universe of fantasy in which we are educated from the first songs and games we learn in our parents' arms to the most recent TV shows and movies we have seen. But this invented universe is not just a storehouse of accumulated data and signs available for use by our developing consciousness, it is more like a matrix that provides the structures in which our consciousness matures. Northrop Frye has given us one map of the literary portion of this world, in a detailed taxonomy of motifs, archetypes, symbols, myths, and genres.[23] This fictional world has been accumulating since the origins of the human race, our history has sifted and laminated it in countless ways, and we are initiated into it as infants and our consciousness of ourselves grows to maturity in and through it. In its content this fictional universe resembles Jung's archetypal collective unconscious, but its transmission through social learning mechanisms seems more plausible than Jung's innate psychic structures.

In its strong forms, this conception of culture as a social artifact would appear to contradict the psychodynamic account of the reader's education we have been exploring. A genetic view of development, after all, conceives of growth as a process that occurs from within the individual, whose skills and capacities flower in adjustments that operate in ever more finely tuned ways on the data of the outer world. A social-construction perspective, on the other hand, locates the significant factors in the social world's ideologies and values, and imagines that the culture imprints itself from the outside on the blank slate of individual consciousness. How can we keep both claims in fruitful tension?

Bernard Lonergan points out that we get both kinds of education simultaneously and dialectically; we grow up as individuals whose capacities unfold and develop, but we are simultaneously initiated into the world's meaning mediated to us by our parents, friends, the communities and social institutions we live in, and the culture that embodies our values.

These are not two different movements. There is a two-way traffic between them, and a forward movement toward an equilibrium. This kind of dialectical view of development enables us to hold together all the different kinds of data that are potentially relevant to a description of how a reader's sensibility changes across the life span: the maturing central nervous system, the evolving psychodynamics of our inner lives, the changing social roles available to us as we mature, the values we absorb from our families and communities, the kinds of books we read, the kinds of readers our educational institutions encourage us to be, the fictional universe that is the cultural matrix in which our development occurs, and the judgments and moral commitments by which we shape our lives as we mature. Our development as readers is no less complex or subtle a matter than our development as human beings, and simple theories will not do it justice.

FIVE ROLES READERS TAKE

This long argument can be summed up in terms of five roles that a reader seems to learn in a fairly predictable sequence. These roles are no more than shorthand labels for a cluster of distinctive responses, a set of attitudes and intentions readers bring to reading and of uses they make of it, which appear to shift as readers mature. These roles constitute the framework of this book and its division by chapters:

1. *The Reader as Player.* In the preschool years the child, not yet a reader but a listener to stories, becomes a confident player in a fantasy world that images realities, fears, and desires in forms that the child slowly learns to sort out and control.

2. *The Reader as Hero and Heroine.* The school-age child is the central figure of a romance that is constantly being rewritten as the child's picture of the world and of how people behave in it is filled in and clarified. Stories here seem to be an alternate, more organized, and less ambiguous world than the world of pragmatic experience, one the reader easily escapes into and becomes involved with.

3. *The Reader as Thinker.* The adolescent reader looks to stories to discover insights into the meaning of life, values and beliefs worthy of commitment, ideal images, and authentic role models for imitation. The *truth* of these ideas and ways of living is a severe criterion for judging them.

4. *The Reader as Interpreter.* The reader who studies literature systematically, typically the college English major or graduate student or teacher, approaches it as an organized body of knowledge with its own principles of inquiry and rules of evidence, learns

to talk analytically about it, acquires a sense of its history and perhaps even a critical theory of how it works.

5. *The Pragmatic Reader.* The adult reader may read in several ways, which mimic, though with appropriate differences, the characteristic responses of each of the previous roles: to escape, to judge the truth of experience, to gratify a sense of beauty, to challenge oneself with new experiences, to comfort oneself with images of wisdom. What seems to be common to these responses is that adult readers now much more consciously and pragmatically choose the uses they make of reading.

Having proposed these five roles and given them names, we have to ask a crucial question. What reality do these labels and their sequence actually describe? We might consider first what they do not account for. They do not describe the unique experience of an individual reader with a particular book. Nor can they capture the gradual, incremental, and multifaceted process by which development occurs in particular readers as they traverse a lifetime of stories and poems and dramas. Nor can they take account of personal history, intelligence, personality traits, and unique likes and dislikes, which are all irrelevant to this schema, yet may explain what is most distinctive about how a particular person reads. Neither can a schematic description of the main lines of development take more than partial account of factors such as gender, race, class, and economic level by which the experience of large groups of readers is socially mediated.

These are further reasons for insisting that the schema of reading development proposed here does not have the kind of universality that Piaget and others claim for their stage descriptions. It depends too much on factors specific to a particular literary culture and, especially in our society, on the length and kind of schooling readers receive. In fact, it can be argued that these roles describe an education in the mainstream culture's values as much as they do an evolution of innate human capacities. In some respects, therefore, they describe what is the case, not what needs to be the case.

However, this does not mean that we have to accept the more fundamental objection to a developmental perspective popular among some Marxists and deconstructionists, who argue that the very notion of an individual person as an autonomous subject of development prescinds misleadingly from the culturally mediated, indeed culturally constructed, discourse that prescribes and limits our ability to understand, even to have our experience. Against this objection I would argue that although the culture and its systems of meaning are certainly prior to the reader in a historical and epistemological sense, nonetheless the construction of any particular meaning (and hence the incremental restructuring of the culture) requires an interaction between an individual reader and the culture. The hypothesis that this interaction has a history across the life of the typical reader and that this history can be described in developmental terms takes nothing away from the part played by the culture in the transaction. Indeed, it can be argued that describing the development of reading responses is an indispensable step in any useful historicist contextualizing of the reader's transaction with a text.

What, then, are these descriptions of readers' characteristic roles good for, positively? I would say, first, that they are useful tools for thinking about much of the observable behavior of readers in the culture we inhabit. Consider them a set of snapshots of related types of responses to stories, which together constitute a heuristic framework for sorting out many of the cognitive and affective issues involved in trying to describe how actual readers read, here and now, in our culture's evolution. Like any theoretical framework, they are most useful when we are beginning to make sense out of a complex and undifferentiated mass of data. They help us make a first pass at the material, and the schema they provide can be refined and nuanced as we learn more about the issues. If the snapshots are accurate, they will also be useful pedagogically, I think, as a chart of the changes students are likely to go through and therefore as a conceptual guide for helping us think about how we teach them.

Furthermore, this schema also implies some conclusions about how readers *ought* to develop. Jerome Bruner (1986b) points out that developmental theory is a "policy science," that is, its object is not simply to describe behavior, but to prescribe alternative optimal ways of achieving certain outcomes. Does this mean simply that the higher roles are better ways of reading? The short answer to this question is yes. In principle, each role exercises capacities that transcend qualitatively the capacities possible in earlier roles.

Thus, the young child's intermittent grasp of the boundary between fantasy and actuality – exciting, but confusing and often scary – yields to the older child's sense of control and identity as the central character of a timeless story about the conflict of good and evil. This role is transcended by the adolescent's ability to see that romance is only one version of life's story and by the discovery that stories can be tested for the wisdom they yield about the world. This way of reading is supplanted by the student's realization that stories are also texts, that they are not just objects that invite us to immerse ourselves pleasurably in them or to think about their content, but also objects that require us to think about the conditions of their production, their effect on us, the issues they raise in the world of contemporary intellectual discourse, and the kinds of meaning they can plausibly claim to offer. Finally, this reading stance is itself transcended by the discovery that all these ways of reading are choices we make and that we shift among them for our own purposes as we discover our mature selves. As developmentalists often say, each role can therefore be understood as standing to the previous role as form to content, each role becomes the material that the higher role subsumes and handles more adequately, and each higher role corrects and improves on the lower one.

But in some ways higher is not inevitably better. What if, instead of subsuming the lower role, the higher role substitutes for it, but inadequately? Then the young child's magical absorption in the world of play may be replaced by the older child's rigid dependence on identifying with a particular kind of hero or heroine; the enlarging possibilities of romantic ideals may be suppressed by the adolescent's insistence on applying standards of truth that are too rigorous to allow imagination any scope; the adolescent's delight in thinking about the vision of life that stories offer may die at the hands of the student who is taught too well to dissect sceptically whatever he or she reads; the confidence of knowing how stories work may yield to the jaundiced adult's conviction that nothing holds any significant meaning anyway. Because there are higher roles does not mean that readers should rush or be rushed into them. Reading works best at every level when it subsumes and integrates the accomplishments that each of the lower levels made possible.

Here the difference between developmental theories like Piaget's and Erikson's is most marked. For Piaget (whose theory concerns only a particular kind of cognitive development), development means improvement that in principle is irreversible; for Erikson (perhaps because he takes a wider view of the factors in development), growth may be halting and uneven, and at later stages the work of earlier ones may need to be repaired. Reading seems to fit better into a view like Erikson's; the higher roles *may* be better ways of reading, if they successfully integrate what is positive in the lower ones, which in principle they should do. In practice, however, the reader's experience will probably always be an uneven process of acquiring, forgetting, remembering, including, and enlarging. Its forward movement may only be obvious in retrospect or at privileged moments of self-awareness. Its untidiness, though, makes some sort of conceptual schema of the large steps in the process all the more helpful.

This schema of readers' roles has other benefits. It sometimes throws a novel light on issues disputed by literary critics. An example is the current argument about the authority of the text to prescribe a single valid interpretation of itself. This is a central question around which traditional rhetorical critics, structuralists, hermeneuticists, deconstructionists, psychoanalytic critics, Marxists, and theorizers of just about any stamp have all staked out doctrinal positions. Yet if we parse it through the different roles a reader is likely to play, we find that the story of its importance as an issue has a plot that resembles the rising-and-falling action of an Aristotelian tragedy.

Thus, for young children the authority of any interpretation of the text is simply a nonissue; indeed, at this age texts are not interpreted, they are only enjoyed or rejected. Interpretation first becomes a matter of concern to older juveniles and adolescents, who are concerned with figuring out the truth about the world and their own lives and therefore with discovering what the writers of books have said about these subjects. But even here the possibility of interpretation is not in doubt; readers are convinced that a text has a meaning, put there by its author, that the reader is meant to discover. Older students of literature start from this assumption and learn more and more skillful ways of dissecting texts and uncovering their meanings. But then a curious thing happens. As they become more sophisticated analysts of literature, they discover that meaning is unavoidably situated in historical contexts and within literary structures and cultural codes. They also discover the conflict of even authoritative interpretations and the conflict of theoretical positions about interpretation advanced by persuasive critics and by their own instructors. This is an inevitable step in cognitive maturity; it is also mightily abetted by the way we teach literature and literary theory today. As Bruner (1986a, 155) wryly notes: "It requires the most expensive education to shake a reader's faith in the incarnateness of meaning in a novel or poem."

But that is what happens, and if this student in turn becomes a professor or literary critic, then it is hardly possible that he or she can talk or write professionally for long without having to take a theoretical position about what it means to interpret a text. Oddly enough, though, if the reader has not gone on to such an expensive education, or has gone through it and out the other side and is now a retired theorist who reads for private satisfaction, it seems that the issue of validity in interpretation and the authority of the writer's intention and the consistency of ideological frameworks and so forth recede in importance. These matters are not irrelevant, but they tend to get subordinated to the reader's purposive and highly personal use of fiction. The older reader turns inward for criteria of value, and their theoretical defense is one battle that is safely enfolded into the history of one's younger self.

An interesting consequence of this point of view is that fashioning literary theories now appears to be only one among several possible responses to reading. However useful it may be for students and teachers and critics of literature, theorizing about texts is one moment in the evolution of reader responses, not more privileged than other ways of reading, especially if it cannot take them into account except by dismissing their authentic satisfactions.

In making these claims about the life cycle of the issue of interpretation, I of course anticipate the detailed discussion to come. I offer them here as samples of the kind of help I think a developmental view of reading can give us. A developmental view suggests that the debate about meaning is not only a debate about the text or about semiotic systems and authorial strategies encoded in the text, but should also be a debate about the evolution of the ways readers make sense of texts. It provides another angle from which to assess the implications of competing theories of reading. It helps us locate and understand the *plot* of our own varied responses as readers. It confronts us finally with the choice of what to do with the power reading gives us.

Much contemporary theory denies the point of this choice altogether, reducing the text to a mere nexus where systems of signs and codes intersect and leaving the reader a prisoner of language. True, it brings to the reader's aid the critic, who can interpret dexterously how this imprisonment works, but is the critic in this guise the reader's comforter or the reader's torturer? Ricoeur takes a more positive view of the reader's role in the transaction that takes place between author, text, and audience. Rather than seeing the inventive power of the mind as constricted by its ready-made linguistic and semiotic materials, he argues that the imagination produces new visions of possibility. Fictional narrative, he thinks, is the most dramatic example of the imagination's power to configure and refigure human experience (Kearney 1989, 17). But narrative is incomplete until it is read. If the author is responsible for configuring the narrative, "it is the act of reading that accompanies the narrative's configuration and actualizes its capacity to be followed" (Ricoeur 1984, 1:76). The reader not only actualizes the story but completes it, by playing with the narrative constraints and by filling in the "holes, lacunae, [and] zones of indetermination" which are part of the author's design (1:77). For Ricoeur this is not merely an act of interpretation, but a step toward social action, because narrative offers us "the freedom to conceive of the world in new ways and to undertake forms of action which might lead to its transformation" (Kearney 1989, 6). A developmental view of reading suits this view, I think, because it permits us to picture the trajectory of our reading experience as a movement from unreflecting engagement to deliberate choice about the kind of readers we will be and the uses to which we will put our reading.

In the end, the precise division of roles proposed here, their names and characteristic features, are less important than the general thesis that the way we organize our experience as readers and the meanings we give to it change significantly as we grow older and that the pattern of these changes can be described. If the apparatus of roles and distinctive responses seems too cumbersome, readers are free to regard it sceptically, but perhaps they will still find here stories about reading that correspond to their own experience and hypotheses that help clarify some of the things we still do not know about the reader's role in the literary transaction.

1

Early Childhood:
The Reader as Player

Most children, we commonly suppose, learn to read when they begin formal schooling around the age of 6. In many respects, though, elements of the experience of reading are already familiar to them long before schooling begins. They are already masters of oral language and have used it to play with, to make up fantasy monologues in their cribs, and to retell their experiences to adults. They also know that written and printed language conveys meaning, and they are likely to know the meanings of many particular signs, from the words on cereal boxes to how their own names are spelled. They watch cartoon stories on television. In families where children are read to and books are common gifts, they will have their favorites and they will probably have engaged in pretend reading, matching the words on the pages of familiar books to the characters and events in the stories. Children who are used to books have familiar expectations as to what constitutes a story: special formulas like "Once upon a time:..," narrative sequence, a central character, and a plot, even if it is only the "basic monster story" of threat-and-threat-averted. Using a book at this age is typically also a rich visual and even tactile experience of vivid images and of an object that can be held, pointed to, turned, opened, and closed.[1]

The most important circumstance of all is that children at this age do not read; they are read to. Consider what we tend to think of as the archetypal bedtime story-listening situation. The child is nestled in the arms of an adult, who reads in the special voice of storytelling and in the rhythms that make even the least formal written prose different from spoken language. Pages are turned over, pictures and words pointed to, and the details of the story are dramatized by inflection and gesture. Typically the reading is accompanied by a running exchange of questions and answers, comments about the story, and references to other experiences of the child and the reader and to people they know. The child falls asleep in the middle of the story or lies awake alone to weave private fantasies and story details into further spells.[2]

Not every experience of story listening involves a lively interaction between text and reader like this, and not all children are read to.[3] Nonetheless, mainstream U.S. culture clearly emphasizes reading as an important part of childhood learning and as a route to school success. And until they learn to read for themselves, whatever experience children have of books will be in the company of adults or older brothers and sisters who mediate the experience for them. Thus, long before children can read a page of print by themselves, reading is apt to be an intensely participatory initiation into a world beyond their own immediate experience, with the most trusted persons in their lives as guides and interpreters.[4]

What is the point from which young children, say age 2, start this reading journey? A general picture would go something like this. They live in a magical, numinous world, where the boundaries between the self, the factual, and the imaginary are permeable and fluid. Everything is charged with intense affective significance. Yet the coherence of this world is fragile and episodic, because young children's thinking is so concrete and imagistic and tied to momentary and shifting apprehensions. It is both a stimulating and threatening experience to live in such a world. A basic issue for children at this age is whether or not they will learn to trust this world in its fullness. As they develop intellectually and emotionally there are different roles that can be learned. One is to play, and especially to be the kind of player who can separate fact from fantasy and still trust the world of fantasy. To achieve this, young children need support from those whom they trust as models.

There is considerable evidence for some of these generalizations, less for others, and some of them are vigorously disputed. Almost all the evidence is indirect. Although we know more about the psychology of infancy and early childhood than of any other period of development, only recently has much attention been paid to children's understanding of stories. Some of the psychological evidence comes from studies where researchers have talked to children about stories, though children at this age have little capacity to reflect on their experience, so the results are necessarily inferential. Much of the evidence has come from investigations about one or another aspect of cognitive development, such as memory, capacity for understanding metaphor, grasp of structural relationships, perspective taking, and so forth. Some of these data are suggestive, but they are specialized skills and extrapolating from test performances of them to natural story listening can be tricky. A large source of evidence is composed of collections of stories elicited from children themselves by researchers. These look like prime data until we reflect that children rarely tell stories spontaneously to adults or to each other, so what these collections illustrate may again be performance on a task devised by adults, rather than what children left to themselves would do. They do, of course, tell us something about what children think a story should be. Some of the most interesting data come from descriptions of particular children, their books, and how they responded to them as they grew older.[5] Finally, there is the evidence offered by clinicians and therapists about the role of fantasy in children's emotional development. The rest of this chapter looks at the varied evidence for these general statements about the imaginative lives of young children and what this evidence entails for understanding how they respond to stories.

THE YOUNG CHILD'S WORLD

Consider some material from three instructive accounts of young children's thinking.

Carol

Carol White, an Australian child growing up in the early 1950s, was two when her mother began to keep a diary of her reactions as they read books together. At one point, just after her second birthday, Carol discovered the word "umbrella." She could pronounce it, and loved to repeat it over and over; it was one of three polysyllabic words she knew (White 1956, 5). Her mother read her *Pitter Patter,* a book about the rain falling and making everything wet, except for a little boy who walks through it with a raincoat and hat and keeps dry. It was intensely exciting to her, and they reread it several times. Two months later it rained one day, after a three-week drought. Carol looked out the window and began to talk about the book. She asked her mother to get out the umbrella and put it up "like the little boy." As they talked her mother realized that Carol was interweaving three experiences: the rain, reading the book, and an incident a month before when they had been caught in a heavy shower, Carol had been badly frightened by raindrops on her bare head, and her mother had calmed her by referring to *Pitter Patter* (White 1956, 13).

Rachel

Rachel Scollon's parents were ethnographers interested in problems of interethnic communication. In 1976, when Rachel was a child, the family lived for a year in an Athabaskan Indian village in northwestern

Canada. Rachel's parents studied carefully the way she dealt with stories and books, because it contrasted so strongly with Indian children's attitudes toward literacy. Even at age 2, she exhibited in her play and talk a marked "orientation to literacy" of a kind that her educated, middle-class parents took for granted, but that even older Athabaskan children did not share. Indian children associated reading with school and church and transactions with the English-speaking culture; for Rachel story listening and pretend reading were intimate play activities she shared with her parents and baby brother at home and a way of imitating approved adult behavior (Scollon and Scollon 1981, 57–80).

At age 2 Rachel already had her own books and a set of letter blocks. She knew the ABC song and often asked to be read to. Before she was three she "wrote" stories, by scribbling letters and squiggles on paper and then narrating them into her parents' tape recorder. Here is my summary of one of her stories (omitting repetitions, fragments, and the apparatus of transcription that the Scollons use to record her exact language):

> Once upon a time there was a girl named Rachel and a boy named Tommy. They went for a walk. And there was Daddy; he went for a walk too. They wrote a letter to Baby Tommy's Grandma. Baby Tommy had a fish and he had a Mom. His Mom told him to read his story, and his Mom tell him No! You go to sleep. And then Baby Tommy went to sleep. He cried, and his Mom and Dad came and they sayed, What's the matter? And he said. . . . My girlfriend gave me a apple. And that's all. (Scollon and Scollon 1981, 72–6)

In spite of the simplicity of this story we can easily see what being "oriented to literacy" means. Rachel uses conventional devices that mark off fictional stories ("Once upon a time," "And that's all"), tells the story in the past tense, and keeps all the events within the third-person narrative framework. Her parents note that she also uses a special voice and rhythm that reproduces the intonation of someone reading aloud.

Even at this age, Rachel clearly knows a lot about what is expected of a storyteller. However, the story she tells lacks coherence; it shifts abruptly from action to action. Events are linked, if at all, only through the characters involved in them. The focus shifts from character to character as the story goes on. There is no conclusion except the conventional formula. Rachel's parents point out that the incidents are a mixture of immediate experiences (a recent walk in the woods with her father) and literary inventions (the letter to Grandma). And the story is by no means as neatly defined and shaped as I have suggested in summarizing it here. In fact it is preceded and followed and interspersed with a great many exchanges with her parents about the process of telling and recording the story and with continuous editorial alterations as she goes along. We might say that the narrative is embedded in a highly self-conscious performance, and that the two are kept distinct only with effort.

Anna

In the United States during the late 1970s Anna Crago's parents set out to keep a more systematic record of her reading than Carol White's mother did, and to analyze her responses in some psychological detail during the years 1.6 to 3.0. One particularly interesting part of the book describes how Anna wove together over a period of eighteen months images from the story *Snow White* and experiences from her own life (Crago and Crago 1983, 94–8). At 3.0 she is told the story at bedtime, but expresses no special interest in it. Two days later, however, reading a story about a farmer, she focuses on some apples lying on the ground in an illustration and asks, "Are they all right?" When her parents tell her the wind has blown them there, she says, "They are red." This begins a complex web of associations, which turn up over the next year and a half, about poison, apples, the color red, stepmothers, sleeping, and dying. When a version of *Snow White* is brought from the library (at 3.7), Anna decides after two readings that she wants it returned, because, "I don't like the stepmother." However, she later looks at it on her own, but puts her hand over the picture of the stepmother because, "I don't want to see that one." This is a time (3.6 to 4.6) when she avoids other books she finds too emotionally involving.

But the themes persist. After seeing a stage version of the story (at 3.9) Anna begins playing Snow White games, assigning roles to her parents, and once during a visit from her grandparents (at 4.5) she puts on her own "play" with the adults in the different roles. In her parents' view, the crucial figure in the tale for Anna is the wicked stepmother, and it is interesting that in these pretend games Anna never takes this role herself, usually playing Snow White and assigning the queen's role to her own mother! It appears to her parents that in these enactments of the story Anna is trying to render acceptable the yoking of the familiar and the harmful (an apple that is poisonous, a stepmother who is jealously murderous). Finally, at 4.6 Anna announces, "The wicked queen is dead [because] I gave her a poisoned apple." Two minutes later she says that her doll is ill and asleep because, "The queen gave her a poisoned apple." This is the last reference Anna makes to the story; apparently she has come to terms for now with the threat of the idea of a stepmother who is wicked and with the special function of poisonous apples. Her parents point out her typical reading behavior at this age (4.6) is to recreate some aspect of the story in her own life, rather than merely to refer to it or query it, as she would have done earlier. In this way reading enables her both to explore cognitive puzzles and to discharge the tension caused by emotionally laden objects (Crago and Crago 1983, 97–8).

The way Carol, Rachel, and Anna think seems to be typical of very young children. They appear to inhabit a world of highly personal concrete images that are loosely woven together in fragile relationship and are intensely involving. It is a timeless world where appearances and identities readily change and where contradictions lie undisturbed side by side, an animistic world where a little boy in a story or a princess sleeping because of a poisoned apple are as real as the rain or toy blocks or a playmate. Mental life here seems to be a tentative process of evolving meaning for these realities out of experience, of sorting out cognitive and emotional responses, and of stabilizing them into something resembling the accepted adult picture of the world.

What value should we put on this kind of thinking? Is it only childish muddle and confusion that these children will eventually grow out of, or is it the foundation on which a rich and promising imaginative life will build? The answer to this question makes a great deal of difference to what we think about young children's responses to stories.

THE COGNITIVE ACCOUNT OF FANTASY

Some of the characteristic responses of young children to stories can be explained by accounts that focus on cognitive development. We shall begin here, though eventually we shall have to go further than these explanations take us. Consider these further reports about Carol White and Anna Crago and their reading.

Carol sometimes has difficulty picturing story events from any point of view but her own, and when evidence conflicts unpleasantly she simply denies the reality of the other point of view. One time her mother reads her a story (at age 3.6) about a boy who wakes up one morning and finds himself the sole inhabitant of his town, free to do whatever he wants to do. But the freedom that older children might delight in is tragic to Carol. "He's all by himself," she says sadly. When it turns out at the end that the boy is only dreaming, Carol is further confused. She goes back to the beginning and simply denies that the unpleasant details are real: The boy's parents are not absent, they are hidden under the bedclothes, and so forth. She often employs this tactic, her mother says, when something contradicts her previous experience (White 1956, 79–80). We have seen Anna Crago react the same way to things she does not want to face, such as by covering the picture of the wicked queen in *Snow White* with her hand. Once when she and her mother are rereading *The Little Red Lighthouse,* Anna cuddles in her arms and pretends to cover her ears when the description of the storm and the tugboat wreck is about to occur (Crago and Crago 1983, 22–3).

Carol is also apt to focus her attention on a single striking feature of a story and ignore others in a way that does not make sense to an adult. One time she and her mother are reading one of the *Babar* books in which the king of the elephants dies. Carol, studying the illustration intently, concludes that the wrinkles on his trunk are the sign that he is dead (young Babar is always pictured with a smooth trunk). She is greatly puzzled, however, on the next page by some elephants who have wrinkled trunks and yet are still alive (White 1956, 131–2). How can this be? This habit of focusing on a single memorable incident is also reported in Applebee's study of how children respond to stories; one-third of the six-year-olds explained why they liked or disliked particular stories simply by citing one striking detail. One boy did not like "Little Red Riding Hood" because, "He eats the grandma," and another liked "Cinderella" because, "She went to the ball" (Applebee 1978, 99).

Carol sometimes fails to connect different experiences of the same event. For instance, at age 3, she sees a picture of a doll with only one arm on one page of book, and on the next page a picture of the same doll with a mended arm and different clothes on. For months afterward, her mother says, whenever they read the book Carol has great difficulty understanding that they are pictures of the same doll (White 1956, 47). Later on she has a similar experience with a real friend she has not seen for months, who is home from school and comes to play. She looks older, has a new hat and coat, and is missing one of her baby teeth. Carol is distraught; "I don't think it really is Ann," she says tearfully, though finally she is convinced and they play together happily enough (White 1956, 180). Piaget gives us an instance of his daughter Jacqueline (at 2.7) thinking the same way. She sees a slug on the road and then another, and thinks it is the same slug. He asks her if it isn't a different one. She goes back to look at the first one. Is it the same one? "Yes." Or a different one? "Yes." Is it the same one or a different one? The question, he says, obviously had no meaning for her (Piaget 1951, 225).

We could generalize by saying that children's responses to what they read seem to be highly, indeed inappropriately, concrete at this age. Carol's friend Ann sees a picture of a little boy holding onto his mother's apron strings, but the drawing stops at his mother's waist. Where is the mother's head? Nothing can convince her that the mother is not decapitated. In another story the children go swimming and there is a picture of one of them standing up in the water. "Where are the little boy's legs?," Carol (at age 2.6) wants to know. They are hidden in the water.

"But where are they?" She presses the paper as if to find them there. Her mother sums up this kind of thinking: "If for a child what is in a picture is, likewise, what is not in a picture is not" (White 1956, 22).

Piaget has no trouble accounting for the accomplishments as well as the limitations of this childhood kind of thinking.[6] He calls it "ego-centric," dictated by the self-centered view of the world the young child has and by the constraints on the child's ability to represent reality successfully. As the examples of Carol and Anna illustrate, this kind of thinking is highly concrete, centered on particular details, tied to images, and unable to sustain the idea of a state that extends through several transformations. It is a tremendous advance on the reflex sensory-motor thinking of the infant, because the child age 2 to 7 is increasingly able to represent objects symbolically, to develop accurate concepts, and to think about them in relation to each other – which for Piaget is the basis of all remembering, inferring, inventing, fantasizing, and the foundation of language. But this kind of thinking is still beset by all sorts of ego-centric limitations, in his view, and is destined ultimately to be replaced by more adequate ways of organizing the information we acquire from experience.

Evidence about other aspects of language and literacy provides some support for this view of the cognitive limitations of young children's thinking. Applebee reports studies of how six-year-old children make literal sense of common sayings such as, "You must have gotten out of the wrong side of the bed this morning." "No, I haven't," is a typical answer. Or, "When the cat is away, the mice will play," which one child interprets to mean that "the mice will play all over the room . . . and when the cat comes back he'll hurry right in his hole" (Applebee 1978, 102–3).

Studies of metaphor (surveyed in Winner 1988, 35–44) offer somewhat ambiguous evidence. Earlier ones appeared to confirm this view that young children's thought is tied to concrete images and that they do not understand words that might be intended figuratively. For example, when six-year-olds were asked to explain the statement, that after many years a prison guard had "become a hard rock which could not be moved," they either constructed an interpretation based on a literal association (he worked in a prison that had hard rock walls), or resorted to a magical but still literal explanation (a witch turned him into a rock), or devised an interpretation that grasped the metaphor in a primitive way based on sensory similarity (the guard had hard muscles). Eight- to ten-year-olds did realize that it was the guard's character that was at issue, but only adolescents could compare the guard and the rock in a variety of ways (the guard was stubborn, unyielding, cruel, etc.). The ability to paraphrase metaphorical language when the metaphors involve stating psychological qualities in physical terms would thus seem to be a late-developing skill (Winner, Rosensteil, and Gardner 1976). However, other studies suggest that children as young as age 3 seem to be able to grasp metaphoric relationships when they know what kind of activity is being asked of them, when the task does not require a linguistic response, when the metaphors are presented in the context of a story or picture, or when the ground of the metaphor is easily recognizable (Winner 1988, 44–59). Winner (1988, 88) concludes that if young children fail to grasp the intended meaning of nonsensory metaphors, it is not because the ability to perceive metaphoric relationships is itself a late blooming accomplishment, but simply because they have not yet acquired enough information about the domains to which the terms of the metaphor refer. These arguments do not seem to undercut the generalization that young children's thinking, complex though our appreciation of it becomes when metaphors are involved, is still largely tied to sensory images and literal relationships.

The stories young children tell offer clearer evidence of egocentric thinking. These stories often appear to be scarcely concealed projections of private meanings and feelings, as in this story by Ephraim H. (2.9), from the collection assembled by Pitcher and Prelinger (1963, 31): "Dog fell in the fence. I got a bit fence. Daddy broke my fence. I hurt my knee. I go bang on the big rock. I go home again." There is clearly some kind of central experience behind Ephraim's story, but short of knowing what the details refer to, it is difficult to figure out how to connect the parts.

Young children have difficulty keeping themselves out of the stories they tell. Ephraim gives up after the first sentence in the story quoted above. Bernice W. (2.11) does a somewhat better job: "Once there was an elephant. The mommy fixed his breakfast. Then he played with his toys. Then he drank his milk. The doggie came into his house. And I had to chase him away. The milkman came. The doggie jumped on the milkman. Then the milkman 'sweetied' the doggie on his back. Then the doggie went away." (Pitcher and Prelinger 1963, 35)

Also quite common are stories whose details contradict one another, as in one where a cowboy kills a bear, then the mommy bear kills the cowboy, then the cowboy has a pistol and kills the bear, and so forth (78–9). It is easy to see why Piaget (1955, 91) says that children younger than seven or eight pass from one point of view to another and forget the point of view they had first adopted. It is not that they actually believe what is self-contradictory; rather they continually accommodate to new situations without sustaining any relationship between them.

The characteristic structures of the stories young children tell illustrate these limitations of egocentric thinking as well, and their evolution between ages 2 and 6 shows what happens as egocentric thinking becomes more organized and conceptual. Although it is widely accepted that even the simplest stories normally contain a structural sequence of equilibrium, disequilibrium, and then equilibrium restored (Todorov 1971, for example), Brian Sutton-Smith (1979b, 61) points out that the stories of young children do not necessarily follow this form. In fact, this is a rather sophisticated form of story telling, implying a grasp of conceptual relationships between parts of the story that seems beyond the capacity of most five-year-olds. The reason for this will become clear if we look at Applebee's (1978, 56–72) analysis of some of the 360 stories that Pitcher and Prelinger collected from children ages 2 to 5.

Applebee examines these stories in terms of two ways of organizing details (borrowed from L. S. Vygotsky): "centering" and "chaining." The simplest form of centering is the "heap" of concrete details whose common feature is simply that they occur together to the storyteller. Thus, one story (Applebee 1978, 53) begins: "A girl and a boy, and a mother and maybe a daddy. And then a piggy. And then a horse. And maybe a cow. And a chair." And it goes on for some time this way. A more complicated form of centering is to connect details on a basis of similarity of relationship to the central element in the story (e.g., a snake ate a monster, ate some "dog dirty," ate an automobile seat, ate some bushes, ate some stairs, and finally ate himself). Still more elaborate (Applebee calls this "primitive narrative") is to join details on a basis of complementarity so that they form a set of parts entailed in the original situation, though concretely rather than conceptually (e.g., a boy dropped a bottle of ink, it broke, he cried, his mommy fixed it for him, etc.). All these forms of organization figure prominently in stories told by children ages 2 to 3.

Chaining is an advanced mode of organizing because it does not depend on relating each new detail to a center; instead the details or incidents imply one another. In the simplest version they form an "unfocused chain narrative," in that the attributes that link the details shift from one detail to the next. Ephraim's story above has something of this kind of structure. In a focused chain the two processes of chaining and centering come together on a basis of perceptual similarity. The result is a story that takes the form of "the continuing adventures of . . . ," a very popular way of organizing stories among four- and five-year-olds. Finally, in a true narrative the details are both centered and chained on a basis of complementarity, so that "each incident not only develops out of the previous one but at the same time elaborates a new aspect of the theme or situation," moving forward to a climax and often a clear "moral" (Applebee 1978, 65–6).

The story in the Pitcher and Prelinger collection that comes closest to this form, in Applebee's judgment, is the one told by Tracy H. (5.8):

> There was a boy named Johnny Hong Kong and finally he grew up and went to school and after that all he ever did was sit all day and think. He hardly even went to the bathroom. And he thought every day and every thought he thought up his head got bigger and bigger. One day it got so big he had to go live up in the attic with trunks and winter clothes. So his mother bought some gold fish and let them live in his head – he swallowed them – and every time he thought, a fish would eat it up until he was even so he never thought again, and he felt much better. (Pitcher and Prelinger 1963, 133)

In this remarkably inventive story the incidents are not only centered and chained but the ending is entailed within the initial situation; the plot, in Piagetian terms, has become reversible. But this kind of organization is rare in these stories, and Applebee (1978, 60) discovered in the 120 stories that he analyzed that even five-year-olds tended to reach only the level of organization he calls the "focused chain."

It seems clear that Piaget's description of young children's thinking can account for many of the egocentric elements in their responses to stories and that his explanation of their progressively maturing ability to organize information is a plausible framework for understanding the simple structures of the stories they tell. Nonetheless Piaget's point of view toward early childhood learning is essentially a description of its limitations. Other accounts of children's thinking – even ones that focus on cognitive development – are not so insistent about its inadequacies.

Margaret Donaldson (1978), for example, discusses experiments in which Piaget's famous demonstrations were altered in significant ways. He had used a toy model of three mountains that differed slightly (they varied in size, and one had snow, another a house on top, and so forth), and asked children positioned on one side of the model to describe what a child represented by a doll would see who was looking at the model from the opposite side. Children below age 6 or 7 tended to represent the doll's view exactly as they themselves saw it. Experiments of this sort led him to conclude that their egocentrism did not allow them to take the point of view of another person at this age. But when the task was altered (children were shown a model of intersecting walls and asked to hide a child doll from two policeman dolls positioned at the corners of the model) even the youngest children tested (averaging 3.9 years) achieved an 88 percent success rate (Donaldson 1978, 13–15).

What accounts for this difference? Donaldson thinks that children may not have understood what they were expected to do with the mountain problem. After all, abstracting a set of relationships involving left-right reversal from a complex and unfamiliar scene would be a challenging task for many adults. The policeman problem, however, made immediate sense to them; they grasped the motives and intentions of the actors with no trouble at all, and showed none of the difficulty in "decentering" that Piaget attributed to them (Donaldson 1978, 17).

Donaldson describes a number of other studies, especially of how young children understand language and how they talk about stories they are told, which also demonstrate that their thought processes are much less egocentric than Piagetian theory proposes. When the situation about which they are asked to think makes sense to them in the light of their own expectations and their understanding of the motives and intentions of adults who are questioning them, they exhibit the kind of competence in thinking that older children and adults show.

These revisions of Piaget do not invalidate the idea that children's cognitive abilities develop, but they suggest that this development is a more holistic process, with dimensions beyond those Piaget took into consideration. The work that is being done on "scripts," for example, suggests that young children (ages 3 to 5) learn words and meanings situationally in particular social contexts. Thus, when asked to tell what happens in familiar experiences, such as eating lunch at a McDonald's or going to a birthday party, they organize the details into scenariolike forms, marked by temporal sequencing of events, distinguishing between central and subordinate details, and using the vocabulary appropriate to the setting (Nelson 1978).

Jerome Bruner (1986a, 61) is a particularly vehement critic of Piaget's picture of the infant learner "going it alone" in the work of developing more and more adequate cognitive schemas out of interactions with the experiential world. Bruner would argue instead for a view of learning like that of Vygotsky, which gives more prominence to the social context that mediates and facilitates the development of the individual. A telling example for Bruner is the kind of interaction that occurs between mother and infant in book-reading routines – questions, comments, exclamations, confirmation of the child's reactions, games with words, and so forth. These are the means by which the mother stays "forever on the growing edge of the child's competence" and the child "borrows" from the mother's consciousness (who is of course a transmitter not just of her own knowledge but of a whole social and cultural context as well) in order to achieve his or her own development (Bruner 1986a, 77).

Another feature of children's thinking that stands out in apparent contradiction to the limitations of egocentrism is its inventiveness. Children are marvelous fantasists in ways that to adults seem imaginative and creative. The story of the boy with goldfish in his head eating up his burdensome thoughts one by one is better constructed than the other stories told by five-year-olds, but many of them match it in fantasy. There are space wars between worms and alligators, a kitten who falls into a clown doll's stomach and later is pulled inside a telephone by a hand that reaches out for her, a little bear who needs a tire around his middle to swim, and a pussycat who wants to be a Christmas present. Several different studies report that the stories of four- and five-year-olds show a marked increase in fantasy and imagination (Pitcher and Prelinger 1963, 158; Applebee 1978, 169; Ames 1966, 392–3).

Inventiveness shows up in other uses of language, too. Though the task of interpreting test metaphors like the one involving the prison guard's "hardness" may expose the limits of their capacity to grasp nonliteral meanings in adult language, in their own use of language children appear to be remarkably fertile in spontaneously using what look like metaphors. At eighteen months a child sees his big toe sticking out of a hole in his sock, points at it, and says laughingly "turtle." A two-year-old picks up a red ball, pretends to eat it, and announces "apple." A four-year-old looks at skywriting and says, "Look, the sky has a scar on it" (Winner 1982, 311). Kornei Chukovsky (1968, 2–3) collected examples of what he called this "linguistic genius" of young children, such as the one who talked about the "barefoot head" of a bald man, and another who called a piece of stale cake "middle-aged." One study discovered that before they are two years old, children can rename objects they are using (calling a spoon "a doll"). Between ages 2 and 3 they can rename objects on the basis of perceptual similarities they share with absent objects (calling a folded potato chip "a cowboy hat"). And by age 3 they can explicitly describe one object in terms of another ("that pencil looks like a rocket ship") (Gardner, Winner, Bechhofer, and Wolf 1978, 16–17). In another study, preschoolers produced some surprisingly inventive comparisons ("sad as a pimple," "quiet as a magic marker," "weather as boiling as your head popping open"). But they also produced some that made no apparent sense (for example, "as tall as an Indian") (Gardner, Kircher, Winner, and Perkins 1975, cited in Winner 1988, 105).

Are these outbursts of fantasy the first stirrings of a creative imagination that will develop into more mature forms of artistic invention? For Piaget (1951, 273) they are merely forms of symbolic play, which is a parallel behavior to cognitive representation in this stage of development and can be accounted for as a manifestation of egocentric thinking. This symbolic play is a consequence of being able to represent objects internally; as soon as children can do this, they delight in it, pretending, like Carol, that the living room furniture is a train she is driving. The imaginative language of children has the same function, Piaget thinks. It is symbolic thinking on its way to shedding its ties to concrete images and becoming genuinely conceptual. At 3.6, Piaget's daughter Jacqueline sees waves on the lake shore pushing little ridges of sand forward and backward, and exclaims: "It's like a little girl's hair being combed." At 4.7, she looks at the sunset and says: "I'd like to go for a ride in the rays and go to bed in sheets made of clouds." She says of a bent twig: "It's like a machine for putting in petrol" (Piaget 1951, 227). For Piaget, these are not examples of linguistic genius, but rather of concrete thought crudely being put at the service of emerging concepts that will more and more accurately come to represent the world of experience.

Winner (1988, 92–102), however, found instances of genuine metaphoric intention in the behavior of one child who was studied from age 2.3 to 4.10. She judged that Adam was engaging in true metaphor when, though he knew the literal name of a physical object, he deliberately renamed it, either at first in conjunction with some kind of pretend gesture during symbolic play (for example, putting his foot in a wastebasket and saying "boot") or later simply by pointing to a sensory property of the object (calling a sewing machine a "table-horsey"). These metaphors, to be sure, lacked the directionality and salience of full-scale adult metaphors (that is, their intent to illuminate a topic by equating it with an unexpected term with which the topic nonetheless shares some common ground), and they were rarely based on nonsensory similarities, but they caution us against taking too limited a view of children's linguistic creativity.

A surprising phenomenon noted by Winner (1988, 103), given this early productivity, is the dramatic decline in children's spontaneous use of metaphoric speech in the early school years, attested to by a variety of studies. Children ages 8 to 10 seem to enter a literal or conventional stage, where they avoid novel language in favor of trite options that they defend by conventional reasoning (e.g., a color cannot be loud). Interestingly, although metaphoric speech declines, the invention of analogies may increase, perhaps because analogies serve the purpose of understanding and explaining, though even here the literalism of nine-year-olds is evident (1988, 103–9).

In general, then, certain features of preschool children's responses to literature are explained fairly well by accounts of cognitive development that emphasize growth toward more abstract ways of thinking: the concrete, image-bound way young children think; the idiosyncratic way they focus on isolated details; why there is so little sense of relationship from part to part of their stories, indeed why contradictions are so easily sustained; the rudimentary grasp they have of even simple narrative structures; the subjective world into which they fit characters and incidents. What this approach does not deal with very satisfactorily is children's proclivity for fantasy. In this view, they invent imaginary playmates, pretend that a doll is a baby or that a set of blocks is an army, and spin out elaborate scenarios with their toys because this is the only way they can think about the world they live in. Because they cannot yet fully distinguish between inner and outer worlds and have not learned very well the collective signs of language, the made-up symbols of imaginative play function as a private language for rehearsing experience and their feelings about it. For cognitive developmentists, this behavior may have positive adaptive value because these fantasy symbols give that experience a reality that verbal signs could not give it at this stage in the child's development, while protecting the fragile ego from too rapid and forced an accommodation to the world of ordinary reality. But, however functional this kind of thinking is at this stage, it is still, in Piaget's terminology, pure "assimilation," egocentric thought making the world what it wants it to be rather than what it is. To develop, in Piaget's (1951, 167–8) view, is to grow out of this dependence on fantasy and to learn more adequate ways of understanding the real world.

The teacher of literature might well feel ambivalent about this version of development. On the one hand, it is undeniable that schooling is to a great extent a matter of teaching children eventually to think abstractly, even about literature, and to express themselves ultimately in the discursively organized prose of the formal essay. Yet so many of the qualities that account for the power of stories and poems and even essays seem to be bound up with the characteristics of childhood thinking that, from this point of view, the developing student is supposed to grow out of: its concrete, imagistic, sensory character, its wealth of personal meaning, its freedom from the constraints of analytic reasoning, and above all its power to involve us emotionally. Anyone who has ever read stories to young children knows how deeply they can engage their feelings and how lasting an imprint they can have on their imaginations. If the world of young children is magical and numinous, it is not only because of the way they think, but also because of how they feel. A theory of development that requires us to leave fantasy behind is a limited tool for analyzing how we read literature.

There is, indeed, something of a lost child between the lines of Piaget's description of development, an orphan who never gets the chance to grow up in his scheme. This is the "autistic" thinker who lives in a dream world of imagination, thinks in images and symbols and myths, and is guided by desires and feelings (Piaget 1955, 63). Unless we can work out a theory of development that gives some weight to this side of childhood experience, we will not have a very useful account of how children respond to literature.

THE AFFECTIVE POWER OF FANTASY

Anna Crago's response to *Snow White* is a good example of what is missing in a mainly cognitive account of reading. As we have seen, the story occupies her thoughts and feelings for a year and a half as she puzzles over the connections between familiar and harmful things (a poisonous apple and a murderous stepmother) and tries to connect them to her own experience. There is clearly a cognitive dimension to her puzzlement, but equally clearly there is a strong affective dimension as well.

The stories young children tell illustrate this too. In the 360 stories from children ages 2 to 5 in the Pitcher and Prelinger (1963) collection, themes of aggression, bodily harm, potential misfortune, death, abandonment and separation, sibling rivalry, sexual fantasy, and Oedipal conflict are surprisingly commonplace. There are all sorts of lost children and homeless animals. Wolves and bears and crocodiles eat people; lions and tigers bite off heads. Trains run over kittens and puppies. Little girls get put in jail. Baby bunnies light fires with matches and burn a house down. A boy kills his mother and daddy and brother with a bow and arrow. Another shoots people's eyes out with his cannon. An old lady bear threatens to eat a little bear for lunch, but the little bear turns into a "pretty man" who chops the old bear up into little pieces. Children end one story by putting "189 knives" into the stomach of a witch. A bear settles down with "a mommy and children" in a place where there are "no daddies." The last sentence of one story says that the boy "lived happily ever after with his mother" (Pitcher and Prelinger 1963, 238). In another, three little babies get shot one after another by a hunter (and one is cooked and eaten), while the "little girl" who is the central character gets all her mother's attention (Pitcher and Prelinger 1963, 231–2). The ubiquity of this kind of subject matter is confirmed by Louise Ames's (1966, 391–5) summary of her study of 270 stories from children of the same age.

Bruno Bettelheim, in his influential book *The Uses of Enchantment,* argues that these are the real issues that concern young children and that contemporary children's books often do not address them. Like many neo-Freudians, he adapts Freud's description of the role of fantasy (in forming dream imagery and neurotic symptoms, for example) and makes it a normal feature of development. Books that aim merely at entertaining children or at teaching them reading skills, he thinks, do not meet their need for this healthy fantasy.

The appeal of traditional fairy tales, in contrast, is that they deal directly with the existential problems of growing up: "overcoming narcissistic disappointments, Oedipal dilemmas, sibling rivalries; becoming able to relinquish childhood dependencies; gaining a feeling of selfhood and of self-worth, and a sense of moral obligation" (Bettelheim 1976, 6). They also appeal because they operate on the young child's level of understanding. The inner life of a child is chaotic, full of transient and ambivalent emotions that the child cannot comprehend rationally as an adult might. To sort out and control these feelings, a child needs the help of fantasy images that fill the gaps in knowledge and speak directly to the unconscious. This is "the only language which permits understanding before intellectual maturity has been achieved" (1976, 161). Perhaps the most important reason for the appeal of fairy tales in Bettelheim's eyes is that they offer in imaginative form a reassuring vision of the goal of healthy development: "the message . . . that a struggle against severe difficulties in life is unavoidable, is an intrinsic part of human existence – but that if one does not shy away, but steadfastly meets unexpected and often unjust hardships, one masters all obstacles and at the end emerges victorious" (1976, 8).

What Bettelheim has in mind can be seen in his reading of the familiar tale "Hansel and Gretel" (1976, 159–66). He sees it as a tale about typical problems of school-age children: fear of being separated from parents, facing in tangible form one's anxieties about the outside world, relying on one's own resources, learning to cooperate with one another, trusting that someday it will be possible to master the dangers of life. The story begins with the children's anxiety taking an oral form; they are abandoned in the forest because their parents are too poor to feed them. The first attempt they make to solve their problem is to regress to dependency, to follow the trail of white pebbles Hansel has dropped, back to their house. But they are abandoned a second time by their father, and this time the trail of bread crumbs fails them. Their regression to dependency then takes the form of the consummate oral fantasy, the gingerbread cottage – a detail that no reader of the story ever forgets, Bettelheim says, because it is so vivid an image of an existence based on the most primitive of satisfactions and of the terrible risk involved in giving in to them. The witch personifies the truly destructive aspects of orality; she is bent on eating not a gingerbread house, but the children themselves. A valuable lesson, Bettelheim says; dealing in symbols is safe when compared with acting on the real thing. To survive, the children have to turn away from dependence and use their own resources and intelligence to escape. The pressures of the id have to be subordinated to the control of the ego. Gretel tricks the witch and pushes her into her own oven, and the children escape through the forest and across the water, guided by the white bird that has figured in the story at several key points. Now they are not the helpless children they were at the beginning of their adventure; they bring back with them the witch's jewels, which are their parents' economic rescue but also images of their own newly won independence and self-reliance. They end up at home.

Nothing has changed but inner attitudes, Bettelheim says, but of course this means that everything has changed: "No more will the children feel pushed out, deserted, and lost in the darkness of the forest; nor will they seek for the miraculous gingerbread house. But neither will they encounter or fear the witch, since they have proved to themselves that through their combined efforts they can outsmart her and be victorious. Industry . . . is the virtue and real achievement of the school-age child who has fought through and mastered the Oedipal difficulties" (1976, 165).

Freud and his followers focus directly on what Piaget downplays: affectivity, fantasy, and the unconscious sources of our behavior. Moreover, they view childhood thinking not as a rudimentary version of mature thought, but as the matrix that permanently shapes adult experience and, in some versions of the theory, the model of the mind at its best. And the account they give of the affective power of fantasy images readily lends itself to discussions of literature. It seems then to be the obvious counterweight to Piaget's discussion of the limitations of young children's thinking.

Two particular aspects of children's responses to stories yield to analysis from a Freudian point of view. So far we have been considering how the Freudian picture of childhood development might contribute to understanding the appeal of certain themes in children's stories that correspond to the affect-laden issues that emerge in each stage of psychosexual development Freud sketched out (they are described in "Five Lectures on Psycho-analysis" and in "The Development of the Libido," Lecture 21 of "Introductory Lectures on Psycho-analysis"). The other line of speculation about the emotional appeal of stories has to do with the mechanism by which the unconscious drives of the id find expression in conscious imagery (see especially Chapter 7 of *The Interpretation of Dreams* and "The Creative Writer and Day-dreaming"). Freud worked out the relationship by studying dreams and then suggested that the same process might also be at work in other forms of fantasy, including art and literature. He did not develop these ideas into any systematic theory of creativity, and he made only scattered remarks about the responses of audiences to works of art. But Freudians have often been attracted to art and literature as subjects susceptible to psychoanalytic analysis, and many literary critics have found Freudian concepts equally congenial, so a body of work has grown up extending these insights about the process by which fantasy images come into existence to the production of art forms generally (for example, Ernst Kris, *Psychoanalytic Explorations in Art*). Like Bettelheim's neo-Freudianism, these applications to aesthetics tend to take mechanisms originally used to explain pathological states and convert them into general theories of the mind's functioning. Of particular interest to us are Simon Lesser's *Fiction and the Unconscious* and Norman Holland's *The Dynamics of Literary Response,* which offer Freudian explanations of fiction's power both to involve us in its fantasies and to control our involvement so that it is unthreatening and tolerable.

Like Bettelheim, they start from the assumption that, although the overt subject matter of literature is the world we live in, human relationships, and social and moral issues, and although much of the manifest meaning of literature will have to do with these kinds of topics directly, nonetheless the underlying and real source of the energy with which we experience literature is emotional, because it really deals with the profound desires and fears we have for ourselves, which these themes can tap.

A work of literature suspends our disbelief, indeed lures us willingly into its world. It does so, Holland suggests, by offering us the promise of gratification on the most basic oral level, of "taking in" in openmouthed wonder the fantasies it contains, of reexperiencing the undifferentiated fusion of ourselves and the world around us that we knew as infants before we learned to separate ego from external world (1968, 74–9). But this fusion threatens to overwhelm us with the loss of self, and so if we are to feel safe literary experience must simultaneously reassure us that in the fictional world we do not have to act. Dreaming, hypnosis, even the experience of psychoanalysis itself are models for Holland of the double state of mind we experience by immersing ourselves in a work of literature; we are both "participants" and "spectators," he says (1968, 84–9), employing a distinction that D. W. Harding first suggested in an account of the psychology of the fiction reader as "onlooker" (Harding 1968a). We both identify ourselves with the characters, incidents, and themes of the work, but also keep them at a safe distance through different devices of "displacement" that are analogous to the defense mechanisms Freud proposed to explain how we transform dangerous fantasies into acceptable ones in our lives generally – repression, denial, reaction-formation, projection, introjection, splitting, sublimation, and so forth (Harding 1968a, 57).

But it is the form of a literary work that, for both Holland and Lesser, most clearly safeguards us from the perils of engulfment by the fantasies we so willingly indulge in. Form – that is, everything from the sound pattern of the words to the structure of the narrative – promises to control and organize the experience, and therefore gives us permission to enjoy our feelings safely, reassures us that they are acceptable and still within our control, and integrates them into a vision of order, a process not unlike the Aristotelian notion of catharsis, to which Lesser refers (1957, 248). The form of a work does this, Lesser proposes, through a double strategy. By telescoping time and sustaining the forward movement of events, form gratifies the part of us that "lusts for the experience of the story" (though that part of us is also immersed in time and therefore is carried toward death). But by simultaneously focusing our attention on one central action and clarifying the pattern of events, form permits the part of us that watches the action "to escape time's dominion," to stand outside and beyond time as spectators rather than participants (1957, 169–70). Thus, though fiction magnifies and intensifies the issues it deals with, its formal characteristics control our anxiety by various devices that distance and frame – in Lesser's term "bind" – the emotions it causes, so that they do not reach disturbing proportions as we read nor threaten to merge with our world after we are done (1957, 183–4). Not only great literature operates this way; allowing for differences of degree it is as true of the detective story and the fairy tale as it is of Sophocles and Dostoevsky.

Lesser draws attention to a special aspect of this binding of emotion by form, namely that the language of fiction is extremely well suited to expressing and evoking the kind of unconscious thought that Freud called "primary-process thinking." It is highly sensory, concrete, almost a picture language, resembling in this respect the earliest forms of infantile knowledge. Because it is so good at simulating the events of our lives, "the language of fiction is an ideal instrument for objectifying and externalizing our desires, fears and inner conflicts" (Lesser 1957, 150), and therefore for relieving our anxieties, because we can project them onto fictional characters, look closely at them from a safe distance, own and disown what we will, and regain a sense of mastery and control over them. The concrete, sensory language of fiction is also like primary-process thought in that it communicates nondiscursively. The speed and economy with which images follow one another means that they bypass conscious response, speaking directly to the reader, but relieving him or her of the anxiety of translating what is understood into words.

This is similar to Bettelheim's point that fairy tales operate on the young child's level of understanding by offering fantasy images that fill the gap in knowledge of the world and speak directly to the unconscious. Bettelheim also echoes Lesser's observation that the imagery of literature operates at a safe distance from the desires and fears it embodies. The formula "Once upon a time . . . " signals to children that they are leaving the world where impulses and actions can have fearful consequences and entering a special time and place where they can enact their wishes imaginatively, but also need experience the consequences only imaginatively. The reader can surrender to the fantasy knowing that it is only a story and that however vivid the sense of involvement is, the listener is always spectator as well as participant and remains in control of the level of involvement.

The Freudian account of the mind's operation and the theories of aesthetic experience based on it take us a good part of the way toward understanding why fictional stories can involve us so intensely. But these views have their limitations, too. Do we need to accept the whole system of childhood sexuality in order to understand the appeal of the themes of young children's stories? Does the model of the mind struggling by various defensive strategies to reduce the tension of biological drives give us an adequate description of the normal enjoyment of reading? Particularly from the point of view of trying to account for children's responses to stories, we might echo the standard criticism of Freudianism; theories of neurosis, however effective clinically, are too reductive when they are turned into general pictures of the mind.

An instructive argument has occurred between Bettelheim and cognitive-developmental psychologists over his claim that fantasy is indispensable for children's development because it is the natural way of dealing with the presence of emotions and unresolved conflicts at an age when rationality has such fragile control over the unconscious. Howard Gardner and others have replied that there is no research evidence showing that preschool children have mastered the mental processes that are presupposed in Bettelheim's description of how they respond to fairy tales. On the contrary, some studies suggest that young children have little grasp of symbolic content and a poor sense of narrative structure; that they may be drawn to the alluring surface details of stories rather than to their underlying themes; that rather than grasp the lessons about life that Bettelheim thinks fairy tales offer, children may just project their own private concerns onto stories or react idiosyncratically to irrelevant details in them; and that they may even respond by taking the fantasy characters and events not as pretend realities, but as frighteningly real ones (Gardner 1977; Winner 1982, 295–9). Bettelheim has replied to these charges by arguing that when experimental psychologists measure children's performance of specific tasks such as retelling a story, what they learn is not necessarily an adequate picture of how children subjectively experience the stories that matter to them. Clinical experience, he thinks, is a better guide to the impact of fantasy on young children (Winner and Gardner 1979, ix).

So the argument amounts to a standoff between Piaget's persuasive outline of the stages of children's cognitive development, with its implication, however, that the imagination's products are subjective illusions to be finally outgrown, and Freud's striking picture of the unconscious sources of childhood fantasy, with its stipulation that these drives can be controlled only by unremitting defensive strategies that are all too liable to leave their scars on our adult lives.

One way of handling this impasse is to reflect for a moment on the reductionism implicit in both Piaget and Freud. Both want to explain developmental mechanisms in terms that can be experimentally or clinically verified. For both the model is the individual child coming to terms with an environment. Development consists of increasingly effective separations from this environment, more realistic assessments of it, and more effectively controlled responses to it. What needs emphasis is that the direction of engagement for both Piaget and Freud is from inside to outside; the child reacts to the confusing or threatening environment and gradually out of his own resources constructs a personality, over against the environment.

As a model for reading, this view stands on its head our spontaneous assumption that a story is a fantasy world waiting for readers to enter it and that the book (indeed, the whole culture it embodies) is an attractive environment that draws us into it as readers, rather than a problematic environment that challenges us to separate ourselves from it and control our reactions to it. Both Piaget and Freud ultimately seem to favor a view of development as a process of *assimilating* (to use Piaget's term) the environment to the emerging structures of the mind. I suspect that readers and teachers of literature ultimately favor the notion that reading is more like *accommodating* our minds to the shape of the world that literature opens up to us. Perhaps, then, we need to find an account of the power of fiction that does not reduce the matter either to the growing cognitive capacities or to the affective needs and defenses of the individual reader.

Some help comes from the views of one of the earliest dissenters within the psychoanalytic school, Carl Jung. He was unsatisfied with the picture of a conflicted ego barely controlling the sexual drives of the unconscious and proposed instead that the conscious mind grows out of the unconscious psyche in a normal and healthy way. In the process he attached a positive, all but mystical importance to the child's way of thinking and to adult versions of it. His striking contribution to rethinking the mind's operation was his proposal of a collective unconscious, an inner cosmos that contains in its *archetypes* all the psychic experience of humanity, which emerge in the conscious mind as images or symbols (see especially the three lectures collected at the beginning of the volume *The Archetypes and the Collective Unconscious*). Typically, these are the figures of mythology, the forms of primitive nature symbolism, and the motifs of fairy tales and religion. They are simultaneously the forms underlying the unconscious drama of the psyche.

Jung, too, offers a reading of a fairy tale (1959). In an Estonian folk story, an ill-treated orphan boy has let a cow escape and is afraid to return home for fear of punishment, so he runs away. Waking from an exhausted sleep he meets an old man to whom he recounts his story. The old man feeds him and gives him water to drink. Then he tells the boy that he cannot go back but must seek his fortune in the world; the old man says he himself can no longer look after him, but that he will give him some good advice. The boy must continue his wanderings eastward, where after seven years he will reach a great mountain that will betoken good fortune. He says that the boy will lack for nothing, offers his wallet and his flask, and says that each day the boy will find in them all the food and drink he needs. Finally, the old man gives him a leaf that will change into a boat whenever he needs to cross water.

Jung observes that in one sense the old man tells the boy nothing that he could not have figured out for himself, namely that he has acted impulsively in running away, that he is at a turning point in his life, and that his successful growth to adulthood now depends on his own skill and energy. But the old man's intervention has a magic quality about it; the boy feels his situation is no longer hopeless. This is a typical pattern in fairy tales. An old man asks questions that induce self-reflection in the hero (who? why? whence? whither?) and mobilize the necessary moral forces for a solution, and he often gives a talisman that embodies the realization of the unexpected power to succeed. The hero is in a situation where conscious will is not by itself capable of uniting the personality to the point where it is strong enough to succeed. The intervention of the old–man figure checks the purely affective reactions with a chain of inner confrontations and realizations, so that the hero or heroine understands the immediate situation as well as the goal.

For Jung, this story illustrates what he means by the archetype of the *spirit,* of which he found numerous manifestations in the dreams of his patients: an old man, a ghost, a magician, a dwarf or talking animal, who "always appears in a situation where insight, understanding, good advice, determination, planning, etc., are needed but cannot be mustered on one's own resources" (Jung 1959, 216). He cites dozens of examples of this theme in fairy tales: earth spirits like the king of the forest or little men made of iron and ice, figures identified with the sun, demonic figures blind in one eye or half-invisible or who have magical powers (and therefore are in the grip of the darker side of the spirit, with which they or the hero will have to wrestle), and helpful birds and animals from a world not alienated by consciousness from the power by which it lives. The ubiquity of this figure and its consistent function in folk tales and in literature suggest that it is an archetypal image of a primordial human experience of assistance from a power that transcends our ordinary resources. Whether we explain that power as parental or divine or as a personification of the highest capacities of our own psyches, on the level of archetype we experience it as the spirit spontaneously manifesting itself and supplying what is needed for a psychic integration that we are at the moment incapable of achieving by ourselves.

The Jungian unconscious is thus a kind of well that we need to draw on from time to time to nourish our psyches, rather than the prison house of pent-up drives that it is in Freud's system. Not surprisingly, then, fantasy, instead of being the carefully disguised translation of censored fears and desires that it is in Freud, is in Jung's thought an ordinary means of bringing us "into contact with the oldest layers of the human mind, long buried beneath the threshold of consciousness" (1966b, 29). It heals us by putting us in touch with the primordial past in the depths of our psyche: "At such moments we are no longer individuals, but the race; the voice of all mankind resounds in us" (1966a, 82). By translating the archetype into our own language, the artist enables us to "find our way back to the deepest springs of life. . . . He transmutes our personal destiny into the destiny of mankind, and evokes in us all those beneficent forces that ever and anon have enabled humanity to find a refuge from every peril and to outlive the longest night" (82).

A broader claim than Jung's for the imperium of fantasy is difficult to imagine. Through it we have access to the entire psychic experience of the race. In Jung's view, it is the way we thought as children, the way the race thought in its childhood, and the kind of thinking we need to recover to deepen our possession of the spirit. The claim is a beguiling one because it implies the ultimate coherence and intelligibility of human culture, the natural world, and the structures of our minds. Who would not want to find such a vision believable? We sense the rightness of supposing that the images and themes of literature have a transpersonal power. We want to think that literature somehow puts us in touch with the accumulated experience of the past and that beyond the edges of our consciousness lie margins of significant mystery that we are not wholly cut off from.

The very breadth of the claim, though, makes it suspect to many. Like Bettelheim's account of children reading fairy tales, it is untestable, and like the Freudian picture of childhood and of the mind's workings, mainly clinicians and therapists defend its value as an analytic tool. The most disputed point in Jung's system has always been the lack of any persuasive mechanism by which an individual might come into possession of the contents of the collective psyche. But is it possible that the study of children's reading can shed light on this subject? If we let reading stand for all the ways a child interacts with the human environment – in talk, play, meals, games, songs, rituals, and so forth; in the daily family activities that follow conventional scripts and scenarios; in taking in the details of how people dress and what the house and surroundings look like; in learning about the different roles people play – then from the earliest moments of life an infant is absorbing and responding to the vast contents of the culture. The more we know about the astonishing dynamism of children's minds, I suspect, the less we need to worry about a mechanism for transmitting and acquiring the primary images of this cultural life. Thus, Jung's addition to Freud seems so valuable precisely because it identifies some of the otherness in our experience of the world and rescues the child from the condition of "going it alone" (to use Bruner's phrase), which both Piaget's and Freud's versions of development require.

So, although Jung takes the idea of the unconscious far from its Freudian starting point, one element of continuity is the claim both make for the power of fantasy to involve us emotionally. Freud locates this power in the way images are formed in the personal unconscious, Jung in the web of relationships a given image has both as cultural residue and as part of the structure of our consciousness. What would be extremely useful in trying to understand childhood fantasy would be a point of view flexible enough to set accounts of both cognitive and affective development in a framework that did justice to the role society and culture play in the construction of our ideas and values.

FANTASY, PLAY, AND TRUST

I think that the starting point of this chapter suggests a clue to the next step in our argument, in the picture of the child sitting entranced in the arms of someone reading a story. If this child's grasp of the world is so fragile and episodic, if imagination so readily fills it with creatures that embody one's worst fears, why does the child entrust himself or herself to the experience of reading at all? The Piagetian answer is that the child does not know any better (but will), the Freudian answer that it momentarily makes the child feel better. But do we have to see this child engrossed in a tale as a problem? Is it possible to construct a point of view that takes the experience for the happy and stimulating activity that it seems to be and gives it a positive function in the development of the child, without falling over into the Jungian position of saying that the child's experience is the best life has to offer? I suggest that we expand our account of what it is that makes the young child so willing a listener to a tale.

To do this we need to amplify the social and, especially, the interpersonal dimensions of our concept of development, and then to consider the significance of play as a mechanism by which the child might enact a growing sense of the world's potential meaning and of the child's identity in it. It will help if we imagine a slightly different model of reading, not the child cuddled in a parent's arms, but boys and girls sitting on the carpet of a day-care school or kindergarten listening to a teacher read and acting out the roles in the stories. These may be older children than the ones we have been talking about up to now; indeed, because they are in a school they might almost be put into a different category of reader altogether. But nursery school is not that far from nursery, and once we see what the model involves, we can look for its roots in the way younger children respond to stories and in the way they learn to play.

For eighteen months, Marilyn Cochran-Smith (1984) studied a group of nursery school children ages 3 to 5. They were from school-oriented, middle-class families, where books were common and the children had been read to since infancy. She was especially interested in how the nursery school functioned as a milieu that educated them in the cultural attitudes toward reading held by their parents and by the social community to which their parents belonged.[7] The school's explicit policy was not to push the children academically, nor to sharpen their "readiness skills" for reading and writing; rather its aim was to make the children's first school experience one of happy, cooperative, supportive play and learning from play. Nonetheless, as her account of even the opening-day puppet show and tour of the classroom makes clear, print in all its forms, books, and storytelling (and esteem for these) pervaded the school life, as they pervaded in quite routine ways the home lives of most of the children and their parents (Cochran-Smith 1984, 37–59).

She shows in great detail how the activities of the nursery school formed a set of concentric circles of context that supported the primacy of reading as an educational activity: at the center the special times when the children sat on the rug listening to their teacher and talking to her and to each other about a book like *The Night Kitchen*; then all the activities outside reading time that had print and literacy embedded in them (labeling things, making signs, writing notes, filling out forms, making Valentine cards, naming pet animals, etc.); surrounding this the whole organized environment of time and space and behavior in the school; and finally the adult belief system in which reading was a means of access to knowledge and of solitary and social pleasure.

Her study makes clear that nursery school reading activities are an organized education not only in the community's attitudes toward literacy, but also in the culture's understanding of what stories are and of how to respond to them. The teacher's role is crucial in this process. She prompts, questions, explains, summarizes, and connects. She mediates for the children conventions about what books are, how to read them, how to follow a plot and explain a character's activities, what different genres imply, and what appropriate responses are. Of course, this is the role any adult reader plays for a child, but now it has the authority of school behind it. Even in the play of nursery school, the child has begun a new level of systematic instruction in the culture's agenda.[8]

Wally's Stories is a different kind of book, about the kindergarten year of a group of five-year-olds, but it makes much the same impression. The teacher, Vivian Gussin Paley (1981), taped the children's conversations about fairies, the rules for making wishes, how pulleys work, where babies come from, fairness, how to use rulers, whether witches can be invisible, and especially about the many stories they read, invented, and acted out themselves. The extracts from these conversations and their teacher's spare comments provide a fascinating picture of children at a dividing line in their development. "Morality, science, and society shared the stage with fantasy," she says, and in a sense the book traces the conflict of two contending world views, the magical one and the one adults call realistic (1981, 4).

Magic weaves in and out of everything the children do, Paley says; it is the "common footpath" from which new ways of thinking are explored. Wally is the most inventive of the children, explaining how spells work, why God saves his power for harder things and lets fairies take care of the ordinary ones, what the tooth fairy does with the teeth she gets, and what the difference is between magicians and fairies. Paley observes that this is a child-centered view of the world, where if something can be imagined it must exist (1981, 30).

But this is also a view of the world that is becoming increasingly realistic and the realism is part of the children's shared understanding of the world: "Children envision an orderly world in which there are answers for every question" (1981, 36). It is just that they have not yet learned enough to distinguish between realistic answers and magical ones. Early in the year they read a story about an enormous turnip a grandfather, a grandmother, a child, and a black cat cannot pull out of the ground until a little brown mouse comes along to help them. The mouse was stronger than the others, they think, or perhaps he pushed it up from under the ground. Toward the end of the year the teacher recalls the same story. Now most of the children see that the mouse added just the strength needed to pull out the turnip. Wally, though, has a characteristically imaginative version of events – "He could of been right under the turnip in a secret place and then he could of chewed it and pushed it a little and also when the people kept pulling and pulling it got looser and looser" – teetering, Paley says, between the practical reality of people pulling together and the vision of a magically powerful mouse (1981, 202).

In one way or another stories and the group's response to them were a major part of the children's curriculum. The teacher read stories to the children, of course, and the children were also encouraged to dictate stories of their own that she would write down. Few children had done this before in her experience (no more than four or five out of twenty-five), but one day she asked Wally if he wanted to act out a story he had dictated. This proved such a hit that they were soon writing and acting out four or five stories a day. Whenever they read or acted out a story, the teacher encouraged them immediately to talk about it.

They dramatized three kinds of stories, and the differing responses are significant. Least challenging were picture books; though they introduced new topics, they were instantly digestible and frequently the children memorized their entire contents. Then there were the stories the children invented themselves; these had simple plots and situations and functioned as a kind of dramatic play in which the children could behave spontaneously and discover what the others were thinking. Best of all were fairy tales, which had the advantage of superior plot and dialogue and themes which provoked the really "serious" discussions (1981, 66–7). One of them, "The Tinder Box," became the favorite of the year. It is about a soldier who returns from the wars and, by performing a favor for a witch, gains magical power and wealth. The role was one that every boy and half of the girls wanted to play, and eventually the class did it seventeen times, in order to accommodate the children. Paley contrasts these fairy tales, which stimulate the children's imaginations, with the "superhero" stories, usually from television, which the boys especially enjoyed telling and performing. Superhero stories tended to consist of conventionalized formulas and to have nothing of the teller's distinctive personality in them, but Paley does not dismiss them; their very conventionality may be a useful crutch to children reluctant to express themselves, she thinks. Though these superhero stories were a staple in the children's repertory, it is significant that the children never brought them into the discussion of serious matters. There magic and reality were the issues, and even superpowerful heroes could not make wishes come true (1981, 127–31).

Both Cochran-Smith's and Paley's books suggest that reading in school changes children's experience of stories significantly, that reading is now an intensely social activity. In the classroom setting, the teacher can assume with a different kind of authority the central role that we have seen a parent or some other adult take previously. Children's play now centers more and more around the collective task of absorbing the culture's lessons. As they read, they slowly build up repertories of the structures and motifs that are conventional in the world of literature. Now when they dramatize stories, their freedom to invent is constricted by a maturing awareness of plot and character and theme requirements in the story on the page and by the expectations they collectively share about the product.[9]

How do readers get from the arms of their parents to the carpet of the kindergarten? How does reading change from the one-to-one experience of infancy to the collectivity of shared roles and performances in the schoolroom? One way of tracing this development is to see the steps by which children enter the world of fantasy, discover that they are safe in it and will not be overwhelmed by its inventions, and acquire the confidence to play there. Erikson's picture of the social influences on the psychology of growing up and of the transitions children go through as their maturing physical and psychic capacities develop in interaction with the new demands society makes on them is a helpful guide to this process.[10] It enables us to see the child not in terms of conflicts and limitations that will eventually have to be overcome, but as the possessor of a real, though unfinished, identity that will be renegotiated a number of times as the child meets the social challenges of growing up. An important part of growing up is to learn to enter the world of fantasy safely.

Let us look more closely at these transitions. For the child below age 2 the experience of being told a story, of "reading," can hardly be differentiated from conversation, play, and other interactions with parents, older brothers and sisters, and other caregivers. At their most intense, these relationships would seem to have the intersubjective, identity-giving value that Erikson epitomizes in the mutual eye contact and smile of mother and child. Even at less intense levels, storytelling probably still has for the infant the effects that Walter Ong attributes to all aural communication; it establishes a relationship of *presence* between speaker and hearer, it asserts their *connectedness* while reinforcing the consciousness each has of existential *difference,* and it registers the *interior* of the speaker and particularly the *affect-laden qualities* of that interior (1982, 71–4). For the child at this age, just learning to distinguish the outside world from inner experience, story listening would seem to be another route by which trusted adults initiate him or her into what is rapidly becoming the other world outside.

But this role soon changes. We know that between ages 1 and 3 children become increasingly competent managers of fantasy in the form of symbolic play. They play more and more, and as they do the kind of play they spontaneously engage in changes dramatically in complexity and in their mastery of it, from the simplest form of pretend play (a one-year-old using an empty cup and pretending to drink out of it) to the kind of collective play that involves differentiated roles and a script of typical events (such as "playing house").

There seem to be four different steps in this development, according to Greta Fein (1979):

1. First, objects and behaviors are decontextualized from their real-life situations and motivations (the child pretends to drink from a cup when not really drinking or thirsty).

2. Then, imaginary objects substitute for concrete ones (at first the play object has to look like the real thing, but then a stick can be a horse, and eventually children need no objects at all to stimulate their play).

3. Then, roles become differentiated and the relationship of self to other changes (in early pretend play the child feeds himself or herself, then feeds someone else – a doll perhaps, and finally stands outside the action and causes another to act as agent – making the doll feed itself for instance).

4. Finally, the play symbols become socialized (players agree what substitutions and representations and roles will be allowed, and expectations about appropriate behavior – what fathers and mothers do, what babies do – become standardized).

While these are all dimensions of increasing competence in playing, the differentiation of roles is particularly important as a clue to children's willing involvement in the make-believe, "as if" world of stories. It seems to be the case that children even at age 3 still cannot confidently enter the story world on their own and will not be able to until they can separate the special role of fictional narrator from their own role as listener; conversely, the ability to realize what the role of the narrator implies makes it possible for them to enter the "as if" world so enthusiastically as listeners.

This becomes clear if we reflect that even the considerable achievements of three-year-olds as players leave them with an uncertain grasp of the boundary between the fantasy world and the world of pragmatic consequences when they listen to stories. Until they learn to separate the two, children may flee the fantasy situation altogether or intervene in it all too realistically. C., whose growing ability to master the narrative role is documented in one study, exhibits both reactions (Scarlett and Wolf 1979). At age 2.11, she is told a story about a king and a princess by a researcher, who acts out the story with toys and blocks. When the researcher introduces a "mean old dragon," C. breaks off and runs to her mother's lap. "Can she bite me?," she asks. As the story goes on and the dragon threatens the princess, C. jumps off her mother's lap, grabs the toy dragon, and throws it away. "I don't want him. You take him back," she says to the researcher. Similarly, a month earlier C., listening to an investigator dramatizing a story about a fat elephant who can't climb a hill, says "Yes, he can," and pushes the elephant prop over the arched block representing the hill. When the investigator says, "Let's pretend that it was very high and he couldn't do it," and returns the elephant to his struggles, C. becomes confused and angry and moves the elephant back over the arch, saying firmly, "He can go up." (Scarlett and Wolf 1979, 30–1). To be a willing listener at this age, when one has ambivalent feelings about participating in the fantasy and when story images can so easily summon up newly found anxieties and fears, requires something more than simple trust in fantasies or in the storyteller. How does a child get beyond this impasse?

It seems that the child becomes increasingly aware, in practice, of the autonomy of the story world, that this world has a hypothetical, pretend quality that makes it safe to encounter dragons there and, as Lesser and Holland have argued, that events there will be arranged so that they unfold toward a satisfactory resolution. These discoveries make it possible to be confident of one's own role as participant in that fantasy world.

In a sense, the child has to learn how to deal with the difference between fictional and pragmatic worlds. One part of this task is clearly cognitive. The child has to learn through experience that story events occur in a specially marked or framed context, a storytime or playtime that has both internal cues (such as opening and closing and transitional formulas, formal diction, perhaps rhyme and meter) and external signals (the storyteller's tone of voice, tempo, gestures, and bodily movements), which signal fictiveness and allow the child to accept the "as if" world of make believe (B. H. Smith 1980, 126–30). But the task also has an affective dimension; it requires that the child risk crossing the boundary into the fictional world and trusting the rules by which it operates. Or, perhaps we might more accurately say, using Harding's distinction, that the child learns to play both spectator and participant roles simultaneously or, following the line of argument taken by Winnicott, Britton, and Peggy Whalen-Levitt, that the fictional world, mediating between the inner world of our needs and desires and the outer world of shared and verifiable experience, is in some sense a place familiar to us from our earliest childhood experiences (Winnicott 1971; Britton 1971; Whalen-Levitt 1983). It is not the case, then, that we learn how to leave the world of pragmatic experience and safely enter the fictional world, but rather that, already there, we learn the freedom and autonomy to play there confidently.

The evidence for this is inferential, but all that we know of how preschool children learn the narrator role suggests that the listener role undergoes a simultaneous evolution in the direction of increasing competence at managing the boundaries of the fictional world and of increasingly playful exploration of that world. Consider, for example, two subsequent performances of C., the young girl who was frightened by the dragon and anxious that the fat elephant get up the hill (Scarlett and Wolf 1979, 34–6). This time the researcher uses toy animals to begin a story about a purple elephant who is teased by the other elephants because of his strange appearance. At age 3.7, before she is even invited to finish the story, C. jumps into play. She lies down on the floor, looks the elephant in the eye, and says, "I will be your friend, don't be sad." She picks up the toy and hugs it, saying, "Now you have a friend." At 5.2, in contrast, she marches the elephant over to face the other animals and has him tell them (she quotes his words) that they look silly too – the tiger with his stripes, the hippopotamus because he's so fat, the giraffe with his long neck. She has them taunt each other back and forth until the tiger announces that the elephant is right and that it is mean of them to tease him. The tiger says that he is going to be the elephant's friend. Each of the animals moves forward, saying, "Me too," and the story ends with the elephant giving each of them a ride on its back.

The first ending is like C.'s response to the plight of the fat elephant; the boundary between the narrative and pragmatic worlds is nonexistent. In the second instance, the fictional world is wholly self-contained. Not only has C. learned that the conflict has to be resolved within the boundaries of the fictional world, but she has also learned that the way to do it is to unfold the possible implications given in the situation. Thus, she gives the elephant a point of view, makes the tiger amenable to persuasion, and turns the conflict into a lesson about getting along with each other.

C. seems to have learned that one function of the narrator is to make events unfold plausibly into a coherent action. She does this not only by developing motivations for the characters and elaborating on their circumstances, but also by introducing conventional scriptlike structures to give a shape to the action (for example, the argument and reconciliation of the animals). Where do all these details come from that supply the substance of this story? In a sense she extrapolates them from the situation proposed by the investigator, but she also clearly has a repertory from other stories and from her own experience of knowledge about how characters should behave and what relationships might occur between them. The narrative she produces, though, is her own invention. The hypothetical status of this level of narrative could not be made clearer than it is in the dragon story she tells at 4.2, which begins, "Let's pretend he had very big teeth, and. . . . "

C.'s growing sophistication as a storyteller is also illustrated by the linguistic skills she brings to her material (Scarlett and Wolf 1979, 36–9). At age 3 she uses language mainly to describe what she is enacting with the toy props, but a year later she is communicating information about the characters' motives and feelings that could not possibly be enacted. For example, telling a story at age 4.2 about a princess threatened by a dragon, she explains that the dragon has eaten so many people that he has become too fat to climb the tree where the princess takes refuge. She also begins to give the characters dialogue (for instance, in the purple elephant story), and to use metanarrative signals (the most common one is "Let's pretend . . . ") to indicate when she is crossing the boundary from the pragmatic to the fantasy world. These developments are significant in several ways. Freed from dependence on props, C. can now use her imagination to invent material. The kind of information that can be brought to the story, such as the thoughts and feelings of the characters, has been greatly expanded. She can dramatize situations and relationships effectively, and she can instruct her audience as to how the story is to be understood. This last point is especially important, because successfully telling a story depends on the narrator's ability to overcome his or her egocentrism and to assume instead the perspective of the listener, providing the kinds of information (who? what? where? when? how? why?) that orient the hearer to the content and significance of the story. One study shows that this ability develops continually from age 3.5 to 9.5 (Menig–Peterson and McCabe 1978).

The point to be insisted on, however, is that development as a listener seems to parallel development as a narrator. Anna Crago at age 3.1 was listening to a Beatrix Potter story told largely in the third person. When the narrator of the story ended by saying, "And I think that some day I shall have to make another, larger book, to tell you more about Tom Kitten," Anna was startled enough to ask, "Who said that?" Balancing the expectation that a story should be self-contained with the fact that authors occasionally interject themselves into the text or indeed tell whole stories as first-person narrators proved difficult for Anna until she was more than a year older (Crago and Crago 1983, 239–40). We have seen that C.'s performance exhibits similar confusions. At 3.7, listening to the story of the purple elephant, her role as listener was so mixed up with the elephant's plight that when asked to take over as narrator, she simply obliterated the story boundary and spoke to the toy elephant as if it were real. At 5.2, however, she seems to be thinking like a potential narrator. Given the opportunity to finish the story, she now has the skills and sense of what a story requires to dramatize a plausible conflict and solution. No longer are her alternatives simply to trust the fantasy world absolutely or to break away from it completely. Now she knows what the pretend status of that world means, and she knows that the narrator's job is to unfold it and make it come out right in the end, and she can be a confident listener in her own right as a result.

This stance that C. can now take toward a story balances spectator and participant roles. This distinction, we noticed earlier, derives from Freud's description of the dreamer and the patient under analysis, who simultaneously both enact and observe their experience. Both W. D. Harding and Norman Holland use it to describe two aspects of the experience of fiction: on the one hand abandonment to the invented occurrences, on the other the evaluative attitude of the onlooker. When J. R. R. Tolkien describes the "Secondary World" of the story maker's art that we willingly enter without losing our grasp of the distinction between fact and fiction, he appears to be making the same distinction (1964, 36–7). Bruner talks about the mode of thought and discourse that "subjunctivizes" reality, which deals with the contingent, the hypothetical, with possibilities rather than certainties, and invites the listener to participate in "performing" them (1986a, 25–6). To be able to do this safely, though, implies that we can also preserve our grasp of the mode of thought that judges our experience by empirical and pragmatic standards. This is why I think that C.'s ability to hold these two roles in balance requires a real, if rudimentary, trust both in the fantasy world and in her ability to explore it safely.

This autonomy is comparable to the sense of autonomy and initiative that Erikson calls the characteristic achievement of older preschool children as they develop beyond the basic trust of the infant. "Autonomy" in Erikson's sense implies newly discovered freedom of choice, self-control, and being able to meet the expectations of the adult world. "Initiative" suggests undertaking things, trying on new roles, deliberate fantasies, and self-confidence. Differentiating the roles of narrator and listener gives the older preschool child new power and imaginative energy. This is the age when fantasy is in full flower, in speech and in drawings and clay construction (Winner and Gardner 1979). And, as we have seen, the stories children tell at this age are full of invention. If we want one word to describe the role of the child as a listener to stories and as a narrator of them, *player* may do. The term suggests the excitement that comes as imagination is freed from dependence on the familiar objects and realities of immediate experience, it suggests the "as if" status of the fictional world, it suggests that to listen to stories and to tell them is to practice the culture's agenda, finally, it conveys something of the growing sense of autonomy and risk taking that the preschool child acquires.

Play is not very important in some developmental theories.[11] From the Freudian point of view it is a form of release, a way of fulfilling wishes and mastering anxiety-provoking situations. For Piaget the kind of play that involves the practice of past experience can promote the assimilation of that experience, and the kind of play involving games with rules has valuable socializing consequences, but children's symbolic play is simply an egocentric distortion of reality, necessary for a time to protect the fragile ego, but destined to disappear as more adequate ways of assimilating reality are acquired (Piaget 1951, 61–168). Neither of these points of view gives us much of a basis for valuing fantasy, especially in adults.

Revisions of Freud and Piaget have produced much richer conceptions of the role of play in development. The psychoanalyst D. W. Winnicott, for example, considers play an essential constituent of the child's earliest experience of identity. He pictures the infant as enjoying a sense of fusion with the mother and of omnipotence in being able to call her breast into existence to meet its need. The child, of course, has to overcome this illusion eventually, this confusion between what is objectively perceived and what is subjectively conceived. It does so by playing with "transitional objects" – the blanket or toy that is its first possession and is neither wholly "outside" nor wholly "inside." The play area, Winnicott suggests, is the intermediate area of shared reality that the mother lovingly creates between herself and the child. But this task of reality acceptance is never complete for us, because no human being is ever free from the strain of relating inner and outer reality. So we always need transitional objects and this intermediate area of experience, which continues the play of the small child in the "intense experiencing" of the fusion of inner and outer that belongs to the arts and religion, to creative scientific work, and to imaginative living generally (Winnicott 1971, 1–14, 38–52). Fiction clearly occupies this intermediate area. From this point of view its function is to offer us imaginable bridges between the pragmatic world that presses in on us and the world of our longing and fears. The life-long addiction of some readers to the satisfaction of fiction would seem to begin, for Winnicott, in the earliest forms of childhood play.

Brian Sutton-Smith also sees in the expressive communication of mother and infant (turn-taking games, performing for each other, unison routines, contest routines, etc.) the paradigmatic enactment of a human potentiality that plays a crucial role in development (1979a, 300–2). It is paradigmatic because it is a social performance in which the infant discovers new ways of framing its relationship to the world. These will develop from solitary play imitative of the mother–child situation, through rules–negotiated games, into the sports and rituals of adulthood. The essence of play, for Sutton-Smith, is that it "opens up thought" (1979a, 315). Many games and rituals, it is true, merely socialize us to the culture we live in, but in genuinely playful activity we negate the ordinary, and open up novel frames of reference and innovative alternatives to our conventional ideas and behaviors. Play is thus "the envisagement of possibility" (1979a, 316).

Erikson, too, makes imaginative play an essential developmental mechanism. In *Toys and Reasons,* he asks what the connection is between the playing child and the play-acting adult, between the legitimate theater and the theaters of politics and war, between playful vision and serious theory, between make-believe and belief, between the child's toys and "aged reason" (1977, 26). His answer begins with examples of children's play with wooden blocks and toys. Here he sees on the child's scale of time and space "the human propensity to create model situations in which aspects of the past are re-lived, the present re-presented and renewed, and the future anticipated" (1977, 44). The child's toy constructions follow a typical pattern; there is a developmental crisis being lived through by the child, the crisis is imaged in the play constructions, new roles and identities are experimented with, and the outcome of the playful mastery in the present is renewed belief in the utopian promise of the future (1977, 44–5). Erikson is suspicious of the view that assigns play to childhood and seriousness to adult business, because in his view they are continuous:

> Play . . . is a good example of the way in which every major trend of epigenetic development continues to expand and develop throughout life. For the ritualizing power of play is the infantile form of the human ability to master reality by experiment and planning. It is in crucial phases of his work that the adult, too, "plays" with past experience and anticipated tasks, beginning with that activity in the autosphere called thinking. But beyond this, in constructing model situations not only in open dramatizations (as in "plays" and in fiction) but also in the laboratory and on the drawing board, we inventively anticipate the future from the vantage point of a corrected and shared past as we redeem our failures and strengthen our hope. (1978, 51)

This broad view of play asserts a connection between the story listening of earliest childhood, the shared performances of kindergarten, and the complex forms of adult culture. The essence of the connection is the social nature of what we do with our toys and our rituals. I hope that it is clear by now that descriptions of what happens when we read stories are only partly adequate if they account for our individual cognitive and affective responses. We have explained very little if we cannot describe the social construction of the culture that is the indispensable context for every reading response.

Kindergarten children listening to stories together on the carpet of their classroom and performing in their games what they have heard illustrate one of the crucial elements in the development of a reader: the social construction of experience and its playful expression. They also foreshadow another level of this development, because this kind of reading will shortly turn into the demanding work of learning how to decode language and master the information it conveys. The nursery schoolroom may thus be a poignant image of the transition from play to work, when some part of childhood is forever left behind.

2

Later Childhood:
The Reader as Hero and Heroine

Glenda Bissex kept a record of detailed observations about her son Paul's growth as a reader and writer between the ages of 5 and 10 (Bissex 1980). Interestingly, he became a fluent writer (of signs, letters, school exercises, lists, rhymes, "little books," home newspapers, observational notebooks, diaries, and fictional stories) before he became a fluent reader. He was a bright child in a home filled with books and all kinds of printed material, and with parents who were skilled at stimulating his linguistic abilities (his mother was a reading teacher), though he received no particular reading instructions other than being allowed to watch "Sesame Street" and "The Electric Company." I have selected and summarized some parts of his mother's very detailed analysis.

Paul's first steps as a reader predictably involve decoding titles of his favorite books, highway signs, and the labels on cereal boxes. Then he moves on to his first whole book, *Go, Dog, Go!* (at 5.7). Just before his sixth birthday he spontaneously shifts to reading silently a Dr. Seuss book, *Yertle the Turtle*. He still reads slowly and has to work at building his vocabulary, but he also says, "I just love reading" (at 6.7). Soon he is reading longer books, at home (*The Phantom Tollbooth*) and during silent reading time at school (*The Wind in the Willows*). His family moves from the country to a suburb of Boston and Paul makes new friends in the neighborhood; social activities take time away from reading. His reading grows more diversified; he begins to be interested in dictionaries and almanacs (at 7.4) and his father buys him an encyclopedia. His mother says that at age eight most of his mental energy seems to be devoted to the sheer acquisition of information. Otherwise he reads comics (*Richie Rich*), magazines (*Mad, The Electric Company, Wow*), and especially the adventure series *Tintin,* which he loved having read to him as a baby and now rereads eagerly. Around this time (8.4), he writes for a school assignment a book that contains a three-chapter story in which a piece of carpet on the stairway to the secret garage meeting place of Paul and his best friends starts to fly, carries Paul to a desert where he learns the secret of directing the carpet, and then causes all kinds of disruption in his schoolroom. The story is a fairly sophisticated one, with dialogue, description, a sense of audience, a concern for credibility, and, as his mother points out, its central themes are power and control, which run through the other stories he writes this year. His reading speed is increasing rapidly, and now something new happens; the day after Christmas (at 8.5) he picks up a new fiction book and finishes it in two sittings. Two months later he reads two of Roald Dahl's *Charlie* books while spending the day in his father's office, and that summer he stays up until one in the morning to finish *The Mad Scientists' Club*. On a weekend trip to their cottage, he packs hardly any clothes but seven books (fiction, history, and mathematics among them). He rereads a lot of his favorite books, as often as three times, and though he still talks with his mother about the informational books, he does not discuss fiction with her much any more. He reads his first adult book, *Star Wars* (at 9.8), during the universal craze about the movie. He immerses himself in the story for long periods of time, but he also treats it as an object of study and a source of information; he composes quizzes about the movie production and each of the major characters in the novel. Though he still depends on adult input when he does not know what is available, he is now mostly a self-directed reader.

Give or take some of the details, this account of Paul's growth as a reader is bound to sound familiar to the parents of any child who takes to books at an early age. To grasp just why it is so familiar, we might begin with a general picture of the psychological development children undergo at this age.

THE YOUNG READER'S WORLD

The six-year-old child, like the infant, has to construct a meaningful world out of experience, but in circumstances quite different from those of early childhood and with a different set of relationships to them because the six-year-old has changed, too.

A vivid example of these changes is schooling. The child leaves the familiar world of family and home, and enters a wider social world of peers and nonfamilial adults, where he or she is offered systematic instruction in the language and numbers that Erikson calls the "technology" of the culture (1963, 258–61). School thus responds to the child's new and speeded-up cognitive capacity to gather and organize information and to the child's new curiosity about the world beyond immediate experience that for Piaget characterizes development in the years 7 to 12 or so (Piaget and Inhelder 1969, 92–6). School is also the chief arena in which the child systematically encounters the adult world and its rules; it makes new demands, but it also offers a stage on which the growing six-year-old can perform and have his or her industry tested and rewarded.

The growth of peer culture is another way in which the setting of childhood changes. As the child grows older, close friends – "the gang" – become an alternative to the family as a milieu in which a child can learn the collective informal wisdom of the culture and the rules of social relationships as the world beyond the family practices them, and a milieu in which the skills and competences that a newly enfranchised cultural apprentice needs to acquire can be practiced.

These opportunities for dealing expertly with the world correspond to changes in the child's inner sense of self. Before, the child was the victim of impulse, often unable to hold together two perceptions or two feelings about a single thing, only transiently in control of ideas and feelings. But now the intellectual power to organize and relate information is matched by a new sense of being in command of impulses, a sense of independence and power that Robert Kegan calls "agency" (1982, 89) and Erikson calls "industry" or "competence" (1963, 259). This sense of self implies both a newly coherent relationship to other people in one's life (a sense of "role," Kegan says – as "child" in relation to parent, for example), as well as a new awareness of having private feelings, a secret life of one's own.

Thus, the growing child's experience of reading in the years 6 to 12 mirrors these changes in two important and related ways. Reading is a prime tool at one's disposal for gathering and organizing information about the wider world and learning how that world works, which is why teaching children to read is one of the main purposes of early schooling and why from the fourth grade onward primary-school learning consists largely of reading as a means of discovering new facts and ideas. But at the same time reading is a way of exploring an inner world, especially as the child gets older. Margaret Meek aptly says: "Reading is an anti-social activity for most eleven-year olds" (1982, 158). It is a way of testing the growing sense of self-possession that school-age children experience. Reading does so in the obvious sense that it is a skill to be mastered, and one that the school culture especially rewards, but it also focuses on issues of identity, in the image of the powerful or clever hero or heroine who in one guise or another is the principal archetype of most stories school-age children read. The prominence of this archetype suggests that a main reward of reading fictional stories at this age is to satisfy the need to imagine oneself as the central figure who by competence and initiative can solve the problems of a disordered world. This is why I suggest that the distinctive role readers take at this stage is to imagine themselves as heroes and heroines of romances that are unconscious analogues of their own lives.

WHAT CHILDREN READ

Can we talk about readers without talking about the books they read? Hardly. As Andre Favat points out, questions about readers' interests and responses do not make sense except in terms of the *interaction* between readers and books (1977, 5). We miss a considerable part of the evidence about readers' changing responses if we do not take into account the characteristics of the books to which they are responding.

What do school-age children read? Purves and Beach survey studies of children's reading interests going back to the turn of the century (1972, 69–84). Their evidence suggests two generalizations. One is that much of what children ages 7 to 12 read has to do with discovering information about the world they live in (books about nature, animals, adult occupations, how things work). Think of the child who becomes a specialist in dinosaurs or whales, or who follows David Macauley's intricate diagrams of how a cathedral or a skyscraper is built, or who devours biographies of historical or sports figures. The other generalization is that virtually all of the fiction read at this age is what can loosely be called adventure.

The term adventure is not very precise, but it will do for the moment. It can be applied to a considerable range of stories: from the fairy tales and animal fables that are apt to interest the youngest readers to the mysteries, mythic fantasies, and historically realistic stories that the older readers in this age group like, and from the brief and simple narratives that beginners can manage to the almost adult storytelling styles of classics such as Robert Louis Stevenson's *Treasure Island* or J. R. R. Tolkien's *The Hobbit*. There are more similarities than differences among these stories, however, and the structures and themes they share tell us much about how children read stories at this age.

On the one hand, there are the obvious adventure stories in which characters face danger and resourcefully come through it: books like Mark Twain's *Adventures of Tom Sawyer,* Jack London's *The Call of the Wild,* detective fiction like Arthur Conan Doyle's *The Hound of the Baskervilles,* and all the juvenile books whose titles begin with *The Mystery of. . .* or *The Secret of. . . .* The series books of this type – the Tom Swift and Buddy books of years ago, Enid Blyton's Famous Five and Secret Seven books, the Three Investigators series, and the innumerable Bobbsey Twins, Hardy Boys, and Nancy Drew books – are a fascinating phenomenon to which we shall return. Then there are the fantasies that involve journeys to other worlds and heroic deeds that take place there before the hero returns victoriously: older ones like Jules Verne's *Twenty Thousand Leagues Under the Sea* and more recent ones like C. S. Lewis's *The Lion, the Witch and the Wardrobe*, Madeline L'Engle's *A Wrinkle in Time*, and the all-time American best-seller, L. Frank Baum's *The Wonderful Wizard of Oz*.

But even books that involve no exotic settings or crimes solved or heroic fantasy turn out, nonetheless, to be adventures. E. B. White's *Charlotte's Web* is about a year in the life of a pig and a spider and a little farm girl, but its theme is danger faced and overcome. Laura Ingalls Wilder's *The Little House on the Prairie*, Esther Forbes's *Johnny Tremaine*, and Charles Dickens's *David Copperfield* are realistic stories, but they are all constructed around a young hero or heroine, journeys, tests of character, and harm finally defeated. Even the simple growing-up experiences of the very young Tucker children in Elizabeth Morrow's *My Favorite Age* – pulling down on their heads the contents of a shelf in their mother's closet, taking responsibility for a new dog, making gingerbread for the first time – have the motif of character defined by struggle that is the essence of adventure.

These books have more in common than the loose similarities that allow them to be called adventures. In format, plot structure, and conception of character, setting, style, and most of all the horizon of the imaginable world they imply, these books share resemblances that tell us much about just how school-age children do and do not read.

The most elementary and obvious resemblance among them is in physical appearance and format. These books are longer than the books read to pre-school children, and they have smaller print and fewer illustrations. These are not unimportant differences to the growing child; they are features that demand and respond to the newly literate reader's ability to create an imaginary world from language alone and to concentrate attention on a task for long periods of time.

At the same time, most adults would find these books extremely simple. They have uncomplicated sentences, short paragraphs, and little description of people and settings. Similes and metaphors are few (the classics written before the era of children's books, such as *Treasure Island*, or the adult books that older children read, such as *David Copperfield*, are exceptions, but children can easily skip the "boring" parts, as they readily acknowledge doing). Instead, the focus is heavily on dialogue and fast-moving action. The narrative structure of these books is apt to be fairly elementary; within the general framework of problem/journey/danger-overcome, the action is likely to consist of a series of episodes, sometimes quite repetitive, punctuated by suspenseful climaxes, that eventually lead to a decisive confrontation. Often the link between episodes is nothing more than a simple "And then. . . . " Subplots and flashbacks, or other complications of the straightforward narrative movement, are rare, at least in the younger children's stories. Foreshadowings (of who the villain is, for example) are crudely obvious by adult standards. Characters tend to be ideal types of good and bad persons. Like the settings, characters are not described in much detail, but are tagged with easily recognizable traits that are mentioned whenever they appear in the story.

Finally, adventure stories typically employ a standard repertory of narrative furnishings, either drawn straight from legendary and epic and folk sources or displaced into contemporary equivalents: exotic settings ("long ago," "far away," an ancient kingdom, a great forest, a ranch out West, a secret cave or staircase, a locked cellar or tower, an abandoned mine, a house on a wild moor), supernatural agents (witches, wizards, fairies, ghosts, angels, wise elders), semihuman figures (trolls, elves), anthropomorphized animals (calculating dragons, woodland creatures and birds and fish who talk, intelligent pets), magic talismans (rings, amulets, shoes, jewels) and weapons (specially forged swords, laser guns, and death rays), and special verbal forms (riddles, spells, curses, codes, and warnings).

Though these stories are apt to be uncomplicated, repetitive in structure, and often quite boring from an adult point of view, it is not the whole truth to say that they have simple plots and deal with stereotyped characters and settings primarily because children between ages 7 and 12 are limited in what they can cognitively grasp and affectively identify with. Their common features come in an endless variety of transformations, and children seem to be able to read hundreds of these books before they lose interest in them. We have to understand why even the most elementary and formulaic of these stories – books like the dozens of Hardy Boys and Nancy Drew adventures – can be imaginatively satisfying to readers of a certain level of ability.

The reason seems to have something to do with the combination of sameness and diversity that is common to these books. Over and over, in constantly changing settings, the heroes and heroines face new versions of danger or evil or crime, but the structure of the situations, the behavior of the characters, and above all the outcome are reassuringly familiar. The Hardy Boys or Nancy Drew stories are a kind of quintessence, a reductio ad absurdum, of juvenile fiction; the never-changing heroes or heroines and their friends move from setting to setting, continually enacting the same defeat of evil by good. But these must be powerfully appealing to school-age children, judging by their sales. The specific developmental task of children of this age, after all, is to gather and organize information about the new world they have been launched into. They have a strong interest in both its newness and its regularity; they have to keep filling in the blank spaces in their knowledge of the world, while learning the rules that prevent facts from just being random and confusing data. What to adults seems repetitive in these stories must to the child appear as confirmation that in diverse new areas of experience, what counts is still recognizable and familiar.

There also seems to be a large affective dimension in the adventure story's balance of diversity and sameness. Perhaps it has to do with the question of whether the world is going to be a place where the young child will be competent or powerless. What Frye says about romance is pertinent here. It is the literary form that deals with "the search of the libido or desiring self for a fulfilment that will deliver it from the anxieties of reality but will still contain that reality" (Frye 1957, 193). This way of putting it allows us to formulate the double function of the adventure story in the eyes of the reader: to give concrete form to threatening evil and then to assure that it will be defeated. Romance, Frye says, is the nearest of all literary forms to the wish-fulfillment dream (1957, 186). The basic structure of childhood narratives that Todorov and others have described – equilibrium/disequilibrium/equilibrium-restored – seems to arise out of the double wish, to acknowledge anxiety but to be assured of deliverance from it. The task of mastering the instruction that the culture requires the school-age child to undergo is thus not simply a cognitive one. Like the whole enterprise of learning one's way in the adult world (the journey, after all, is the major motif of romance), it involves the fundamental question of whether a child will turn out to be competent and therefore successful or defeated by fearful and evil forces. The continually reenacted victory of the heroes and heroines of juvenile narratives assures the young reader that the adventure of traveling into the world and meeting its challenges can have a happy ending.

A child of 11 or 12 is limited, however, in imagining how the conflict of good and evil can be resolved. Frye does not suggest that romance is a child-centered literary form, but he does propose that the four generic literary modes – romance, tragedy, irony-satire, and comedy – form a cycle of episodes in a total quest myth whose parts are: adventure and conflict (corresponding to romance), catastrophe (tragedy), demoralization in defeat (irony-satire), and restoration in triumph (comedy) (1957, 192). To go beyond romance in this cycle, however, requires being able to imagine wishes and dreams ending in catastrophe and death (the point of view of tragedy), or the permanent discrepancy between dreams and the ambiguous reality of actual experience (the point of view of irony and satire), or the transformation of this limited world into a new community freed from the power of death to undo it (the point of view of comedy). Young children ages 7 to 12 can scarcely imagine these possibilities, which are for the most part beyond their cognitive and affective capacities. They can certainly imagine evil people and bad actions and temporary failure (these are the staples of adventure stories), but they cannot imagine a good person whose life ends in failure (as tragedy does), or that good and evil might be inextricably mixed together (as irony and satire do). So they telescope the cycle and attach the happy ending of comedy to the adventure and conflict of romance.

This may be why so much juvenile literature consists of adventure stories, and why romance in Frye's sense seems to be the first literary form children can grasp and reproduce. It suits the way they view the world. It is the simplest way of envisioning the relationship of good and evil: to acknowledge their conflict and assert the inevitable victory of good. Though children soon outgrow simpler versions of romance that put it this way, the function of romance does not change. Adults never tire of it. Frye would say that this is because it is an essential part of the full cycle of mythic analogues of human life.

NARRATIVE STRUCTURE: COGNITIVE ASPECTS

Children's stories appear to be all plot. This is not necessarily evident in the ones written for them by adults, which often have extended descriptions of settings and of characters and their motivations, but it is clear from the stories children themselves tell that the plot is the story. In the age group we are concerned with, children make rapid advances in their ability to comprehend and construct plots. Something in the way they imagine the world responds to the organization of action in a story, and when they tell stories plot is their dominant feature. Theories of narrative and studies of the structure of children's stories shed some light on this, though the matter is far from being entirely clear.

One group of studies focuses on the structural complexity of children's stories and particularly on the number and relationship of the elementary units in them. It is clear from these studies that children become increasingly adept at both telling and recalling stories that are longer and structurally more differentiated. These studies thus confirm in a general way the Piagetian view that organizing concrete information by grouping it into classes and by relating the classes to one another hierarchically is the characteristic way of cognitively structuring experience at this stage of development, which Piaget calls the *concrete-operational stage* (roughly 6 to 11 years).

An example of this kind of study would be Botvin and Sutton-Smith's analysis of the structural complexity of stories told by children ages 5 to 10 (1977; summarized in Sutton-Smith 1981, 24–7). The Russian structuralist Vladimir Propp, in *The Morphology of the Folktale* (1968), worked out a schema of the fundamental components of the action of folk stories.

Botvin and Sutton-Smith adapt his categories to the analysis of the structural units of children's narratives. The primary units or functions represent both the motivation and the resolution of action – for example, the two basic kinds they find in children's stories at this age: villainy/versus/villainy-nullified, and lack/versus/lack-liquidated. The secondary functions are the varied concrete ways by which the primary functions are mediated, such as threat, attack, chase, defense, escape, defeat, and so forth. Using these categories Botvin and Sutton-Smith find that below age 3 children's narratives are devoid of any manifest structure; typically they are concatenations of nouns with actions only implied. Children age 4 to 6 tell stories based on a single primary function. For example, an astronaut goes into space, is attacked by a monster, but gets into his spaceship and flies away.

As children get older, the stories often have secondary elements arranged in increasingly systematic ways. A young girl is lost in the woods when night comes; an owl discovers her crying, discusses her plight with her, offers to help her, flies off and looks for the route, then leads her home, where she kisses him and promises her parents she will never go walking in the woods by herself again. At ages 7 and 8 children can expand this pattern by adding further primary functions to the story. A lion is captured and brought to a zoo, but he escapes; then a truck tries to run over him, but he gets out of the way; then he begins to get hungry, so he eats a rabbit. This one simply stops; the teller says, "The end."

By ages 9 and 10 children are able to develop appropriate secondary elements for each of the new primary functions, so that there are two or more well developed episodes. Thus, in one fairly elaborate story, Batman and Robin are in a haunted house. Robin falls through a trapdoor into an underground river, but manages to signal for help and Batman rescues him. Then they hear a scream, think it is a girl in distress and run up to the attic to rescue her. They discover that the scream has come from Spiderman, who throws an extra strong spider net over them, and says that he intends to kill them and run off with Wonder Woman in the Batmobile and live in the Bat Cave. Batman says that he needs a special key for the Batmobile and Bat Cave and when Spiderman comes to get it they overcome him and put him in jail. The step to embedding true subplots within the primary story structures is not made until later.

These results show why the ability to construct complex stories is related to cognitive abilities that develop in a systematic way. They also suggest why in the years from 5 to 10 children's stories are apt to seem episodic and repetitive; having mastered only the primary-function structure, the only way children know of expanding a tale is to repeat with slight variation the secondary elements (attack-and-defense followed by another attack-and-defense, for example), or eventually to string together more secondary elements (attack-and-defense followed by chase-and-escape). More material can be dealt with, the tale can be longer, but the available structure does not allow much internal differentiation.

Another kind of investigation that supports this conclusion about the relationship between structural complexity and cognitive development is the analysis of narratives done with "story grammars" (Rumelhart 1977; Thorndyke 1977; Stein and Glenn 1979; Mandler 1984). These are descriptions of the basic components of a story and of the logical relationships that link them, which closely match the cognitive structures (or story schemas) by which readers encode and retrieve story information. The Stein and Glenn story grammar is one of these. It conceives of a simple story as a setting plus an episode that has a structure of specific components – for example, the tale they invented about "Melvin, The Skinny Mouse." It begins with a statement of the *setting*: "Once upon a time, there was a skinny mouse named Melvin who lived in a big red barn." The basic structural components of an episode then follow. They are an *initiating event,* which changes the environment: "One day, Melvin found a box of Rice Crispies underneath a stack of hay. Then he saw a small hole in the side of box." The event is followed by *internal responses* of the character, which may include affective states and cognitions, and result in formulation of a goal: "Melvin knew how good the cereal tasted and wanted to eat just a little bit of the cereal. He decided to get some sugar first so that he could sweeten his cereal." Next come *attempts,* which are goal-directed behaviors: "Then Melvin slipped through the hole in the box and quickly filled his cereal bowl." These are followed by the *consequence* of attaining or not attaining the goal: "Soon Melvin had eaten every bit of the Rice Crispies and had become very fat." And then comes the *reaction* of the character to the consequence: "Melvin knew he had eaten too much and felt very sad." Each of these five component categories logically follows the preceding one, and the categories always occur in this specific temporal sequence (Stein and Glenn 1979, 265–6). Most stories, of course, are more complex; they consist of several episodes, and different logical relationships may connect the episodes ("meanwhile," "then," "therefore," etc.).

Story grammars have led to some interesting conclusions about children's comprehension of what they read. It is clear, for instance, that children, like adults, do expect certain types of information to occur in stories in specific temporal sequences (Stein and Glenn 1979, 282). Even preschool children can recall the correct order of events in a story, provided they correspond to the expected sequence (1979, 268). But young children do not remember deviations from the expected sequence as well as older children (1979, 274). When faced with a story that does not match their expectations, first-graders will add new information and even reorganize the story structure so that it conforms to the expected sequence (1979, 283). These younger children expect the story to follow an anticipated structure; they have not yet acquired a set of rules that will enable them to recover information from stories that do not (1979, 274). Fifth-graders also have a developed set of expectations about the kinds and sequence of information a story will contain, but they can deal with deviant structures much more readily than younger children; they can, for instance, recall information presented in inverted sequences in stories (1979, 284), suggesting that they can make correct inferences about causal relationships among parts of stories even when they do not follow the expected order. This would imply that unlike younger children who can construct a sequence only in a forward direction, the fifth-graders here can reverse logical operations (e.g., from effect to cause), a significant advance in cognitive development that Piaget ascribed to children in the concrete-operational stage.

Some of the salient components of a plot structure also emerge from the studies done with story grammars. For instance, taking the setting and the five parts of the typical episodic structure in the Stein and Glenn grammar, both first- and fifth-graders recalled the setting, the initiating event, the attempt, and the consequence just about equally well. They did not recall as accurately the character's final reaction or any of the internal responses of the character, except for the statement of the goal (1979, 276). It appears that both younger and older children remember the parts of the plot structure that relate directly to the action.

Even fifth-graders in one study (McConaughy 1982), when they were asked to rate the most important elements in a story, tended to emphasize the causal relations in the action sequences of stories and especially physical causality. That is, they focused on the initiating events and the resolutions, and on the salient attempts and outcomes that happened between the beginnings and endings. Here is one child's typical summary of a story: "A wolf had a bone in his throat and a crane helped him get it out and the reward was getting his head in and out safely" (1982, 583). In contrast, adults emphasized psychological causality, focusing like the children on initiating events and resolutions, but adding the major goals of the characters that provided a motivational tie between the beginnings and endings. Adults also made more inferences about the internal responses and dispositions of the characters. For example: "The wolf, a 'ferocious' animal, was in need of help and offered a reward for someone to help him, possibly because he knew no one would do it without a reward. The crane volunteered and did help the wolf, but obviously didn't think of any danger involved. The wolf was being quite egotistical, I feel" (1982, 583). Story grammars clearly describe more structural components of a narrative than younger children are able to take account of and respond to. But the path from action-oriented responses that emphasize the physical causality of plot to insight into the psychological roots of characters as the true motive for action is one that the developing reader must learn to walk.

NARRATIVE STRUCTURE: AFFECTIVE ASPECTS

Studies of story grammars have usually focused on the cognitive aspects of children's responses to narrative structures. Much more interesting than the purely cognitive aspects of these studies are their intimations of an affective basis for the specific plot structures of young children's stories. The Stein and Glenn grammar might be restudied from this point of view. Though its components are conceived of as categories of information, related in terms of their logical relationships, the grammar also seems to be a picture of a person trying to achieve a goal and succeeding or failing.

All discussions of plot acknowledge that what is at stake is not events, but events arranged in a significant order, incidents given some kind of intentional formal coherence by a storyteller for an audience. This crucial distinction has been formulated in a number of ways. There is E. M. Forster's early comment, that a story is "a narrative of events arranged in their time-sequence," whereas a plot "is also a narrative of events, the emphasis falling on causality": " 'The king died, and then the queen died' is a story. 'The king died and then the queen died of grief' is a plot." (1927, 130). Then there is the more technical terminology of structuralists such as Tomashevsky, Benveniste, Gennette, Chatman, and Prince. Though their terms vary, Tomashevsky's distinction between "fable" or "story" (which is the causal and chronological order of supposed events that constitute the preliterary material) and "subject" or "plot" (the narrative as actually told or written) gets at the basic difference they are all concerned with (Martin 1986, 108). It is the difference between events and events organized, in Scholes's phrase, "so as to engage the emotions and develop a theme" (1974, 78).

Even the most reductive structuralist schemas, such as Todorov's equilibrium/disequilibrium/equilibrium-restored, imply some kind of metalogical, dynamic relationship between the fundamental parts of the structure. They must be connected by value and intention; the disequilibrium is undesirable, restoring the equilibrium is a goal worth a struggle.

In a way, this is to say that plot necessarily implies character, someone for whom the actions have value and meaning, who therefore formulates a goal, who attempts to achieve it, and who reacts to success or failure (to use the terms of the Stein and Glenn grammar). Yet, as we shall see, children's stories make very little use of developed characters, their motivations, thoughts, or feelings. My point is rather that as soon as you go beyond schematizing plot elements in terms of logical relationships and envision them as the actions of *someone,* they have dynamic and affective relationships as well, even if the character is a conventional stereotype. Thus, if increasingly competent narrative skill is the mark of the 7-to-12-year-old child, it may be in part because of the child's growing ability to control not only structural strategies, but affective relationships as well.

Sutton-Smith's analysis of stories told by children ages 5 to 10 illustrates what I mean (1981, 19–24). He borrows a schema from folklorists who used it to describe levels of plot development in terms of what happens to the characters (Maranda and Maranda 1971). It is not unlike Propp's or Todorov's or the Stein and Glenn schema or Leondar's. At the lowest level of plot development, the central character is threatened or overcome by a monster, or there is some lack or deprivation and nothing is done about it. One such story (told by a girl, age 5) simply says that once upon a time there was a jungle and a lot of animals and a little girl who was scared: "Then a crocodile came in. The end" (1971, 20). The level-two stories are about escaping or being rescued, but the original threat is not nullified. For example, a girl, age 10, tells a story consisting of a series of episodes in which a tick named Henry first escapes from a hippie's hair just before it is cut, then narrowly misses being stepped on, then is almost flushed down a toilet, and so forth. In level-three stories, a character defeats the threatening force or supplies what is lacking, sometimes with the help of another character, as in the story (told by a girl, age 9) about an abandoned kitten who after a number of unpleasant adventures finds a home as a birthday present for a little girl. Finally, at the fourth level, not only is the villain defeated or the threat nullified, but there is a complete transformation of the original circumstances of the hero. A boy, age 10, tells the story of an owl named Henry Hoot who wants to get married, goes through various adventures, and in the end meets a childhood sweetheart; they have "the most beautiful wedding you can imagine," go to Niagara Falls, settle down, have two children, and "lived happily ever after" (1971, 24).

That the ten-year-olds in this sample tend to tell the higher-level stories is hardly surprising. As soon as one formulates the basic plot components as a dialectic of things feared and desired, and in terms of the ability of a character to take action against evil or to remedy a lack, the parallels with Erikson's description of the main developmental task of children in the years 7 to 12 become obvious. The levels of plot development can then be seen as phases in the ability to imagine effective agency. It is inconceivable that moving through these four levels is only the result of cognitive development. The structure of plots implies a logic of emotion as well.

One of Sutton-Smith's incidental findings also gives some support to this conclusion. He discovered that there were no sex differences across the four levels in ability to manage plot development, but that there were stylistic differences in how the solutions were arrived at; boys tended to reach level three or four by having the hero overcome the villain, whereas girls reached a solution more often by having the central character make an alliance with someone else (1981, 24). This seems to be a clear instance of affective rather than cognitive style influencing plot structures. Sutton-Smith also points out that the Marandas' data show that in cultures where there is no belief in one's ability to overcome fate, children's stories do not rise above the first or second levels (1981, 24). This too suggests that more than cognitive development accounts for the evolution of plot structures.

A more fundamental argument for the connection between plot and desire may be found in Paul Ricoeur's suggestion that narrative is inseparable from dream. He proposes that a dreamlike, fairy-tale vision of returning to the origin, a vision whose form is the circle, is prior to the heroic tale of action, whose form is linear, and that true narrative sustains both dimensions simultaneously, each episode both expanding and deepening the originary vision. He offers this idea as part of a criticism of the kind of structuralist analysis of narrative Propp and Barthes have made. He argues that taking the quest story as their paradigm of narrative has led structuralists to focus one-sidedly on the linear dimension of stories (the sequence of episodes from the challenge of the hero to the outcome), to the neglect of their "metatemporal" dimension. His argument is worth looking at in some detail, because it makes a point that is relevant to understanding both the motivations of older children reading romances and the limitations reflected in the kind they read.

Ricoeur's analysis is part of his larger project of exploring both fictional narrative and the writing of history in relation to the human experience of time, in the multiple volumes of *Time and Narrative*. The part of the argument that is pertinent here is more accessible in a 1981 essay, "Narrative Time." Here Ricoeur begins with an exposition of Heidegger's notion of the existential specificity of the human experience of being "thrown" into time, which is so poorly represented by the abstract notion of time as a linear succession of events (1981, 168). The nature of this being "within-time" can be seen in expressions such as "taking time," "having time," "wasting time," and so forth, which indicate the fundamental intentional quality of our experience of time. This leads Ricoeur to say that every narrative combines two dimensions: one *chronological*, the episodic dimension of a story as made out of events, and the other *configurational,* the pattern that makes a significant whole out of successive events (1980, 174). This pattern, which of course is the plot, he also calls the "thought" or "theme" (equivalent to Aristotle's *dianoia*) or the "point" (as in a biblical parable) (1980, 175). It differs from a one-directional linear succession of events, because not only do its episodes lead to an ending, but its end is implied in its beginning, so that we can read the story time backward as well as forward (recall that this was the most complete kind of plot structure described by Applebee – see Chapter 1).

Adding this configurational dimension to the chronological dimension discloses why the narrative experience of time cannot be reduced to the kind of atemporal formula sought by the structuralists. Plot does more than move events forward. It "repeats" (repeats thematic motifs, I would think Ricoeur means) and therefore "deepens" our thematized experience of time. Even quest stories, Ricoeur says, work this way. When the hero or heroine goes astray in a dark wood at the beginning of the tale and meets a devouring beast (as in "Little Red Riding Hood," for example), we are not just introduced to the mischief that is to be suppressed, rather we are brought into a primordial space and time that is more akin to the realm of dreams than to the sphere of action. And as the tale unfolds this dimension deepens with it, so that "two qualities of time are thus intertwined: the circularity of the imaginary travel and the linearity of the quest as such" (1981, 181).

Ricoeur's proposal of the psychological priority of dream to action and their simultaneous combination in narrative does not at first seem to be confirmed by the stories that interest, say, ten-year-olds. The general picture of their development suggests that they have made the transition from a world organized largely as a dream to a world imagined in terms of action. Though romance is their preferred form of story, most of the stories they read and all of the ones they tell have rather simple plots in which episodes repetitively enact an elementary structure such as challenge-attempt-response until the final goal is successfully achieved. And, though these stories leave no doubt about the goodness of the starting point and the badness of the challenging evil that is to be remedied, there is very little sense in the Bobbsey Twins or the Hardy Boys books of an originating dream vision that is deepened or expanded (much less changed or darkened) by each episode of the action. Dream has simply been replaced by action, not fused integrally with it. Is this a complete picture?

It may be that Ricoeur is describing a mature kind of narrative that is beyond the capacity of young children to recognize or enter into, one that depends on a reader's or teller's ability to take more complex views of good and evil, to hold together more potential meanings, to have a more fully reversible sense of the causal implications of character and action than ten-year-olds can master. We know that children organize their world spatially before they can do it temporally, and that the acquisition of a time sense during the concrete-operational period requires that they de-center from their dependence on a spatially concrete understanding of the world. Does the linearity of the romance plot reflect the young child's new grasp of time relationships? Then the reason that this kind of plot is not more than linear (in Ricoeur's sense, that is, that the only way of elaborating the space between the challenge and the outcome is by repeating simple structures that do not deepen the original vision of the goal) is not because the child of ages 7 to 12 is indifferent to the desires and fears of the dream world that was the only world the child once knew, but because he or she cannot yet make the kind of intentional connection between events and developing character that a complex plot requires.

One might wonder too whether the quest story is not inherently more limited – by the kind of organization that the structuralists have accurately described – than Ricoeur allows. Perhaps his ideal narrative is something like Frye's complete cycle of romance-tragedy-irony-comedy and the quest story reflects only the first part of this cycle. If so, we can readily understand why it is within the grasp of ten-year-olds and why it has the elementary structure it does.

Nonetheless, the suggestion of a relationship between dream and narrative is important. The plots of the stories children tell and many of the ones they read at this age may not be skillfully built out of episodes that expand and deepen a central vision of primordial wishes and fears. Still, it helps our understanding of narrative to see that even the simplest ones have both chronological and configurational dimensions, and that plot is always in some sense the working out of desire, even if only of the most conventional kind. The best children's adventure books sustain both dimensions, and the routine ones at least offer practice in the apprenticeship of reading at this level.

Ricoeur's analysis suggests one further observation about the relationship of plot to children's cognitive grasp of the world in the years 7 to 12. Scholes and Kellogg argue that among the Greeks narrative developed out of myth when two things happened: a linear concept of time began to replace cyclic time and literature got separated from religious ritual and began to respond to aesthetic criteria (1966, 22ff.). Does this parallel the shift in the child's imagined world, from dream to action?

CHARACTER

When we first meet Dorothy in L. Frank Baum's *The Wonderful Wizard of Oz*, she is standing in the doorway of Uncle Henry's and

Auntie Em's farm looking at the Kansas prairie. We are told what she sees – the broad sweep of flat country, the gray plowed land, the blistered paint on the house – but we are not told what she thinks about it. The anonymous narrator tells us that Dorothy came to the farm as an orphan and that Auntie Em was startled by Dorothy's merry voice and surprised that she found anything to laugh at. One of the things that makes her laugh, we are told, is her dog Toto, whom she loves dearly. When the storm comes, Dorothy is halfway across the room on her way to the cyclone cellar, when suddenly she loses her footing and the house rises into the air. The events are described but all we know about Dorothy's reactions is that she sat very still; a bit later we are told that she had been frightened and now felt lonely, but that because nothing happened she stopped worrying and resolved to wait calmly and see what the future would bring.

What it brings in the second chapter, of course, is an abrupt landing among the Munchkins. We are told what Dorothy sees – the fair countryside and the people (no taller than she is) and what they are wearing. She is astonished to discover that the house has killed the wicked Witch of the East, but her conversation with the Munchkins is a model of just how a polite little girl of 1900 should talk to strangers. She says that Aunt Em has told her that the witches were all dead years and years ago, but when the Witch of the North explains that that may be true of civilized countries like Kansas but not of Munchkinland, Dorothy is quite willing to believe her. And when she discovers (from a magic cap that turns into a slate with a message on it) that the only way of getting back to Kansas it to undertake the journey to the City of Emeralds where the Wizard lives and that she has to go alone, Dorothy calmly sets out on the yellow brick road with Toto for company and the dead witch's silver shoes on her feet.

From then on we learn about Dorothy's character in the same three ways we have in the first two chapters: through what she does, what she says, and (to a much lesser extent) what the narrator tells us about her thoughts. And what we learn about Dorothy's character can be summed up in three statements. She is a perfectly good little girl, not unusual in any way except in the unusual things that happen to her (though perhaps being perfectly good also counts as unusual). She is exactly the same kind of person at the end of the story as she was at the beginning. And we know next to nothing about her inner feelings, thoughts, or motivations, because the narrator gives us only the briefest and most conventional glimpses of her reactions.

In short, to use one set of critical terms (Rimmon-Kenan 1983), the method of characterization Baum uses is to tell us directly some things about Dorothy, but for the most part to let us see her indirectly, by what she does and what she says during her unusual adventures (1983, 59–67).

And so far as the kind of character Dorothy is, we can say that if characters can be classified along three polar axes, then in terms of *complexity*, she is a rather simple character with a few distinctive traits, in terms of *development*, she is a static character, and in terms of *penetration into her inner life*, she is a character seen mostly from the outside (1983, 41–2). This approach to fictional characterization suggests some ways of thinking about how children ages 7 to 12 imagine the characters in the stories they read.

It is only a slight exaggeration to say that in children's stories characters are what they do. They are presented almost entirely in action and dialogue. Nancy Drew is occasionally described in a kind of photo caption style, in *The Secret of Shadow Ranch*, for example: "Titian-haired Nancy was a trim figure in her olive-green suit with matching shoes. Beige accessories and knitting bag completed her costume." We are given brief glimpses of her reactions: "Nancy's eyes sparkled with interest." We even read about her thoughts, though these are scarcely introspective and center almost entirely on the events of the story: "Was it a threat or a well-meant warning? Nancy could not make up her mind. Although Dave was gruff, Nancy liked his straight-forward manner." What really defines Nancy, though, are a few idealized traits (she is good looking, well dressed, can buy whatever she needs, and has permission from her widowed father to do just about anything she wishes), a set of equally idealized personal relationships (she is popular with her friends, their clear leader, well liked by the good adults, and attractive to all the most handsome boys), and especially all the things she can do (drive a sports car, ride a horse, fly a plane, bake a cake, use a compass, win a square-dancing prize, and, of course, solve crimes).

There are good reasons why characters in these stories are presented in terms of a few distinctive traits and many incidents. Children ages 7 to 12, Piaget would say, are concrete, dualistic thinkers; a thing is either in one category or another. The idea of a complex character, with shades of light and dark, is difficult to grasp. For example, the inner feelings of fictional characters do not seem to be of great interest to children at this age (Winner 1982, 299). Young readers can understand them if they are presented directly in the story by the narrator, but children don't appear to be interested in assigning them much causal value in explaining behavior; this does not happen until ages 8 and 9 (Leondar 1977, 181). The reason may be that children at this age have just succeeded in disentangling from their undifferentiated experience a sense of themselves as being able to take a role and have their own inner lives (Kegan 1982, 89), but this newly emerged self-concept is still unitary and concrete – a specific acting person, not yet a unique and authentic inner self with opinions, beliefs, and values (Broughton 1978, 80) – therefore a doer rather than a reflector. And so, as Scholes and Kellogg observe, if as a writer you do not develop the inner life of a character, then your only other resources for developing a story are plot, commentary, description, allusion, and rhetoric (1966, 171). Other than plot, these are all unlikely to be appealing strategies to a ten-year-old reader, for obvious reasons.

Scholes and Kellogg might have added dialogue to their list of strategies used to develop a story. It deserves attention because in children's stories what is not action is apt to be dialogue. But in a sense dialogue is a kind of action. More precisely, it is a means of presenting interaction among the characters. Its chief purpose seems to be to establish social relationships, which of course in these stories are presented as simple, unchanging, and based on external behavior, as the characters themselves are. *Manners* would seem to be an important aspect of children's fiction, as of course learning the rules that govern social relationships, especially among peers, is an important part of the life of the school-age child. This explains the prominence of chums, buddies, "the girls," and "the guys" in these stories, the gang of friends that surrounds the hero or heroine, a displaced version of the band of warrior companions in epic tales. The intimate relationships of family and lovers are not the subject of these stories, nor are the larger social relationships that will later be created by work or citizenship. The issues in these stories are learning to get along with peers and learning how to talk to them.

Is it fair to call the characters in these stories flat or stereotypes? Or to say that character is a negligible element in children's stories in comparison with action? Hardly. If children are limited in their capacity to imagine and identify with complex characters who develop and change as the story goes on and have elaborate inner lives, the converse is also true; they can readily imagine and identify with a character defined by the right traits and relationships and skilled at the right tasks, and they do not tire of seeing this kind of character repeatedly exercise these traits and skills in the kind of episodic tale that most adult readers would find tedious. Good children's stories illustrate as well as adult fiction the point behind the much-quoted questions of Henry James, "What is character but the determination of incident? What is incident but the illustration of character?" (1986, 174). Martin offers a formula, borrowed from Genette, to describe this relationship: $A \times C = k$ (action times character equals a constant). That is, if the emphasis is on plot, there is little room for complexity of character; if a character is complex, then even everyday incidents become interesting (Martin 1986, 117). We might alter this slightly by saying that attention to plot *requires* characters who are constants or that a strong stable character seen from the outside *requires* the elaboration of incident.

A simply drawn character can be a very powerful one. Scholes and

Kellogg point to Homer's portrayal of Achilles in *The Iliad*. The very
clarity of this kind of character and the predictability of his behavior is
a virtue in the eyes of the child. He needs to be right and to act correctly,
rather than be drawn in detail (1966, 161–3). The adult reader of Tolkien's
The Hobbit can find in Bilbo Baggins enough touches of complexity and
ironic coloring to make him entertaining, but his usefulness to the tale
is not because of his domestic idiosyncrasies or the nursery satire he
makes possible, but because once the adventure is launched he has all
the virtues of the quest hero: bravery, skill, leadership, and supernatural
protection. The fact that these virtues are almost identical with Nancy
Drew's or Dorothy's or Sherlock Holmes's suggests that the type is
important, not the individualized character.

The type raises some interesting questions. Why is Dorothy an orphan,
Nancy Drew motherless, and Bilbo Baggins's ancestry mysteriously
tainted by the Took connection? One answer is that the mysterious-
birth-of-the-hero archetype so common in mythological literature (explored by Otto Rank, Lord Raglan, and Joseph Campbell) has found its
way into the common store of story-telling themes. There is also a
Freudian explanation, that this is a residue of the Oedipal conflict; young
children readily fantasize that they should have the full attention of the
opposite-sex parent or that as foundlings they can begin their lives again
with the parents they deserve rather than the ones they have (Lehrman
1927). Davis gives this Oedipal situation a Marxist turn by interpreting
parentlessness or the fantasy of adoption as a defense against the conviction of being alienated from the kind of ideal family community that
the conditions of modern life no longer allow (1987, 132–3). There is
also a modified and more obvious psychosocial explanation – family
issues are not the subject of the books children ages 7 to 12 read; the
heroes and heroines of these books have to be at least psychologically
parentless if they are to be convincing models of world mastery – that
is, if they are to be what the young reader wants to become and has
started on the way to being, but realistically cannot yet be. There is also
a cognitive explanation in the fact that children's idealized views of their
parents' authority and omniscience are often discovered to be wanting
just in these years when they go to school and begin to acquire skills
and learn information on their own. Their new cognitive abilities often
lead them to be certain about what is really fragmentary knowledge, to
make assumptions about what they know and what their parents do not
know. This "cognitive conceit," as Elkind calls it, is the source of the
theme, common to many children's books, of the smart child who gets
the better of stupid adults (1981a, 80).

Why are the characters in these books simple when children themselves
at this age are undoubtedly complex? Two possible explanations appear

to go in different directions, but are quite compatible, I think. The obvious one is that fictional characters represent what children at this age *want to be*; they are the fantasized embodiments of the unambiguous virtue, skill, popularity, and adult approval that will resolve confusion about identity. The other explanation is that they represent what children *were* and are reluctantly giving up. Elkind points out that children are apt to have ambivalent feelings about the transition to adulthood, an attitude embodied so vividly in Peter Pan, who has never abandoned the clarities and certainties of childhood (1981a, 81). Similarly, Favat thinks that the reason children ages 6 to 8 eagerly read fairy tales (and then contemptuously abandon them when they are a year or two older) is that these stories preserve a simpler magical world view that the developing child is painfully learning to abandon (1977, 49). These two functions may obviously be divided among the characters in a story (it is easy to imagine a child admiring Dorothy or Nancy Drew or Bilbo Baggins, while feeling superior to the Cowardly Lion and the Scarecrow, the rather dull friends and collaborators of Nancy, and the hesitant comrades of Bilbo Baggins). But in a deeper sense, the central characters in these stories may themselves *simultaneously* represent both what children want to be and what they once were (Berg illustrates this point with some good anecdotes of children reading, 1977, 38–40). Every developmental advance is a new perspective on the way one used to think; the most persuasive ideal that a child can conceptualize at this age may be a reimagining of what he or she used to be.

It is important to notice, however, that the idealized characters that young readers identify with may not always be ideal in any sense that their parents and teachers would approve of. The point has often been made that a large measure of the appeal of a book to any reader is its capacity to satisfy impulses for wish fulfillment and instinctual gratification. Both Lesser's and Holland's psychoanalytic accounts of the appeal of fiction, cited in the previous chapter, employ this notion. It is also a central topic in one of the most thorough and thoughtful accounts of the appeal of books to young readers, chapter four of the study Frank Whitehead and his colleagues did for the Schools Council in Britain in the 1970s (Whitehead, Capey, Maddren, and Wellings 1977). Wishes, of course, may go toward a range of potential satisfactions, but critics of the quality of children's books and of their motives in reading them who take the wish-fulfillment point of view often argue that the gratifications offered by many popular books are frivolous, if not wholly debased. One of Whitehead's own studies offers some support for this view. It concludes that ten of the most popular secondary school books in Britain (including *Treasure Island, A Tale of Two Cities,* and *Silas Marner*) appealed to readers to the degree that they could identify with the central characters, that the wish-fulfillment element was strong, and that the themes were emotionally immature (1977, 213–14). However, Whitehead and his colleagues are reluctant to settle for this view of the matter. They introduce D. W. Harding's reservations about the notion of "identification" as an explanation of a reader's involvement with a work of fiction, and especially Harding's observation (cited in the previous chapter) that as readers we take both a "participant" and an "onlooker" stance, which allows us simultaneously to be involved in the action and to evaluate it from a variety of perspectives that go beyond simply identifying with a central character (Harding 1968a). Moreover, they argue, as children get older they tolerate outcomes that are more realistic than wish fulfilling and indeed expect to encounter in stories unpleasant and even disturbing material – a conclusion that, I think, the evidence about adolescent reading in the following chapter strongly endorses. The Whitehead group (1977, 225) concludes that any satisfactory account of the appeal of reading fiction will have to include both the imaginative sharing of a character's experience, which is generally called "identification," with its strong suggestion of wish fulfillment and the evaluative judgments made in the name of a realistic acceptance of experience by the reader in the role of spectator. We shall come back to these issues later. For the moment, it is enough to see that for young readers the appeal of a character in a story can be grounded in powerful affective affinities, even when the character is sketched in terms that, cognitively speaking, are far from what a mature reader would demand.

FICTION AND INFORMATION:
TWO POINTS OF VIEW

To the five-year-old child reading is a form of play; its content is a world of images undifferentiated according to whether they are real or made-up. The ten-year-old, however, has begun to learn to read books in two different ways, some for the satisfaction of being able to imagine oneself in this world, but others for a much different purpose: to acquire information. Is this the root of the distinction between fiction and nonfiction? And, though school-age children can operate with increasing competence on both levels, what does the distinction mean to them? Let us go back for a moment to a circumstance mentioned at the beginning of this chapter, that these are the years when children begin formal schooling. This change has enormous consequences, even though it has been intensively prepared for. One result is that activities that before were entirely play now become skills to be mastered. Being read to was entertainment; learning to read for oneself is work. It is a long and arduous process and by no means a successful one for every child who begins it. And it seems that the more competent a child becomes at reading, the more likely he or she is to read in two different ways. And the nonfictional way of reading even may eventually change the way the child reads fiction.

Chall's description of the process of learning to read will help to make this point clear (1983, 13–26). She divides the process into six stages. In the prereading stage (ages 0 to 6), children mainly learn the syntax and words of spoken language, but in a literate culture they also accumulate considerable knowledge about written language; they can name the letters of the alphabet, print their names, recognize words on road signs and packages, and pretend to read books. In the first stage of actual reading (grades one and two), children learn the relationship between the arbitrary alphabet system and spoken language. Chall calls this the "decoding" stage. In the second stage (grades two and three), children consolidate this ability, interiorizing their decoding skills, gaining speed and fluency by reading many books whose stories or subjects are familiar or whose structure is recognizable (as in fairy tales). The greater the practice and the greater the immersion, says Chall, the greater the chance of developing the fluency needed to advance to the accomplishment of the next stage. The third stage (grades four to eight or nine) is the beginning of the long course of reading to learn new knowledge, information, thoughts, and experiences – of relating print to ideas. In the early years of this stage, what children learn is largely conventional information about the world and about how things in it work (the fourth grade is traditionally the point where children begin to study subject areas such as history and geography), but gradually their range of knowledge and ideas increases, as does their ability to analyze what they read and to react critically to the different viewpoints they read. In this stage, prior knowledge and experience become important for understanding new ideas, and children have to learn the process of finding information efficiently in what they read. The fourth stage (high school) differs from the third in that it involves the ability to deal with multiple points of view and with complex information and concepts that technical textbooks might present. In the last of Chall's stages (college and beyond), reading is essentially a constructive and reconstructive activity involving the analysis, judgment, and synthesis of ideas into one's own point of view. This requires knowledge of the subject and broad general knowledge, as well as the ability to construct knowledge on a high level of abstraction and generality.

It seems that the direction of this process is toward a kind of reading that consists of sophisticated decoding (and eventually reorganizing and constructing) of information and ideas. A literate culture obviously puts a premium on this skill. Indeed, a literate culture may structure our consciousness to produce this kind of direction once we start to learn to read. Walter Ong points to some of the changes involved in the historical shift from an oral to a literate culture. One of the chief changes is that writing presents words decontextualized from the setting in which they occur when spoken – that is, they are not the words of a real person speaking to other persons in a specific setting. Without the expressive connotations of a context, written words lack the full emotional tone they have in speech (Ong 1982, 101). Instead they achieve their power by means of precision, analytic exactitude, and nuance of meaning (1982, 105). (Note that in Chall's description the age at which the child begins to read for information corresponds to the age at which the child also stops sounding words and reads silently and privately.) Writing thus leads us to treat words as signs to be decoded, Ong says (1982, 75), as things rather than as events (1982, 91).

A literate culture teaches a child to read from this point of view. Donaldson makes a similar point; a technological culture values "disembedded" thinking, the manipulation of symbols abstracted from the concrete circumstances in which they occur in ordinary experience. Learning to read language that is free of nonlinguistic context encourages self-conscious reflection about one's thinking and therefore control of the directions one's thinking takes, characteristic features of the kind of thinking that logic, mathematics, and the sciences will employ (1978, 95–7).

From age 6 onward, then, all of the child's study of reading, and much of the actual reading a child does, will be done under the auspices of school. And especially as a child moves through grade school, school reading turns increasingly toward information and explanation. Later, self-consciousness about the rules of thinking will be added as a norm, but in grade school facticity is the primary norm for this kind of reading. Yet children also continue to read fictional stories in school (though more and more in reading class primarily), and out of school many are avid readers at this age. In fact, the reading peak, when children do most voluntary reading, seems to occur at about ages 12 and 13 (Purves and Beach 1972, 85). How does their increasing competence at informational reading affect the way they read fiction?

It is probable that children who are good readers manage, in the grade school years, to read from both the informational and fictional points of view without much trouble and without feeling any need to resolve what older children and adults may think are contradictory implications in these points of view. The egocentrism of concrete-operational thinking readily allows children to live in the realms of both fact and of fictions that they would like to be true. It is also true that both fictional and informational reading exercise many of the same reading skills children develop during this period. However, there is some evidence that as children read more widely, especially under the influence of school, they are likely to become increasingly aware of the distinction between fiction and nonfiction. And sometimes by the end of this period children have developed judgments about the relative value of one kind of reading against the other.

We have already seen from the stories they tell that children as early as age 5 or 6 have some grasp of what is involved in the fictional point of view. That is, they can establish a boundary between events inside the story and those outside it, and keep themselves out of the stories they tell (Winner 1982, 319–21). They use the conventional markers to indicate the special status of the story (opening and closing phrases, such as "Once there was..." and "The End," and consistent past tense) (Applebee 1978, 36). They use a special tone of voice when telling a story (Sutton-Smith 1981, 31–2). They have firm expectations about stock characters and situations, which suggests that they are learning the repertory of archetypes that the culture supplies to storytellers (Applebee 1978, 47–51). They get better at distinguishing between fictional and real-world facts; quite a number of six-year-olds are still apt to think that a favorite character like Cinderella was a real person who lived far away or a long time ago, but by age 9 they hardly ever say this (Applebee 1978, 43).

Most interesting of all – we have seen the early traces of this development in the first chapter – they are clearly able to take the point of view of an *implied narrator,* someone who reports objectively and impersonally the events of the story, who can follow the characters and the actions wherever they lead across space and time, and who maintains a uniform distance between the story events and the real-world concerns of the storyteller and audience (Leondar 1977, 177–9). They also get better at managing the point of view of this narrator in several ways. Whereas their early stories are limited to one kind of impersonal narrator, who knows only the kind of facts and events that an external observer could see, the stories of older children provide information about the inner lives of characters. And the distanced, impersonal observer often yields, by age 10, to a first-person narrator who tells the story from inside his or her own experience – a development closely correlated, Leondar notes, with the appearance of psychological motivation in characterization (1977, 184). Of course, this anticipates the later accomplishment of mastering much more complicated narrative points of view, such as Booth explores in *The Rhetoric of Fiction.* Other developments in reading fluency include mastering stories where the narrative point of view shifts from one character to another for extended periods of time, or where the distance shifts regularly from long shot to close-up.

From what we have seen of plot structure, we also know that children become increasingly adept at telling, and therefore even more so at comprehending, longer and increasingly differentiated kinds of stories. A related fact is that children are increasingly able to disengage a story from its concrete form and to grasp it and talk about it as a whole. Whereas six-year-olds who are asked to discuss a story often simply retell it in a form as close as possible to the way they heard it, nine-year-olds are more likely to synopsize it or summarize briefly "what it is about" (Applebee 1978, 92–4). Here is one written comment Applebee records, from a boy age 9.3: "I think that the Famous Five stori's are quite good. In the storis there is a lot of adventure and a lot of things happen. They get bad luke at the beginning and thing all kam out all right in the end" (1978, 94). Because these summaries are usually in the present tense rather than the past tense of typical narration and often involve, as in this example, elementary generalizations about the kind and quality of the story, it seems that this nine-year-old can at least in a rudimentary sense conceive of a story as an artifact that can be described and evaluated. Finally, it seems obvious that as children reach the stage where their reading turns from the familiar to the new, fiction serves equally well as nonfiction as a source of information about the world and how it works and how people behave in it.

Still, the groundwork seems to have been laid for some kind of separation between factual and fictional reading. In interviews with readers at every age from early adolescence onward, I have found that almost everyone at some point spontaneously distinguishes between reading done out of a sense of duty and reading done for fun. The obligatory reading is associated with school by students of all ages and with professional work by teachers and librarians, but even adults who have no academic or professional reasons to read say there is a difference between what they read because they ought to and what they read for enjoyment. The obligatory reading is usually nonfiction or the kind of fiction that demands close attention and analysis; the pleasure reading is usually romance fiction or travel or autobiography, forms often not very far removed from romance. The roots of this attitude are no doubt complex, but one seems to be that early schooling turns reading into work and that it gradually gives priority to facticity as the criterion of successful reading.

THE PROCESS OF GROWTH

So far, this chapter has attempted to describe how children read stories in the years 7 to 12. Focusing on a six-year span like this requires making some large generalizations about the period as a whole. Yet it is obvious that children go through a number of transitions within this stage of their development: entering it, maturing to the point where they embody its characteristics most visibly, and then by degrees leaving it for another. What does the reading of school-age children look like when viewed as a continuous process of change?

In the early part of this period, the young reader is acquiring a new point of view toward reading. What before was a kind of magical play in a world where the boundaries between dream and reality were easily and pleasurably blurred becomes a much more organized task. School demands that the child master the task, but of course it also offers the opportunity to control an experience that others had to provide before. The child who begins school is also an apprentice learner about the world and an apprentice performer on that world's stage who has to learn how to organize vast amounts of new information and what rules people follow to relate to one another. Reading is a tool of discovery that can be adapted to the service of this need to learn and organize information. But reading not only images the world; in story form, it also images the reader's role in the world. And at this stage, the role it offers is the story version of the role of performer on the wider stage of school and neighborhood that the culture now calls on the child to fill. So it is not surprising that the young child's view of reading (say in the years 6 to 9) mirrors both of these preoccupations – learning and mastering – and does so in the simple forms suited to beginners: uncomplicated structures, unambiguously good and bad characters, clear issues, an easily identifiable and admirable protagonist. The characteristic literary mode in these years is romance, because it is the simplest version of the fantasy of competence, a story about having one's wish to be successful come true because of the way one skillfully acts.

The reader between the ages 6 and 9 does not discover this story all at once; some of it he or she already knows from infancy, but as an independent reader and as an apprentice learner about how the world is organized the child now has to assemble the parts of the story anew. The child is thus a kind of collector, systematically adding to and rearranging the jumble of images acquired as a little child. He or she needs to acquire the whole repertory of images and themes that the culture has gathered around the primary form of storytelling called romance. Breadth of reading and repetition have a lot to do with this increasing competence, as they do with all learning at this age.

If the first years of this way of reading are marked by establishing and consolidating its most elementary forms, what does the midpoint of the movement through this process look like? I suggest that a useful index of what is typical at this stage of development are the juvenile series books, those numerous installments of the adventures of the Rover Boys,

Tom Swift, the Bobbsey Twins, Ruth Fielding, Nancy Drew, and the Hardy Boys and more up-to-date heroines and heroes, which have been part of the scene in the United States since the late 1800s.[1] Though educators and librarians have argued about their literary merit, sales numbers and research clearly testify to their popularity. They sell in millions of copies annually,[2] and surveys and studies have shown that at various times they have been the most popular books read by fifth, sixth, and seventh graders (Soderbergh 1980, 69). In addition, the students with the highest IQs are often the heaviest readers of these books (1980, 69). Interestingly, one group of library science graduate students at Columbia turns out to have been devoted to series books as children (Vandergrift 1980, 118). Written to formula by stables of anonymous writers, the most popular books are regularly revised and updated so that the surface details will match their readers' experience; yet they are about as far from what teachers of literature think of as books as one can imagine. No grace of language, no subtlety of characterization, no individual authorial voice distinguishes them. Yet as often happens with mediocre or indeed banal literature, they can be a more useful guide to how a child midway through this stage conceives of a story than unique books that earn the praise of literate adults.

They are useful because you can chart children's growing interest in these books, the peak of their involvement with them, and their waning fondness for them. One thirteen-year-old boy said of the Hardy Boys books: "They're all the same." When asked how many he had read before he came to that conclusion, he answered: "I don't know, fifteen or twenty maybe." This number does not come anywhere near Bobbie Ann Mason's claim that she had read "all forty" of the Bobbsey Twins books "at least a dozen times each" by the time she was ten or eleven (1975, 29).

Mason's discussion of the series books about girl detectives is a shrewd analysis, which invites one or two qualifications from a developmental perspective. She has contradictory feelings about these books; they were the sources of her childhood dreams, yet it is clear to her in retrospect that they present undiluted the conventional sexist, racist, and materialistic values of the mainstream culture, that their characters are superficial and thin, their plots elementary and repetitive, and that the idea of women they offer to the children who read them is fundamentally false. In hindsight, all these charges have merit. Popular literature mirrors popular values; it does not call them into question. And children's books are written by adults whose values are transmitted in them. Mason's comments are symptomatic of a fairly widespread effort to scrutinize the social and political attitudes children learn from their reading (see, for example, Dixon 1977; Dorfman 1983; Green 1979, 1984; Zipes 1984). This is potentially a very promising line of inquiry, if it alerts parents and teachers to the implications of what they encourage children to read and provided it does not encourage narrow-minded censorship on the one hand or the proliferation of naively didactic books with *good* values in them on the other. In one sense, though, criticism of the inadequacy of children's books misses an important point. Conventional values, type characters, simple plots and one-sided ideals are exactly what ten- or eleven-year-olds expect to find in stories. Indeed, they are what they need to find in them if the stories are to be at all satisfying or meaningful to them, because this is the way the world looks as far as they have succeeded in putting it together for themselves.

Repetitive reading of these stories is a clue to their attraction. Not only is one book very much like another in the series, but the true fan may reread the same book "at least a dozen times." We tend to suppose that mature readers reread to discover subtleties and relationships missed the first time through, but that does not seem to be involved here. Mason compares reading the Bobbsey Twins to an addiction, a repeated attempt "to assuage a confused longing, only to have it deepened" (1975, 47). Perhaps the wish to be reassured about one's image of oneself and the world drives the series fan forward. Indeed, this may be a more general motive for reading at this age. Favat speculates that the repetitive, patterned quality of fairy tales and the symmetry of structure that Propp discovered in folktales may appeal to growing children precisely because these qualities suggest the reassuring orderliness of a stable and reliable world at a point in children's lives when their own views of the world are changing so quickly: "It does not take children long to learn that having had the kind of experience they had with one tale, they can have it again with any tale. The reassurance is there from tale to tale, as it is not necessarily from one art story to another" (1977, 53). Inglis talks about his own childhood reading of Enid Blyton's series books:

> Partly I read them for their utter unreality. The adventures were such as to hurt no one, and I wanted to be sure of painlessness. Partly I read them for the untaxing safety of their stereotypes – the facility with which the children won the day to the amazed acclamation of parents and police, the unrufflable, wholly impossible calm of big boys, the clinging unreliabilty of little girls. Indeed, I was hardly troubled by the notion of 'character' at all. I wanted the placid, predictable turn and return of events, and Enid Blyton, who, as George Orwell said of Frank Richards, could only be a syndicate of writers packed into one body, served up the looked-for safety of stories essential to the regular repair-time which we all of us take out of dealings with the difficult world. (1981, 65–6)

Adults who repetitively read one kind of book may be expressing a resistance to change that, as Davis argues, we ought to counter by a self-conscious, politically resistant kind of reading (1987, 18–19), but in school-age children, repetition may better be thought of as a transitory phase that serves the positive function, as Favat suggests, of reassuring young readers of the potential stability of the world precisely when so much of what they discover puts that notion in question.

It may not even be the content of the book so much as the experience of it that counts for the addict. Why otherwise would children reread the same simple book? One study of comic-book readers discovered that children who are fans (distinguished from moderate readers or those indifferent to comics) often could not even recall the plots of comic-book stories they had just read. What satisfied them apparently was being absorbed in a mood or "aura," escaping into a world where they could imagine themselves as powerful heroic figures (Wolf and Fiske 1949, 13, 29). Nell reports a vivid case of "reading gluttony": a text gobbler who speed read books hoping that he could forget them so as to be able to have exactly the same experience when he read them again (1988, 238–9).

A further clue to this response is C. S. Lewis's essay "On Stories" (1966) and the distinction he makes between "excitement," arising from the alternate tension and appeasement of anxiety that a good plot provides, and the "atmosphere" of a powerfully imagined world – in his case, the world of "redskins," giants, pirates, epic figures – that a reader can get lost in. The former pleasure, though real, can necessarily be enjoyed only once, because in rereading surprise is gone. Atmosphere, though, can be enjoyed over and over: "It is the *quality* of the unexpectedness, not the *fact* that delights us" (1966, 17). This is not a distinction between good and poor quality literature; Lewis sees that "sensational" literature like H. Rider Haggard's *King Solomon's Mines* may for some readers have more atmosphere than classics do. The experience of involvement, which slightly older readers often identify as their most characteristic response to a good story (see Chapter 3), may be composed of both these reactions that Lewis identifies.

One further comment about repetitive reading of series books. Mason says that the trappings of the mystery genre – the crooks and clues and gothic settings – are there "to glamorize the trespass into adulthood" (1975, 16). Literate and technological cultures postpone the child's entrance into real adulthood and multiply the tasks and credentials to be mastered along the way. The juvenile romance about the girl or boy detective is a fantasy of what maturity will be like; it may need repeating dozens of times in dozens of variations before a ten-year-old is satisfied that it is a possible future.

Of course these stories offer a false ideal to boys as well as to girls. That is one reason why children outgrow them. They begin to find them unrealistic. What leads to this discovery?

Curiously, one of the factors that builds up and consolidates the child's view of the story world in the early part of this stage undermines it in the last part of the stage: wider knowledge and experience and wider reading. The more he or she learns about the world, the more a child realizes that the vision of romance is an inadequate picture of it. People are more complicated than the heroes and villains of adventure stories. Events and characters are connected by more subtle links than suspense. There is more to becoming an adult than solving crimes or slaying dragons. It is not simply that romance pictures the world imperfectly; the child's view of the world enlarges, and what was an adequate way of making sense out of the world no longer is.

To put it briefly, character becomes more important than action. A boy or girl age 10 to 13 is interested in and can imagine the thoughts and feelings of others in ways that are beyond the capacity of children ages 7 to 10. Their growing self-consciousness about their own inner states, their contradictory and unresolved feelings, and their confused thoughts find no mirror in the underdeveloped characters of adventure stories, certainly not in the eternal juveniles of the series books. So they look for stories about people who are not simply good or bad, stories about intentions and motives and points of view and how they might conflict even in well-meaning people. In short, their own role as readers changes and the attitudes toward stories that satisfied them as juveniles no longer work for them as adolescents.

Is it only the growing child's wider experience of the world and more subtle view of human character that stimulate the transition through and out of this stage of reading? Or can it be speeded up by the challenge of more sophisticated books? The assumption of education is that it can be, and parents and librarians are frequently disturbed by children's fondness for what they consider frivolous reading. But is it a good idea to push children beyond what they like to read?

A simple answer to this question can only be: yes and no. Yes, because the kind of development involved in reading is not genetically pro- grammed like bodily growth, but needs the stimulus of challenge. No, because challenge without readiness may be counterproductive.

Cognitive and affective development parallel the movement from one stage of reading to another. A young boy or girl who is not ready to advance beyond concrete-operational thinking will not bring to reading a point of view more complex than what is needed for simple romance fiction. Furthermore, it may take a long time and much experience to consolidate the gains of a developmental stage. Especially in the early part of the concrete-operational stage, a reader may learn more from the series books typical of this kind of reading than from the unique books that win the Newbery Prize (for the best children's book of a given year as chosen by the American Library Association). This is an argument for quantity instead of quality. Children need to find their way through a developmental transition at their own speed. Too much challenge can result in the frustration of the "hurried child" (Elkind 1981b). A good case can even be made for complacency in the face of children's predilection for a certain amount of "rubbish" in their reading (Dickinson 1973).

Still, if challenge is appropriate, how should it be provided? What is challenging is what requires a child to reimagine a view of the world to include the new point of view. It is an attractive and acceptable challenge if it is about something that the child has just gotten interested in and is curious about. Challenges, in other words, have to match individuals. This, of course, is an argument for quality of reading over quantity. And though some children may discover their own challenges, clearly this can also be construed as an argument for the importance of guidance by the adults who care about them. But though adults may guide, will children be guided in something as personal as reading?

Norma Schlager did an interesting study of why children ages 7 to 12 read certain books and not others, why a Nancy Drew book would have the same popularity as a classic like *Tom Sawyer,* or why some Newbery Award winners languish on library shelves while others are in constant circulation (1978). She found that the books most asked for in libraries reflected a perception of the world that corresponded to the developmental level of the child. Seven- to twelve-year-olds were no longer interested simply in magical stories of childhood, however well written, nor yet in books about adolescent issues like falling in love. But a book like Scott O'Dell's *Island of the Blue Dolphins,* about a young Indian girl who has to survive alone on an island off the coast of California, deals with the intermediate realities of the older child's world: how to imagine being independent, making decisions, and solving problems. It scarcely got put back on the shelf, she says, before someone asked for it again. We might guess from such accounts that the books that will be read – the books we ourselves remember years later – offer a child vivid images of how to deal with these concerns, of how to be the one who acts, takes over, comes through, and deals competently with the challenges of growing up.

It is interesting that Schlager's empirical test of popularity was how often a book was withdrawn from the library. The case has been made for noticing that children, because they are naturally active learners, often form a very effective "community of readers" (Hepler and Hickman 1982). Why do books like Judy Blume's *Superfudge,* Roald Dahl's *James and the Giant Peach,* or Shel Silverstein's *Where the Sidewalk Ends* pass from hand to hand until everyone in the class has read them? Because the children talk about what they read. They not only exchange information about books they like, they also help each other work through meanings in what they read, teach one another how literature works, and model for one another how to think and talk about books. If this community of readers exists, then perhaps adults need not worry so much about how children will be guided in their reading development. Parents and teachers do not have to stand outside this community. They too can be models of how to read and talk about books. The teacher's role especially is to help young readers learn new strategies for comparing and evaluating what they read, to introduce them to books appropriate to their interests and level of development, and to help them connect new books with old favorites so that their shared knowledge of the literary world is constantly being reorganized and reabsorbed (see also Hickman 1981, 1984; Mikkelsen 1984).

What does a reader look like who is beginning to shed the need to read about heroes, but has not entirely found a new way of reading yet? Stephen is fifteen, a bit old for this chapter chronologically, but poised between two different ways of enjoying books and his own writing, as vicarious adventure on the one hand and as an opportunity to reimagine the world on the other. He is a fan of science fiction and especially of sword-and-sorcery books. He retells with enthusiasm the plot of a five-volume series called *The Chronicles of Amber* by Roger Zelazny. He summarizes at even greater length the plot of a book he is writing himself, 120 pages long already, about another planet inhabited by a superior race during the eleventh century. Then he relates the gist of a group of short stories he had just finished writing about an evil warlord called Spector, who fights off the nuclear weapons of the U.S. armed forces on his Maine island stronghold; a rebel lieutenant of his named Wardrex, who has a magic ring and animated gold statues of warriors to fight for him; and Sansmore, "the foreseen one," a normal human being (of incredible intelligence, however) who gets involved in the fight against Spector, but Spector by his power destroys them, though they are not really dead, and then. . . .

In one sense Stephen seems to be looking backward, at the magical world of childhood, at heroes and villains involved in struggles between good and evil, where power settles everything. There's not much ambiguity in this world and no overt sex: "The biggest things I stay away from are romantic stuff and things that have to do with humanism . . . like *Ordinary People*," he says. And character development does not interest him very much: "That just slows down the story." But in another sense Stephen uses literature as a source of ideas for rethinking the world in ideal terms. His stories are exuberantly if somewhat conventionally inventive and draw on a supply of literary experience ranging from James

Bond to J. R. R. Tolkien. His intelligence makes special demands on a book. Magic in science fiction, for example, has to be consistent: "Like, it isn't right if you have guys that are running around with laser guns, and one second they're shooting each other, and the next second they're fighting a duel with sabers. I mean, that doesn't seem to make sense. It's an anachronism." And then there is science, which requires a kind of acknowledgment: "In *Star Wars* you've got actual physical laws broken, such as the fighter ships dancing around the skies. I mean, you've got to remember that even the one that's sitting still is moving at thousands of miles a second. Simple. And if you ever tried maneuvering at that speed, you'd crash into yourself. Now, *Star Trek* was a bit better because it was dealing with a large ship, and there wasn't all these little intricate movements and it seemed more realistic."

School does not challenge Stephen the way this stuff does. He plays "Dungeons and Dragons" on computers on his own time, but Steinbeck bores him. In class he's currently reading *Of Mice and Men*: "This is so easy I could read it with my eyes closed. I was reading more difficult books than this when I was in the third grade." Difficulty to Stephen at this point seems to be entirely a matter of plot complexity; the emotional intricacies of the Steinbeck characters' lives or the moral issues they face do not count. "I'm always trying to find intricate, complex stories," he says. "For instance, *The Odyssey* – the rest of the class had difficulty with it, but I loved it, the blend of mythology and the human aspect, the realism of that world."

Though in some respects Stephen is still a concrete thinker, in other respects he already thinks in the kind of hypothetical way Piaget associates with adolescence and formal-operational intelligence. Asked where he gets the ideas for his stories from, he says: "I see this thing, and I'll say 'Well, all right, if this is this way, what if this happened?' . . . I'll take one basic concept and think about it, and I'll eventually change it entirely until the finished product is nothing like what I started out with." Stephen can put the power of thinking this way to use in sword-and-sorcery inventions. He does not yet seem to be interested in imagining his own or other people's actual lives this way. That is still to come.

A NOTE ON SEX ROLES

The repertory of images and themes through which young readers picture themselves and the world is not value-neutral. It necessarily embodies the mainstream attitudes of the adult culture. A vivid and much discussed example is the understanding of sex roles that a child acquires. Some theorists, like Robert May, associate distinct sex roles with fundamental biological and psychosexual givens: the different bodies boys and girls have and the asymmetrical experiences involved in being cared for and raised primarily by women. These differences show up even in infancy, May argues. Boys are restless, vigorous, impulsive, and poorly organized in their movements; girls are more controlled, apt to sit still and watch, and more responsive to social influence. By ages 4 and 5, observed bodily differences become part of a child's understanding of what being male or female means; a girl maintains a continuity of identification with her mother whom she physically resembles, while a boy defines himself by separation from her and identification with his father (May 1980, 109–18).

Erikson similarly notices that in playing with toys and blocks boys and girls build distinctively different constructions, which he associates with their distinctive bodily organs. The boys tend to picture outward and upward movement in towers or channeled activity, the girls to picture interior spaces that are closed or open, intruded upon or safely protected (1963, 97–108). Of course, the culture surrounds and supports these behaviors with its own direct and indirect instruction in the expectations of parents and elders.

Whether or not we accept this kind of physiological and psychosexual explanation of the origins of sex-role differences, it is clear simply from observation that distinct sex roles are familiar and important even to very young children. Raphaela Best studied peer-group attitudes among children in grades one to six in an affluent suburb and found that, in addition to the academic curriculum, there was not only a "second curriculum" in which the teachers communicated the culture's assumptions about proper male and female behavior, but also a "third curriculum" in which the children, largely unnoticed by adults, educated themselves in matters of sex and sex-role behavior (Best 1983). Vivian Gussin Paley also found that children's conceptions of distinct sex roles were already firmly in place among the five-year-olds in her classroom. "Kindergarten is a triumph of sexual self-stereotyping," she says in the opening sentence of her study of the process of social definition of "boy" and "girl" that goes on in the fantasy play of young children at school (1984, ix).

Given this consciousness by both children and their elders about different roles appropriate to each sex, it is not very surprising that in studies of what elementary school children read, boys prefer stories of male heroes involved in adventure and mystery and girls prefer stories about female characters in home and school settings (Purves and Beach 1972, 70, 93–4). These distinct preferences are less clearly marked, however in younger children, and in earlier studies especially they may have been a consequence of the kind of books that were available for boys and girls to read (Hawkins-Wendelin 1983, 402; see also Segel 1986). There is evidence that these preferences are also less marked in older children;

boys in grades eight to ten are less interested in male protagonists and more interested in female ones, while girls' interest in male protagonists increases steadily from grade five on (Johnson, Peer, and Baldwin 1984).

Does the matter of sex-role distinctions go beyond content preferences to *how* boys and girls read stories? This is a much harder question to answer, though some feminist critics want to make the case (see Crawford and Chaffin, 1986; Flynn 1986; Schweickart 1986; and Bleich 1986).

There is some evidence that boys and girls *tell* different kinds of stories – thus Brian Sutton-Smith's discovery, mentioned earlier in this chapter, that boys ages 5 to 10 resolved their plots more often by having their hero overcome a villain, whereas girls tended to avert a threat or supply what is lacking by having the central character make an alliance (1981, 24). Paley provides some details:

> Boys exult in superhuman strength, girls seek gentle relationships. Boys talk of blood and mayhem, girls avoid the subject; a character in a girl's story simple dies, no details given. Boys fly, leap, crash, and dive. Girls have picnics and brush their teeth; the meanest, ugliest character in a girl's story goes on picnics and keeps his teeth clean. Boys narrate superhero adventures filled with dangerous monsters, while girls place sisters and brothers, mothers and fathers in relatively safe roles. If lost, they are quickly found, if harmed they are healed or replaced. Boys tell of animals who kill or are killed; girls seldom involve animals in violence. A bear or lion encountered in the forest is likely to lead a girl home and will not be shot and eaten for supper. (1981, 203–4)

These kinds of data would seem to support the claim that Schweickart makes (citing the work of Jean Baker Miller, Nancy Chodorow, and Carol Gilligan) that in reading men value autonomy, separation, and the arbitration of conflicting rights, whereas women value relationships with others and are more apt to be interested in negotiating between opposed needs to maintain a relationship (Schweickart 1986, 54–5). This thesis, plausible as a generalization about adult readers who are the products of a long socialization process, would also seem to fit the stories children tell. How much of this is learned and how much natural? How much of it is better unlearned? Or, as Gilligan argues, are these complementary attitudes that both sexes need to cultivate? These questions, on the level of reading anyway, would seem to need much more detailed investigation before they can be confidently answered.

Is it possible, while thinking along these lines, to suspect that the generic mode of romance as Frye describes it, with its emphasis on the quest-adventure of the central character and the defeat of evil by good, may be fundamentally a *male* child's version of what adult competence is? Certainly the features of romance can be summarized to stress physical danger and the armed conflict of hero and villain. However, the task of venturing into the world and of coming to terms with the good and evil there faces both girls and boys. If the struggle with danger draws the male reader, we must not forget that an essential of romance is the reconciliation and restoration of the ending, which may be the female reader's priority in the story. Paley points out that both superhero stories and doll-corner play are variations on the same underlying theme: vulnerability and fears about safety (1981, 135). Perhaps Ricoeur's notion (mentioned earlier in this chapter) is relevant here, that quest stories involve both a linear and a circular dimension, the movement of the adventure through time, but within a primordial space that is more like the realm of dreams than the sphere of ordinary action (1981, 181). Even if we decide that boys and girls take notably different perspectives as readers because of the sex roles they have learned to play, the romance genre seems to give scope to the imaginative needs of both.

3

Adolescence: The Reader as Thinker

Chris is fifteen, a high school sophomore, slight, dark-haired. He is slouched in a chair, his eyes alert and suspicious. We are talking about books he has read and some particular stories and an essay I have asked him to look at. Here are some of the things he says, in a slightly abridged form.

> I never read much when I was, say, ten or eleven. I knew kids that read, but they didn't read novels; they just read the Hardy Boys or whatever. I never read those books. I really didn't like reading. I never really tried reading, actually. It was a labor to pick up a book. I never could sit still long enough to read. Then all of a sudden . . . I don't know. I read a book that I liked and one thing led to another. I just kept reading.

When was this?

> In the seventh or eighth grade. We read *The Outsiders,* by S. E. Hinton, and that was one of those books that has a lot action, and I thought it was a pretty good book. It gave me a lot of information about New York streets [the story is actually set in a nameless city "in the Southwest"], a lot of information to think about. And so I just picked up other books like that.

I had asked him to read George Orwell's essay, "Shooting an Elephant," a first-person narrative about Orwell's experiences as a young British policeman in colonial Burma: "There's not a lot of action, but he writes it so you can relate to the situation he's in. He's uneasy because he feels he doesn't belong there." Why does Chris relate to this feeling? "Maybe because I tend to think like that. I think that I don't belong where I am. . . . I'm ill at ease . . . this [he gestures to the high school building where we are talking] isn't the place for me . . . that sort of thing. I generally like this kind of story where the person isn't liked or isn't, ah, you know, comfortable where he is and he has to adapt to it or leave it, and where he thinks about it throughout the story."

What makes this kind of writing enjoyable to read, rather than unpleasant? Orwell's essay, he says, is "not a story you just pick up and read for leisure. You have to sit down and read it and think about it. It's more of an insight story." So what frame of mind would you have to be in to pick it up? "When you feel like...," Chris mumbles something. When you feel like thinking? "Well, I didn't want to say that, but maybe that's what I mean. It sounds foolish to say: 'when you feel like thinking.' But in a sense that's what it is. I mean, you're sitting down and reflecting or something, and you want to find somebody who has maybe the same problem.... The situation he's in: the Burmese people are looking at him, and laughing at him or maybe looking up to him, and he doesn't know what to make of it. It seems true, something that's not like a fantasy.... It doesn't give you any answers. A story that doesn't give you the answers is better than a story that gives you a solution but doesn't leave you with anything to think about."

This idea leads Chris to some ambivalent thoughts: "This summer I read *On the Road,* by Jack Kerouac. I was really disappointed at the end. I didn't know what to make of it. The main character is just left there and he doesn't know if the last five years of bopping around the country was worth it, if any of it was worth it." But didn't he just say that he liked books that did not provide neat solutions? Why was he disappointed? "Well, maybe I don't mean that. I really liked the book. It made me think, which is what I usually like to do. It didn't disappoint me in that sense, but it was hard to think up what could happen after that ending."

Chris's reading is expanding in different directions. He's just read Hemingway's *A Moveable Feast,* and he's thinking of reading some of the authors mentioned in the book. His most demanding book so far ("almost no action and all thinking") is Dostoevsky's *Crime and Punishment*: "It took a long time to read, but I really enjoyed it. Not enjoyed it in the sense of 'oh, wow! isn't it great,' but afterwards I thought that. Reading it was very slow... you have to pay the price... but afterwards it gives you a lot more insight about how people think."

At the end of our conversation, I asked him how he was doing in school, how he compared to other students in his English class. He seemed uncomfortable about answering and he groped for words. "This quarter I'm probably in the top ten students, maybe, but I didn't really do great. I'm not... an intellectual or something like that. I don't... I wouldn't like to be... I don't know... I haven't experienced it."

Let's see to what extent Chris is typical of adolescent readers.

THE ADOLESCENT'S WORLD

Of all developmental transitions, adolescence is perhaps least in need of defending as a distinctive stage, for a twentieth-century audience at any rate. Patricia Spacks points out that although adolescents have always existed, the myth of adolescence has a short history. It was invented, she says, by the psychologist G. Stanley Hall in 1904 with the publication of his massive study of the subject and reinforced in the 1950s by Erik Erikson when he called attention to the crucial role of adolescence and its identity crisis in the developmental cycle (Spacks 1981, 228ff., 257ff.) Hall's romantic description of adolescence and its conflicts has combined with Erikson's darker but still optimistic picture of youth struggling to achieve a mature identity amid the problematic choices offered by adult society to give us our conventional image of adolescence and its characteristic features: sudden and erratic physical growth, intensified sexuality, idealism that is often grandiose as well as naive, self-consciousness, romanticism, moodiness and ambivalence, ambition and drive, rebellion and crisis. We take for granted now that any or all of these features might be found in a boy or girl between the ages of 13 and 17.

Spacks makes the point, though, that the importance of this picture may not lie in its accuracy as a description of the behavior of the young so much as in its power to express the conflicting attitudes of adult culture about its own experience (1981, 11–13). This observation cautions us once again to weigh the explanatory value of schematic generalizations about development against descriptions of actual behavior as well as we can and to be alert to distortions that discover in evidence what we would like to be there rather than what is there. Reading is certainly one area where we can test developmental schemas against the behavior of real readers. Therefore, we shall first look briefly at the psychological accounts of adolescence to see how the conventional characteristics of adolescence might be said to form a coherent process of development and then look more closely at the way actual readers respond to the books they read.

One way of relating these phenomena is to see them as manifestations of one central phenomenon: the discovery of the subjective self and of subjective experience as something unique (Kolhberg and Gilligan 1971). A child age 7 to 12 has only an inchoate notion of self; it is "me" or "you," the specific person who perceives an objective reality and acts on it. The younger child can be aware of subjective feelings and thoughts, but experiences these as directly caused by objective things and events. An adolescent, on the other hand, experiences an inner self as the locus of unique feelings, opinions, and thoughts that can have a greater reality and importance than the objective events that occasion them. The inner self is seen as authentic, the outer self a social role to be played, an appearance put on for others (Broughton 1978, 83–9). The discovery of the subjective self is concomitant with an intensified emotionality and often ambivalent and conflicting feelings; it seems to be the necessary condition for aesthetic feeling, for the contemplative experience of nature, for religious mysticism and romantic love (Kohlberg and Gilligan 1971, 1060–4). The discovery of subjectivity and the relativism of points of view can also lead to a sense of isolation and loneliness in the young adolescent (Chandler 1975). But the sense of a divided selfhood, of a split between a secret, authentic inner self ("the me nobody knows") and a changing personality needed to deal with the outside world, need not be proof of alienation, as the psychiatrist R. D. Laing, for example, sees it in *The Divided Self* (1960). It can also be viewed as an attempt to come to grips with a philosophical truth about existence – that inside and outside differ and can be at odds – and to lay the necessary dialectical foundation for subsequent development (Broughton 1981).

Piaget's account of adolescents' cognitive development complements this description of the discovery of the subjective self (Inhelder and Piaget 1958). Whereas the seven- to twelve-year-old child reasons concretely (in terms of objects and their classes and their concrete relationships here and now), the young adolescent begins to reason in terms of the formal or logical relationships that exist among propositions about objects. Thus, he or she is not limited to thinking about real objects, but can think hypothetically about possible ones and therefore can imagine that present reality is only one among many hypothetically possible alternatives and can deduce the consequences that these other hypotheses imply. This opening up to the possible is what allows an adolescent to think about the future, to construct theories and ideological systems, to develop ideals, to understand others' points of view (see Moshman and Neimark, 1982, for a discussion of the adolescent as developing logician, scientist, philosopher, and artist). Correlative with this is the ability to think about thinking, to reflect critically about one's own thoughts. This is the source of adolescent self-consciousness and introspection, of the egocentrism of much adolescent thinking, of the sense of discrepancy between one's authentic self and the roles one plays for an imagined audience (Elkind 1981a, 90–5).

Cognitive and self-concept approaches to adolescence entail the risk of emphasizing the solipsism and isolation to which some teenagers may come. It is important, therefore, to fill out this picture by stressing the social context in which adolescent identity develops and is supported, as Erikson does (1968, 128–35). For Erikson, the significant circumstance is that although adolescents undergo a rapid physiological maturation, society (especially a technologically advanced one) postpones their taking genuine adult roles by keeping them in school. So they have to work out a set of balances between their newfound sense of possibility and the restrictions with which adult society often appears to be threatening them. Thus, although they look for people and ideas worth having faith in, their fear of foolish commitments may express itself in cynical mistrust. Similarly, although they want to choose freely the roles they will play, they are mortally afraid of being forced into activities that might expose them to ridicule or self-doubt. Again, they are ready to put their trust in peers and elders who will give imaginative scope to their aspirations, yet they violently object to anyone who sets limits to their self-image and ambition. Among such competing impulses – which, we must not forget, offer support as well as challenge – the young man or woman has to integrate an identity. No one should be surprised that the process can take a while and have its ups and downs. As Winnicott says, of course the adolescent is immature, but immaturity is an essential element of health at this age (1971, 146).

Nor is it obvious that the solution to negotiating these conflicts of adolescence is simply to mature in the kind of abstract, decentered, and relativistic thinking that Piaget's cognitive schema favors. Some of the challenges of youth yield to this kind of thinking, but Chandler and others (for example, Blasi and Hoeffel 1974) argue that adolescence also presents young men and women with challenges that are better met by recentered styles of thought grounded in concrete personalized experience that is affectively meaningful. Assessing one's own experience of a work of art, for example, or making one's way in an affective relationship, or committing oneself resolutely to a chosen course of action are situations where relativistic perspectives and abstract conceptualizing may inhibit a successful outcome rather than advance it. Dialectical solutions that do not sacrifice the particular to the general, but preserve both, may eventually contribute to a fuller maturity (Chandler 1975, 178–9).

Adolescence is least stormy, Erikson thinks, when the young are gifted, well-trained, and ride the wave of whatever technological, economic, or ideological trend is dominant. When this is not the case, the adolescent mind is apt to become ideological in a sense that fits the analysis of Broughton and Piaget: looking among various possibilities for an ideal that will express the authentic inner self. This search may be especially arduous in a society like ours, Erikson thinks, that brings its young people up to value autonomy and choice and self-realization – promises not easy to fulfill in the complex and centralized systems of industrial, economic, and political organization where they will have to work.

"Moratorium" is Erikson's term for the postponement – deliberately chosen or involuntary – of commitment. Schooling is the institutionalized form of moratorium for middle-class youth in our culture. It is the major setting for the adolescence we have been describing. The home, the part-time job, peer hangouts, all contribute to development, but certainly from the point of view of reading the school is the principal context in which changes occur in adolescence and from now on.

WHAT ADOLESCENTS READ

The general picture of adolescents' reading habits is fairly well documented.[1] Reading for enjoyment typically reaches a peak in the junior-high-school years and drops steadily from the ninth grade onward. Indeed most teenagers do not voluntarily read much at all. Nearly half of the thirteen-year-olds and one-third of the seventeen-year-olds in the 1979–1980 National Assessment of Educational Progress (NAEP) survey could not name a novel they had read on their own outside of school (Mellon 1975, 93). In the same survey, though more than half the nine-year-olds said that they read for enjoyment every day, only one-third of the seventeen-year-olds did, and 75 percent of them read for less than an hour when they did read (but 60 percent reported that they had watched television one to three hours the previous day) (Petrosky 1982, 9). Most of these students think it is important to read, Petrosky says, but few read for enjoyment and when they do it is for short periods of time. Given the opportunity, they would rather spend their spare time watching television or going to a movie (1982, 9).

What voluntary reading is done, however, is largely fiction (as much as 75 percent) and most of that is novels. Among the younger junior high students, mystery is the preferred type of fiction, along with ad-venture, romance, historical fiction, and science fiction. High school students have similar interests as to genre, but they also read more stories about adolescents and their problems and they increasingly read adult fiction as well. Sex differences are more marked here than at any other age – hardly surprising because, as May points out, the formation of a self-conscious sense of identity, a central theme of adolescence, is heavily influenced by the bodily changes of puberty and by the need to imagine acceptable versions of adult maleness and femaleness (1980, 120–9). The distinctive modalities that psychologists summarize in terms such as "male autonomy" and "female interpersonal empathy" show up in the books adolescents voluntarily read; though there is considerable overlap of categories, especially mystery and humor, girls choose romantic stories and boys choose adventure, science-fiction, war, and sports stories. Girls read more than boys here, as they do at all ages.

Looked at in terms of conventional genre classifications – adventure, mystery, and so forth – much of the fiction adolescents read does not differ notably from what younger children read. In one sense this should be no surprise; at every stage readers continue to read the kinds of books they enjoyed earlier. But there is a further problem with classifying what people read by categories that loosely describe subject matter and genre. They do not tell us much about the real sources of appeal that such books have for readers. J. P. Wyss's *The Swiss Family Robinson* is an adventure story about a shipwreck and survival, so is William Golding's *Lord of the Flies*. Louisa May Alcott's *Little Women* is about a girl growing up, so is *The Diary of Anne Frank*. The Hardy Boys books are about teenagers dealing with crime; so is S. E. Hinton's *The Outsiders*. The difference is that the juvenile books all deal with an innocent world, where evil is externalized and finally powerless, where endings are happy. The adolescents' books deal with sex, death, sin, and prejudice, and good and evil are not neatly separated but mixed up in the confused and often turbulent emotions of the central characters themselves. This is true of classic novels long popular with teenagers, such as Charlotte Bronte's *Jane Eyre,* more recently popular books like Harper Lee's *To Kill a Mockingbird,* and the young adult novels that have been raising parents' eyebrows, such as Judy Blume's *Forever.*

One can say in a general way that adolescents read these books because they are growing up, but it is more useful to look closely at how these books fit the teenagers' way of making sense out of the world. For example, when questioned about their reactions to particular stories, teenagers tend to give three kinds of responses.

1.   They explicitly mention the experience of *involvement* with the book and *identification* with the character ("it was just like I was there," "you can sort of lose yourself in it," "it could have been written about me," "I couldn't get into it").
2.   They talk about the *realism* of the story ("it was true to life . . . believable," "the characters have flaws like a normal person," "I know kids just like that").
3.   And they say that a good story *makes them think* ("I like things that force me to think," "a story that keeps you reading and constantly thinking about what's going on").

These three responses appear to be interrelated as a sequence of deepening penetrations into the relationship between previously unquestioned experiences and the newly discovered need to understand and judge them. It is as though involvement and identification (which really are characteristic of the way younger children read stories) somehow need to be explained and justified now that the characters are mixtures of good and bad and the situations they find themselves in are so problematic. The adolescent turns to the realism of the book as the criterion of its acceptability. But realism is only one part of the whole question of truth, whose multiple versions (as competing values, beliefs, and behaviors, especially about emotionally painful subjects) the adolescent boy or girl is just learning to confront. So a further criterion of a story, especially for older adolescents, is that it helps them think about the claims of competing truths in their own lives.[2]

Thinking about the implications of a story may seem to be at the opposite pole from being wrapped up in the experience of it, but the connection between the two responses lies in the adolescent's new way of making the world meaningful. The adolescent has become what the juvenile was not, an observer and evaluator of self and others, so it is an easy step from involvement in the story to reflecting about it. A closer look at each of these three responses will clarify some of the strengths and limitations of this stage of the reader's development.

INVOLVEMENT AND IDENTIFICATION

How many adult readers can summon up an image of themselves as teenagers, stretched out on a porch glider, totally absorbed in a novel the whole of a long summer afternoon or staying up long past bedtime with an engrossing book? Diane (16), a high school junior, says of a novel she has just finished, "I was so into that book that I read it in one night. I stayed up until two o'clock in the morning, I was so glued to that book." Rina (17), a classmate, remembers doing it even when she was younger: "I can remember going up to my room in fifth grade with my books and staying there all day."

Nell offers a helpful distinction for thinking about this kind of reading. It is not simply a matter of absorbed attention, of being abstracted from our surroundings while we read. This is no more mysterious a state, Nell suggests, than that of a clerk adding a row of figures or of a driver negotiating a busy intersection (1988, 76–7). The true "reading trance," being "lost in a book" or caught up in the fortunes of the hero or heroine, is harder to account for. It involves a total immersion in the experience, so that the distinction between the subject and the object of the experience breaks down. It is a kind of hypnosis or altered state of consciousness in which the reader is, in J. R. Hilgard's words, "transformed or transported by what he reads . . . swept emotionally into the experience described by the author" (quote in Nell 1988, 211) "Attention holds me," Nell says, "but trance fills me, to varying degrees, with the wonder and flavor of alternate worlds" (77).

Not surprisingly, this response often goes together with intense emotional reaction to the story. Rina, asked what she expects of a good story, says, "I like stories that bring me on the edge of my seat, that stir my emotions." She mentions J. D. Salinger's *Catcher in the Rye* and Margaret

Mitchell's *Gone with the Wind*. She says she likes "romances," but dismisses Harlequin romances as "stupid . . . the same plot." However, "*Love Story,* that was good. That made my emotions come on. . . . They were from two different worlds and they came together and they were happy. And then when she died, it showed that it could happen to anyone. . . . If she had lived, I still would have liked it, but it wouldn't have brought the extra emotional response you have at the end. I like to have a good cry with a book." Diane says, "I like sad stories. I like love stories too, but most of them end up sad."

The more common expression of involvement is not so explicitly a matter of emotion, but rather of identification with the characters and the situations they are in. Lesleyann (15), a high school sophomore, appeals to this criterion in several different comments she makes. She likes Frank O'Connor's story "Guests of the Nation" because "you can relate to it better and at the end you could sympathize with them and see that that could happen to you." Later, when asked what makes a book enjoyable to read, she says, "If it's real to life. I don't like fantasy. I do, but it's better if it's real to life, and you can relate to the characters and they're believable, and their . . . I don't know . . . their experiences are more like yours, not something totally strange." When asked whether she has noticed changes in the kinds of books she has read over the years, she says, "Yes, I guess. I was never into mysteries or stuff like that . . . or horror. . . . When you were younger you read about typical little kids and then the whole series of Ramona books [by Beverly Cleary], and then in the sixth or seventh grade you got into Judy Blume stuff. I liked those a lot." Why? "Oh, because they were real to life and there were situations you could relate to and things you could see happening to other people and to yourself."

Often a reader will mention a strong personal motive for identifying with a character or a type of character. We have already heard Chris saying that he can relate to Orwell's situation in Burma "because I tend to think like that. . . . I don't belong where I am . . . ill at ease . . . this isn't the place for me . . . that sort of thing." Ravi (17), a senior, says he likes biographies because they show you people who do not know where they are going, who start off in one direction and end up in a completely different direction, and you can follow them through all those changes and see how they managed: "I can identify with that because right now [as a high school senior], you know, you're in a state where you have to make a lot of decisions. . . . You get to see how these people made their choices and you see that even these great people didn't know what they wanted to become, or they had troubles too like everybody else, so that's good to know."

A reader can identify positively with more than one character in a story. Charlie (17), a senior, who is quite observant about his responses to what he reads, says that Ayn Rand's *The Fountainhead* is one of his "all-time favorite psychological novels." Why? "I'm interested in going into architecture, that was one thing. But I could definitely identify with Howard Hawke, the main character, because he had sort of an ideological . . . not commitment, but he was very idealistic. I could really see, you know, in myself what he was feeling. Then, also, this is funny too, I could see the point of view of some of the other people too, and they had the opposite point of view from him. So for me it was a test of my objectivity, you know, being very objective." For Charlie, identification seems to be a way of articulating and trying out potential aspects of his identity that are still competing for priority.

As we have seen in Chapter 2, Holland and others argue that we do not just identify with one character in a story or only with their good qualities. We might identify with several characters or with several aspects of a single character, Holland says, because the drives we satisfy through identification are balanced in an "economy" of relationships created by the work as a whole (1968, 278). He cites a case described by psychoanalyst Edith Buxbaum of a twelve-year-old boy, a compulsive reader of detective stories. The stories, she found, allowed him to express not only his manifest fears (by identifying with the victims in them) and his aggressive impulses (by identifying with the criminals), but also his determination to keep these drives under the control of his ego (by identifying with the detectives) (Buxbaum 1941, 380–1). We do something similar in every story where multiple characters and their relationships deeply involve us, Holland thinks (1968, 279).

A college freshman says something similar. Dan (17) talks about the books he reads almost entirely in terms of "identifying" with the characters or not. During the conversation he mentions that since high school he has been a dedicated player of "Dungeons and Dragons." This leads to a discussion of the game, and of how players build up characters which they then set against the characters developed by other players: "I have a new character I'm playing . . . actually two characters. One is a Paladin, a 'lawful-good' character. He has to fight all evil and always gives a fair chance to whoever he's fighting. My other character is a 'chaotic-good' character; you can't always tell what he's going to do. . . . The Paladin character is my ideal. It's what I'd like to be, but that's a fantasy world and I think the other character is a little bit more like I am. He's not always good. Well, he's always good but you can't predict. Say a lady's getting a purse stolen, my other character would chase the guy right away, but this guy might just walk past and say 'I'm not going to risk my life for this lady.' Sad but true. I think he's more like me and the other character's what I'd like to be."

Identification may be a somewhat misleading term here because, as both Charlie and Dan illustrate (and as I have argued in the previous chapter), there is often something unfinished about the identity the reader is claiming. Sometimes it is very clear that the identity is something wished for rather than something already shared. Rina says that she could identify with Holden Caulfield in *The Catcher in the Rye*. Why? "Well, I guess he's a little self-conscious. He loves his sister a lot. I liked him, the character. He'll . . . he's not afraid to do what he wants; he walked out of school and didn't tell anyone. I guess because I'm a pretty shy person, so I don't usually . . . I do what I'm told [she laughs], so when I read things, you know, about people who do what they want, that kind of appeals to me because I usually don't."

D. W. Harding, as we have already noted, questions the aptness of the term identification, in the sense of vicarious experience or wish fulfillment, to describe a reader's involvement with a fictional character. Rina's response illustrates his view that although the reader empathizes imaginatively with a character as a "participant" in the story, he or she also evaluates or reacts to the character in the role of "spectator" (1968a, 308–16). Even while Rina admires Holden Caulfield, she seems to be well aware of the difference between who he is and who she is. Perhaps this awareness of difference is an indispensable part of the appeal of characters who embody ideals for us.

In a study of Plato's presentation of Socrates, Charles Altieri advances the notion of an exemplary character who can be a model of a more noble way of life, with whom we identify not just because of his cogent teaching (which our contemporary ironic analyses can always undercut), but because of the principled life he lives in exemplification of them. Thus, his life enacts values that connect philosophy to practical life and creates a space in which we can imagine these connections in our own lives (1985, 255ff.).

In some ways this seems like the notion of an inspiring or edifying life, the kind of idea that contemporary critical theory would translate into a matter of authorial ideology or of misplaced reader interest in deriving a moral lesson from what we read. But from what adolescents say it does seem that one reason they read biography and fiction is to imagine real lives to help them understand the possibilities in their own lives. Don't older people often read from the same motives? Booth points out that although much of mainstream culture in the past 150 years has tended to substitute a social notion of the self for the romantic idea of the unique individual, nonetheless the idea of an individual personality as an undividable center – however much affiliated to others and constituted by these affiliations – survives tenaciously, especially in literature (1988, 237–40). Perhaps we have to acknowledge both the power of fictional models to embody versions of what we can imagine ourselves being – Rene Girard calls them embodiments of "triangular desire," images that mediate between the desiring subject and the desired object and so enable us to imagine the kind of life which will achieve the object of desire (Girard 1965, 1–52) – and to represent equally well the difference that yet separates us from our ideals, a realization that Altieri calls, after Kant, the "tragic sublime" (Altieri 1985, 265). And perhaps awareness of this difference grows slowly – from undiscriminating identification in childhood to a sense in adolescence of both the power of the ideal and the pathos of the gap, then to a more realistic appreciation of what the disparities mean in adulthood, or even to an ironic rejection of idealism altogether.[3]

Denise (18), a high school senior, shows how mixed together both of these realizations can be. She talks about the different kinds of books she likes: science magazines and books about psychology and current issues such as teenage suicide and abortion. Then she says, "You'll probably laugh, but I like to read romances, I really do." She says they all have practically the same plot, but what appeals to her is that they're not realistic: "It's an escape more than anything. You're wrapped up, and you become, I guess, this woman who's in this love affair or, you know, is infatuated with this man. They're not real people. Everybody's always perfect, you know. The guy is handsome, the woman is beautiful and she can play the piano and she sings beautifully and she can cook right and all the men are crazy about her. . . . Everybody has an ideal image of what they should be, you know, even though they're not really that. . . . When you're reading about this woman, you sort of identify with her, you know. It makes you feel good for a while" [she laughs]. She knows that her reactions are ambivalent. She says about Harlequin romances: "There's some pretty images in them. . . . I don't know, I wish I had that kind of life that a lot of those people do have. But I couldn't read the same thing all the time. I couldn't read a romance, you know, every day of the week. I'd get pretty tired of it." A few seconds later she interrupts the interviewer to add: "You know, it's funny, when we did *Huckleberry Finn* last year, I really liked it. The teacher was saying that usually it doesn't appeal to girls, but I was crazy about it. . . . Girls don't have that kind of adventurous attitude, but I wouldn't mind sailing down the Mississippi River, no problem. It was kind of nice because . . . I mean, what little boy that age here in Somerville lives that kind of life, that exciting? He's sort of his own person." One may wonder whether a reader who talks about identifying with a character may be implying a mixture of "the me I am" and "the me I'd like to be" and whether involvement does not operate on the promise of straightening this uncertainty out.

Identification succeeds when the characters of adolescent novels match their readers' newfound sense of complexity, but do not exceed it. The chief difference from the characters of juvenile stories is that the main characters of teenage fiction have inner lives. The reader has full access to their thoughts and feelings, their anxieties and self-questionings. This does not mean that they are necessarily well-developed characters. Holden Caulfield's appeal to both young and older readers is not typical of adolescent novels. Most of their characters are stereotypes by adult standards. The difference is only partly a question of whether they are well drawn. Rather more pertinent is the adolescent version of the phenomenon of cognitive egocentrism. Adolescents want characters like themselves or their ideal selves, with inner lives, but those characters also have to be recognizable and therefore conventional by their standards. One does not have to read many successful adolescent novels to discover that the fantasy of being unique is inseparable from the fear of being different. So the central characters of these books tend to run together into a composite adolescent self-image: the sensitive, misunderstood outsider, no longer a child and not yet an adult. That seems to be the most successful formula for securing the reader's identification.

Adolescents talk about their involvement with stories almost entirely in terms of identification with the characters and the situations they are in. They make occasional references to the "fast-moving action" of a story, and a common criticism of disliked books is that they are "long" or "drawn out," but in general unless they are talking about the kind of adventure stories they could have read at an earlier age, they make few references to plot or narrative structure. Yet it would seem plausible to suppose that some part of the experience of being caught up in a book should be due to the more complex structure of the stories they read and to their maturing ability to be receptive to this complexity. Perhaps the explanation is that genuine plot complexity is not a matter of subplots and flashbacks, but of the causal interrelationships between character and action, and that adolescents, although they are now aware of this relationship and eager to see it worked out in a story, are temporarily one-sided in focusing on character when they try to explicate it. After all, exciting stories have been familiar to them for some time; the inner lives of characters have not. One might also speculate that even for adults – unless it is a mystery, a spy story or a historical novel we are talking about (all, of course, romances) – plot is generally subordinated to the unfolding of character in our appreciation of a book.

There is a paradox about the whole matter of teenagers' involvement with a story. As Applebee shrewdly notices, to say that you are involved means that you no longer are, at least not in the unself-conscious and spontaneous way that you were before you identified and labeled your involvement. The truly involved reader is the preadolescent, absorbed in what C. S. Lewis calls the "atmosphere" (1966) and Nell "entrancement" (1988); once the experience is named, it becomes a *possible* response, one that may or may not occur, a response that is psychologically distanced by the recognition that it is only "like I was there" (Applebee 1978, 112). This is wholly consistent, of course, with the adolescent discovery of the self. It suggests, too, that Harding's distinction between participant and spectator roles in the reading process reaches a new level of self-consciousness in adolescence and that all subsequent responses to stories will be marked, to a greater or lesser degree, by some sense of the division between the experiencing and the judging self. That an adolescent thinks a good story is realistic and that it "makes me think" are the most immediate of the reactions that evidence this split.

REALISM

In one study, the most common critical yardstick that a group of ninth and tenth graders applied to stories they read was whether or not they were "true to life" (Squire 1964, 44). This is a response one regularly meets in talking to teenagers about what they have read. A story is praised because it is "true," "normal," "like how people really act," "valid," "something that's not like a fantasy."

The criteria of realism take different forms. Sometimes it is the fact that the story reflects the reader's experience accurately. Rina (17) reacts to "Samuel," a short story by Grace Paley about four boys who dare one another to ride on one of the swaying platforms between two subway cars: "It was sort of depressing but . . . real to me too because they were young kids and to me it seemed like something a kid would do just to show off, like riding on the backs of streetcars. . . . This was . . . like . . . close to home, 'cause kids around here do a lot of stupid things to show off and everything."

Or the story is realistic because the reader can easily imagine similar situations. Rina says that she thinks Frank O'Connor's "Guests of the Nation" (about two young Irish militia volunteers who are ordered to execute the British prisoners they have been guarding for several weeks) is a good story: "I think people have probably been in that situation. These men became good friends, and then they just had to do their duty . . . probably like the Vietnam War too. A lot of kids went into that not really sure why they went. They took the first step and they had to follow through; that's what's expected of them."

Another proof of realism is that the characters are not ideal types or one-dimensional. Lesleyann (15) when asked what kinds of books would appeal to her, says: "I think they'd have to be realistic, but not too. . . .

The characters would have to be, I don't know, normal, I guess. Not be ideal, but have flaws like a normal person, not like a perfect character."

For one student the possibility of identifying with a character depended directly on the amount of information the author provided: "You don't get involved with this character . . . because you don't know anything about him. That's what I like about Dickens. For example, in *David Copperfield* you get . . . you can identify with him because you know all his feelings and how he identifies with each situation. When you end up going through a life cycle, you know, you really care for the person and what's going to happen to him" (Ravi, 17, a senior). This requirement for information is like the demand for "good description," which Squire also found was a frequent critical attitude of ninth and tenth graders (1964, 45).

Why is the realism of stories important to adolescent readers? After all, it is younger children, in Piaget's concrete-operational stage, who are characteristically curious about the world around them and intent investigators of its phenomena. The difference seems to be that for adolescents realism is now an issue; they have discovered that a story's truthfulness to life is not something a reader can take for granted but must make a judgment about. This may not be an explicit attitude, but it is one they employ over and over again in practice. Consciously or not, they have adopted what Harding calls the "spectator" role, the psychological position not of the participant in the events but of the onlooker, for whom the reading of a novel is a process of attending to the representation of imagined events and of evaluating their significance and the adequacy of their representation as well. It is important to repeat that adolescents may be scarcely aware that they are making explicit judgments about the realism of stories. As Harding says, the full grasp of the fictional status of fiction is a sophisticated achievement, and many adults have only a precarious hold on the distinction between fiction and factual narrative (1968a, 307). But the consistent use of realism as a criterion of a good story implies that, however spontaneously and unreflectingly, adolescent readers make judgments about the truthfulness of what they read to their own experience.

And therein lies a problem. The adolescent notion of what is real is quite distinctive. Consider, for example, the prominence of illness and death in books popular with teenagers. Cancer is a staple (Erich Segal's *Love Story*, Richard Peck's *Something for Joey*, Barbara Conklin's *P.S.: I Love You*, Doris Lund's *Eric*, John Gunther's *Death Be Not Proud*, William Blinn's *Brian's Song*), and so are suicide or its aftermath (Judith Guest's *Ordinary People*, Judy Blume's *Forever*), psychological disorders (Joanne Greenberg's *I Never Promised You a Rose Garden*, Flora R. Schreiber's *Sybil*, Ken Kesey's *One Flew over the Cuckoo's Nest*, James Reach's *David*

and Lisa), mental retardation (Daniel Keyes's *Flowers for Algernon*), crip-
pling accidents (John Knowles's *A Separate Peace*, E. G. Valens's *The
Other Side of the Mountain*), and murder and other violent crimes (Judy
Blume's *Tiger Eyes*, S. E. Hinton's four books, *The Outsiders, Tex,
Rumblefish*, and *That Was Then, This Is Now*).

Why should these dark themes be so prominent in adolescent literature?
One reason is that teenage readers have discovered that the conventions
of juvenile literature do not match the complexity of their new experience. And as a result they demand that stories not just embody their
wishes and fantasies, but also reflect realistically the darker parts of life
and the newfound limits on their idealism, as Whitehead and his colleagues have argued (1977, 223–6). Defending her enthusiasm for a story
where boy meets girl and girl dies of cancer, Lesleyann (15) says, "Life
isn't just to live happily ever after; it has its ups and downs." This
comment poignantly captures the view of someone who has discovered
that not all boys and girls are good looking or popular at school, that
not all encounters with the opposite sex are romantic, that not all families
are happy and not all quests end satisfactorily. Illness and death are only
extreme versions of this whole side of the adolescent experience.

In Frye's terminology, the generic literary mode we are dealing with
here is tragedy, which acknowledges that an originally heroic destiny
can end in catastrophe. Tragedy is the second part of the full cycle of
Frye's unified myth, the marvelous adventures of romance being followed by the defeat and death of the hero, then by the demoralization
reflected in irony and satire, and finally by the restoration of comedy
(1957, 192). It seems plausible to think that the preference of developing
readers for the realism of stories about suffering and death has something
to do with the discovery that romance is not an adequate image of life's
possibilities. The tragic point of view may be the next step in the normal
evolution of a literary sensibility.

When we think of tragedy some of the great masterpieces of literature
come to mind, but it is instructive to see how well some of the characteristics of tragedy also fit the adolescent world view. Thus, says Frye,
tragedy concentrates not on a social group, as comedy does, but on the
single individual, who is somewhere between the divine and the "all too
human" (1957, 207). In fact, tragedy tends to oppose the isolated individual to the social structure, and one of our deepest fears that tragedy
plays on is the terror of being excluded from the group and therefore of
being pathetic (1957, 217). The plight of the tragic figure is that, isolated,
one may make the wrong choices and discover too late the shape of the
life one has created for one's self in comparison with the potential one
has forsaken (1957, 212). But there may be no right choice either. The
two reductive formulas for tragedy – that it exhibits the omnipotence of

external fate or that it is a result of a violation of the moral law – are complementary, not antithetical, truths about the existential predicament of human life (1957, 209–11). If this sounds all too much like the picture we often have of adolescents – yearning to discover an authentic individuality, conceiving great ideals, agonizing over their relationships to others, burdened by a sense of fate beyond their control, wondering whether the life choices they make will be the right ones, aware of the seemingly inescapable ambivalence of their feelings – it may be because tragedy is the literary genre that suits the adolescent's realization that the real world is not the green world of romance but a much darker and more dangerous place.

Of course, adolescent versions of tragedy do not face all the implications of this realization, nor do they work out the issues in very complex ways, and if anything they are apt to be one-sided in what they emphasize. *Love Story* is not *Othello*. Adolescent novels seem rather to be something like primers that introduce their readers to how they should feel and think about these troubling new phenomena. The mimetic yardstick for measuring a story's quality, though it may begin in the adolescent's need for a verisimilitude corresponding to experience, has a long way to go before it will satisfy a reader with a mature experience of the world. And, of course, even adolescent stories with tragic themes do have happy endings, though they are not necessarily the triumphs of romance. At the very least, the character through whose eyes we see the events survives; life is not over yet and happiness is still possible. And even if the hero or heroine dies, a central archetype of tragedy is sacrifice, as Frye points out, the death that draws the survivors into a new unity (1957, 214–15).

The discovery that the world is a complex and not wholly innocent place can be a daunting experience, and some readers may even mourn a bit for the simpler way they used to look at things. Rob, a college junior, describes reading *The Lord of the Flies* when he was much younger:

> In my *Old Yeller* phase, the good guys all wore white and the bad characters were in black. Now it was not so simple. Many new shades of grey had entered the scene which made it difficult to find 'myself' in the story.... No one character was the perfect hero I had been accustomed to playing... I was becoming a realist.... At first I disliked this way of reading... I had to decide where the different characters stood according to my values and beliefs... I remember that I longed so much for a "mindless" novel which would carry me away, that I tried to re-read a Hardy Boys book.... It was too simple, too foreseeable, and too unbelievable.

Growth does not always feel comfortable when it is happening. Realism promises truth to experience, but it sometimes delivers disillusionment as well on the way to its larger wisdom.

THINKING

The step from saying that a story is good because "I can identify with the character" to saying that it is good because "it makes me think" seems to be an easy one for an adolescent to make. Both reactions are grounded in the new way the inner self examines and evaluates the different possibilities that experience offers.

What does this "thinking" mean? At times it almost appears to mean simply that adolescents are enjoying the novel experience of being aware of their own thoughts and feelings as they read. But let us give this activity some content and say that the most obvious meaning is that the reader reflects about the characters, their motives and feelings, and how these do or do not resemble his or her own motives and feelings (for some vivid examples, see the accounts of Phil, Jeannie, and Linda, in Coles 1989, 31–66).

Readers who have this response often retell or synopsize the story and provide a running interpretational commentary as they do, frequently discussing the characters and their reactions to them as though they are real people. One high school student begins to talk about Robert Coover's short story "The Brother": "I think he's telling the story because it's raining . . . it's the impact on his life . . . it's ruined. As it starts off, already his fields are ruined. It's having an effect on his life, so he's going to say something. I mean, he's kind of upset that he's being used by his brother, and he really has no idea why."

A more developed way of thinking about fiction shows up when adolescents talk about the "meaning" of a story. This represents a higher level of abstraction, because a statement of meaning requires a generalization about the significance of the story taken as a whole. Meaning is often perceived as expressing the author's purpose or what the author is "trying to say" and is formulated as a metaphysical or ethical statement about the way things are. Charlie (17), a senior, struggles to state his reaction to William Carlos Williams's story "The Use of Force": "I don't know what he was saying other than . . . let me think . . . I don't know, unless . . . I guess sometimes it's necessary to use force to achieve a goal which is essentially peaceful or to achieve a goal . . . like in saving someone's life sometimes you might have to use force to get . . . I don't know if the end justifies the means, but in the end, to get a certain goal which is positive, maybe you might have to do something which you wouldn't approve of in other situations." A reader who has this kind of response can clearly separate the characters and actions of the story from its significance to him. The usual way of putting this is in terms of an image of depth; the deeper meaning is somehow waiting below the surface to be discovered. Frequently, of course, the generalized significance of a story is described as its moral or its lesson.

There appears to be a sequence of ways of thinking about the meaning of a story. The first impulse seems to be to think of it in concrete terms as a given of the story, a single summary formula that the reader has to get out of it ("Did you get the meaning?"). To see the meaning as originating in the author's intention is probably an advance on this point of view, because it conceives of the meaning not as a thing concealed somewhere in the story, but rather as a dimension of the whole story. The image of a deeper level of meaning makes much more sense from this angle. Thus, Charlie says that he read *Oliver Twist* and *David Copperfield* in the sixth or seventh grade, but when he reread them in the tenth grade he found out that "there's so much more in them than just the story," that Dickens was also writing an elaborate criticism of Victorian society and its class system. Denise (18) has just had a similar experience discovering religious symbolism in Joyce's "Araby." This reminds her of what happened earlier with *Gulliver's Travels*: "When I read it when I was a kid I loved it. Then I come up into the high school and it says something else. It's on a much deeper level." Significantly, both Charlie and Denise did not stumble on this way of reading unaided. Charlie says the social criticism in Dickens was "pointed out" to him, and Denise says, "You know, it just passes right by you until you get in English class and you start to dissect it."

This notion that literary meaning is something "hidden" in the text can be seen as an extension of the adolescent's new-found awareness that there is a disparity between the inside and the outside of experience. If this is true of oneself, why should it not be true of others and of things like texts insofar as they embody an author's point of view? This discovery marks a fundamental aspect of literary apprehension, Michael Steig says, the perception that a literary work is not only a "representation" of an imaginative world but also in some sense an "utterance" of another person who speaks to us (Steig 1989, 32).

The discovery of multiple levels of significance deriving from authorial intention is perhaps the limit of an adolescent's ability to deal with the idea of meaning in a story. It is an extension, to the story as a whole, of the metaphoric or figurative principle that sees one thing simultaneously as another. But the adolescent version of this principle still wants this meaning to be a set of objective and decipherable facts. To go further would require taking the point of view that meaning results from an act of interpretation by the reader, which is the issue faced in the next stage of development. Adolescents interpret, but they do not have a theory of interpretation. They debate about interpretations, but the point at issue is which one is the right one. The answer is assumed to be a fact of the text, put there by the author, known by expert literary authorities – among whom may be the teacher – because they have mysterious skills of reading and special sources of information. Many high school and college students do not get any further than this in their attitude toward the meaning of a story.

Some do not get this far. Squire (1964), for example, found that certain reading difficulties were widespread among the ninth and tenth graders he studied. They failed to grasp the most obvious meanings of words and implications of details and then they clung tenaciously to their misinterpretations; they relied on stock responses and stereotyped patterns of thinking to interpret what they read; they wanted fairy-tale solutions and so they distorted details of the story to get happy interpretations; they came armed with critical yardsticks for evaluating stories, such as a narrow notion of realism or descriptive accuracy; their reactions were distorted by irrelevant associations to personal experience or to other stories, films, or television shows they had seen; and they often insisted on rushing to clear and definite interpretations, even when the evidence demanded a tentative and exploratory approach to the story's meaning (Squire 1964, 37–49).

But even readers who have arrived at the notion that a story may have layers of meaning are only partway along the road to an adequate resolution of the problems posed by inquiring about the meaning of a text. The concept of the author's intention, for instance, also implies that a story has a design, which in turn implies that its meaning is a function of its design, which can be analyzed in an evidentiary way, and ultimately that this is part of the process of reading (which by now means studying) the book. The adolescent reader is entering the foothills of this whole new range of thought. For now it is fun just to be here, thinking about the characters and about one's own life as it is mirrored in the story. Perhaps it is possible to sum up a meaning and to defend it by pointing to what characters say and do in the story. To get beyond this into techniques of analysis and the categories of literary criticism is something the best students may get a glimpse of and some may appear to be good at because they are clever at imitating the language of their teachers, but it finally requires a new way of looking at a story – as a problem of textual interpretation – that is substantially different from the adolescent's impulse to think about a story, even about what it means.

READING AND STUDYING LITERATURE

The places where adolescents do almost all their reading – alone in some private space or in English class and study hall at school – symbolize two aspects of reading at this age: that it is both a highly personal exploration of feelings and thoughts and at the same time a training in the social processing of meaning according to norms prescribed by the larger culture. These two kinds of reading, not in principle opposed to one another, seem in fact often to create a split in the way adolescent readers learn to respond to stories.

After all, if the experience of being involved in a story and identifying with its characters eventually leads a reader to think about its meaning and to develop an interpretation of it, it would seem plausible to assume that studying literature in school would stimulate and systematize this kind of analytic response and that older high school students would generally be good at it. This does not seem to be the case. Petrosky's review of the data from the 1979–80 NAEP survey makes this clear. Seventeen-year-olds did quite poorly when asked to explain or defend the meanings they drew from what they read. They were weakest in explaining the inferences they made about the themes of selections, better about characterization and mood, but even the answers judged adequate on these points tended to rely on summary or synopsis rather than on any systematic analysis of the text or of the students' own ideas and values (Petrosky 1982, 11–12).

Another part of the study assessed the criteria students used to evaluate what they read and how they applied these to specific texts. The two most cited criteria for stories were their content and subjective reactions, such as whether the stories were "interesting" or "adventurous." (For poems the most prominent criterion listed was form, followed by subjective reactions, and then content.) When they came to explaining how they applied these criteria, the responses were either vague assertions unsupported by evidence or they were synopses or summaries of text based largely on content as a criterion (1982, 12–13).

Finally, when the students were asked to write free responses to stories and poems, their reactions depended overwhelmingly on the type of selection (thus, a Houseman poem produced inferential responses, a story about a son leaving home produced personal-analytic responses). Common among all the responses were retellings, subjective evaluations, emphasis on feelings, and simple inferencing (all fairly elementary approaches to a text). And even the most sophisticated responses were generally superficial, abstract, undeveloped, and lacking in specifics (1982, 14–15). Petrosky quotes from the final NAEP report:

> The most significant finding from this assessment is that while students learn to read a wide range of material, they develop very few skills for examining the nature of the ideas that they take away from their reading. Though most have learned to make simple inferences about such things as a character's behavior and motivation, for example, and can express their own judgments of a work as "good" or "bad," they cannot return to the passage to explain the interpretations they have made. (1982, 15–16)

Petrosky attributes these results to multiple-choice testing and to the kind of classroom discussion and textbooks that aim at quick easy answers. In their place he would like to see analytic skills developed by extended discourse – both speaking and writing. Because the seventeen-year-olds, when measured by multiple-choice tests, did fairly well in literal reading and in inferencing (75 percent), but were poor at using evidence in their arguments (22 percent), and judging by the writing they did demonstrated almost no ability to analyze a passage, Petrosky argues that only extensive class discussion and substantive writing assignments will develop the problem-solving and critical-thinking skills students need to be able to read literature carefully and interpret it intelligently (1982, 16–18).

If schools followed Petrosky's advice, the abilities of high school students to interpret what they read and to explain their interpretations would undoubtedly improve. But there is another factor influencing how students respond to stories: what their teachers assume about students' ability to read stories and therefore what they assume the goals of a high school education in literature ought to be. The 1970 International Association for the Evaluation of Educational Achievement data on reading and literature education in ten different countries allow some interesting inferences on this point. Purves wrote one part of the original report in 1973; when he reviewed this material in 1981 he devoted a chapter to what teachers reported about themselves (Purves 1981). One of his conclusions is that the U.S. junior high school and high school teachers queried tended to fall into two groups, depending on which kinds of responses to literature they regarded as important. One group took a *personalist* approach, valuing questions that relate to the life of the reader, such as "whether the reader finds a connection to the work, whether the work resembles the reader's perception of the world, the lesson of the work, the emotions aroused by the work and its success in involving the reader, and whether the work is serious and significant." The other group took an *academic,* text-centered approach to literature, focusing on "literary devices, language, the relation of technique to content, structure, evaluation of craft, symbols, genre, and tone" (Purves 1981, 38). Purves suspects that these critical stances toward literature arise less from perceptions about students' needs than from the kind of training the teachers had – in reading, language, English literature, or literary criticism, for example – and whether it was recent or in the past (1981, 45).

These conclusions suggest a new approach to the poor ability of students in the 1979–80 NAEP study to explain their interpretations of the literature they read. Is it possible that personalist teachers have too low an estimate of students' analytic abilities and academic teachers have too high an expectation of what they can do? And that what is missing in between is the kind of response that ought to be most suited to high school students' way of thinking: a critical evaluation of what the work of literature seems to say about the world?

Personalist and academic approaches to literature do not seem to be simply choices about how to read. A sophisticated reader, it is true, might think of them as options, depending on one's reason for reading a particular work (a detective story, for example, might be read for relaxation or as material for a semiotics course). But for a young reader they are more like steps in a sequence, which have to be taught and learned – except that an important ingredient is missing. An adolescent's first experiences as a self-conscious reader are wholly personalist: being involved on the level of feeling with the story, identifying with the characters, being aware of this involvement and identification, judging stories according to their realistic resemblance to one's own experience, thinking about the characters and their motives and feelings. But if we make students proceed directly from this way of responding to a story to academic talk of literary devices, symbols, genres, ambiguity, point of view, and so forth, then we risk passing over the adolescent's crucial involvement with the whole world of meaning and significance. We should be more afraid of introducing such matters too early, Britton says, than too late, especially when the voice of the teacher or literary critic seems to be the voice of authority (1978, 108–9). There is good reason, in fact, to think that readers who are more emotionally involved in a story when reading it are more likely to make informed literary judgments about it after they have finished it. Conversely, a demand by the teacher for more analysis, judgment, and interpretation is likely to inhibit the proper affective responses of younger readers and even undergraduates. Harding's sensible comments on this whole topic deserve study. He cautions above all that in teaching adolescents and even university undergraduates, "It is literature, not literary criticism, that is the subject" (Harding 1968b, 390). How do we strike a balance?

When adolescents say that they like a book because it makes them think, they appear to be saying something like this; they have discovered that their own judgments and feelings, the motives of other peoples' actions, indeed the whole intelligibility of the world are up for grabs and that they need to sort these things out and that reading helps. If we reduce this reading only to personalist terms or go in the other direction of substituting for it a technical analysis of how a literary work functions, then we deprive adolescents (so far as reading is concerned) of what they most need: the tools to deal with the world of ideas and values as they have recently discovered it.

But aren't the techniques of literary analysis precisely the tools a student needs to interpret and evaluate a text intelligently? Yes and no. Yes, if we mean that one cannot really resolve ambiguities in the interpretation of a text without understanding something about how texts are put together and work, and if we mean that as adolescents become more experienced readers they will be drawn to the challenge of figuring out how stories create the meanings that speak to them. No, if we mean that an adolescent's interest in interpreting and evaluating a text will be satisfied simply by learning how literary critics think texts are put together and work. What falls through the cracks here is the reader's sense of connection between his or her personal and emotional involvement with the work and the stance the work takes toward the whole world of ideas and their history, the debates about what men and women should and should not believe or value or do, the attitudes and feelings it is permissible or desirable to take toward the experiences of life, and all the ways poets and storytellers have interpreted their experiences. This sense of connection cannot be achieved by focusing on either the reader's private response or the textual strategies the author employs, yet these are the dangers posed by the tendency of many teachers toward the personalist or academic critical stances discerned by Purves. Something seems to be missing.

Scholes's outline of the kinds of competence students need to become good readers of fiction may shed some light here (1985, 21–4). He proposes three related skills. The first he calls simply "reading," the largely unconscious activity of constructing an imaginary world out of our knowledge of the narrative codes we have been learning since our first childhood experiences of stories. Any hitches or problems in reading – words we cannot understand, for example, or the sense that some concealed meaning is operative – cause us to shift to the second skill, the active and conscious process of "interpretation," which requires us to formulate the themes of the story and the attitudes the writer takes toward them and, concomitantly perhaps, to explicate the strategies the writer uses to accomplish the thematizing. Scholes says pithily that typically some excess of meaning in the text or some deficiency of knowledge in the reader pushes the reader into this activity of interpreting. But the reverse situation – some deficiency in the text or excess in the reader – will lead to the third kind of response, "criticism." The reader's human and ethical and political responses, having been shaped by a social context, by membership in groups that share values and interests, ultimately require a critique of the themes of the text or a critique of the codes out of which a given text has been constructed. This act of criticism does not privilege extraliterary values over literary ones, but it creates an indispensable dialogue between them; it opens the way, Scholes argues, between the literary text and the social text in which we live.

The more educated reader will eventually learn to balance all these reading strategies, but their full employment is probably beyond the grasp of most adolescents. Nonetheless, teachers ought to find ways of helping them practice all three of these competences, however imperfectly. Adolescents are, at very least, passionately principled about the world and its meanings. Classroom approaches to reading that emphasize mastering analysis of literary techniques and fail to relate this kind of competence to students' experiential involvement with what they read on the one hand and with their convictions about the larger world on the other fail to do justice to the adolescents' need to find a usable wisdom in the books they read and study.

One does not have to look far to discover why meaning in the sense of useful wisdom about the world disappeared from official view. The history of English education in the last few decades has been against it. The dominant critical theory, formulated as the New Criticism in the 1930s, made its way from the graduate schools into the undergraduate training of English majors during the postwar years, and into secondary schools in the 1960s. Its principles were stated in the beginning of Brooks and Warren's influential 1938 college textbook *Understanding Poetry*. Teachers were warned to resist the temptation to study, in place of the poem, one or another substitute: a paraphrase of the poem's logical or narrative content, biographical and historical information supposedly pertinent to it, or readers' inspirational or didactic interpretations of it. Instead, emphasis should be on "the poem as a poem." Its treatment should be concrete and inductive. And its poetic quality should never be understood as inhering in one or more factors taken in isolation; rather the poem should be treated as "an organic system of relationships" (Brooks and Warren 1938, xi–xv).

Several things can be said about this point of view toward literature. It certainly was a useful corrective to sentimental and moralistic ways of reading poetry and to the philological and historical study of literature. Furthermore, it was and is a useful point of view to take toward literature, if your object is to begin to understand how a poem works internally as a certain kind of linguistic structure; therefore, it may be well suited as a way of beginning the formal and systematic study of literature – say, as a college English major. It also has the advantage of appearing to be empirical, indeed scientific, and of prescinding from issues of meaning and value, which makes it an attractive point of view to take in a pluralist educational setting where questions of value and meaning are often handled by being assigned to the realm of private judgment. However, it has the disadvantage of suggesting to more extreme practitioners than Brooks and Warren that poems not only should not but cannot be paraphrased, that biographical and historical information is not pertinent to understanding them, and that it is naive and misleading to talk about a poem's meaning. One can talk about the way poems mean (New Critics did so at great length), but not about what they mean.

One thing that tended to disappear from view in New Critical doctrine was the writer. To suppose that it is desirable to draw conclusions about what the maker of the poem or story meant us to think or feel was to commit "the intentional fallacy." To try to understand the work as a product of a particular life in a specific time or place was to give way to "the biographical fallacy." To read a poem or story as an expression of the writer's point of view about the work's subject was to commit "the heresy of paraphrase." Yet why is it that we spontaneously take all these attitudes toward literature and have to be coaxed out of them by training in critical analysis? One reason we are inclined to think that poems and stories have meanings (leaving aside for the moment the question of whether this is an adequate way of talking about the hermeneutic problems involved) may be that as adolescents we discover that meaning is an issue, that the things we read cannot simply be taken for granted as pictures of the world, that they offer us points of view and ways of feeling that ultimately have to be evaluated.

These realizations go together with the adolescent's discovery of the author. Younger children scarcely know authors' names or think of them as no more than labels to identify books they like. But adolescents discover that a person has written this book and begin to think of the writer as someone like themselves, with a point of view, speaking out of his or her experience, saying something to the reader about the way the world is. Recall Holden Caulfield's memorable comment in *The Catcher in The Rye*: "What really knocks me out is a book that, when you're all done reading it, you wish the author that wrote it was a terrific friend of yours and you could call him up on the phone whenever you felt like it" (Salinger 1951, 20). Harding points out a fact about readers' responses that literary critics often disparage:

> Any but the most naive kind of reading puts us into implicit relation with an author. A novelist (or a playwright) may be directing our attention mainly to the action and experience of his characters, and part of our job is to enter imaginatively into them. But he is at the same time conveying his own evaluation of what is done and felt, presenting it (to mention simpler possibilities) as heroic, pathetic, contemptible, charming, funny . . . and implicitly inviting us to share his attitude. Our task as readers is not complete unless we tacitly evaluate his evaluation, endorsing it fully, rejecting it, but more probably feeling some less clear-cut attitude based on discriminations achieved or groped after. (1978a, 201)

We want to feel (perhaps, I would add, especially in adolescence when we are trying out and shaping our convictions) that someone else has contemplated certain possibilities of experience and evaluated them in such and such a way and that when we share the author's point of view "some mutual sanctioning of values is occurring" (1978a, 206) or that when we reject it we know ourselves and our feelings and convictions more clearly for doing so.

Adolescent readers may even be quite disappointed when authors fail to meet their requirements for conclusiveness: "I wanted to know more about what the author thought about duty and friendship, more about his feelings," one seventeen-year-old boy said about O'Connor's "Guests of the Nation": "At the end I wanted to find out the truth about these things, and all he did was describe what was going on." Older and more sophisticated readers may require different conceptions of the meaning of stories, but adolescents first need to exhaust the possibilities inherent in the critical stance that looks for truth and understanding and wisdom about the world in what they read.

High school textbooks often illustrate the confused critical attitudes that the English profession has about teaching literature. Most of them awkwardly straddle the gap between meaning and technical analysis. The typical study questions after each selection fall into two unrelated groups; one implicitly acknowledges that the text's objective meaning can be ascertained by careful study, whereas the other encourages text-critical analysis of symbol, tone, point of view, and so forth. The problem is that these approaches are seldom related to each other or to the emotional responses of the reader. Textual structures are not seen to be the vehicle of meaning, perhaps because of the thin conception of both meaning and technique prevalent in these books. Meaning is the kernel to be ascertained from this poem or story. Metaphors and symbols and instances of personification are technical facts to be identified and labeled. There is little sense in these textbooks that a writer wrote this way because of a passion or a concern for something, that skill was at the service of feeling and ideas, that these works mattered once and still may because of their influence on us, and that the reader has a personal stake in understanding all of this.[4] But if high school encourages the attenuation of this attitude toward reading, college presents an even stronger challenge to the student.

4

College and Beyond:
The Reader as Interpreter

When Susan Sontag wrote, "None of us can ever retrieve that innocence before all theory when art knew no need to justify itself, when one did not ask of a work of art what it said because one knew (or thought one knew) what it *did*" (1966, 4–5), she conveyed both the truth about a particular moment in our development as readers and the nostalgic regret that we may feel about it in looking back. All experience of art is a matter of interpreting, however, as Sontag herself concedes, quoting Nietzsche: "There are no facts, only interpretations" (1966, 70). But there is a difference between the innocence of interpreting without knowing that you are doing so and the self-consciousness of interpreting after it has become a problem. The mode of reading that we now want to consider is the kind of response that does not take the story for granted as a direct experience of an imagined world, but sees it as a text that someone has made, as something problematic and therefore demanding interpretation.

It seems unlikely that anyone will come to this attitude without considerable schooling. Indeed, many of the crucial experiences necessary to produce the changes in attitude involved in this mode of reading stories seem to be connected with the study of literature on the college or university level. Readers who do not go beyond high school will of course engage at some level in acts of interpretation and criticism, in the sense Scholes gives to these two terms – that is, they will construct thematic understandings of works they read and they will evaluate the thematized works by reference to their interests and commitments (1985, 22–4). But these acts of interpretation and criticism embrace a range of behaviors and skills, from generalizations and judgments based on very global responses on the one hand, to complex analyses that depend on a wide experience with different kinds of literature and on a sophisticated understanding of how codes and literary structures operate. Readers who do not become students of literature probably will not face the full implications of the problem of consciously interpreting and criticizing what

121

they read, in this latter sense. And even college students, unless the study of literature forms a considerable part of their work, may not face the problem or face it only in its simpler versions.

In other words, the transition to this mode of reading marks a split among adult readers that is by no means easy to describe or to evaluate. Is it likely that readers who go no further than high school will continue to read in their later years in the same way they did as adolescents? Is it desirable that college and university students of literature be led in the direction of analysis and interpretation as the preferred mode of reading? Can it be said that wrestling with the difficulties of interpretation is an advance over the more unself-conscious immersion in the story and the world it pictures, and over global kinds of interpretation and criticism, which are the uncritical adolescent and adult responses to a work of fiction?

This split among readers may seem to mark the point where a developmental account of reading gives way to a culture-specific account, or where a pattern of development that up to now looked natural and common to all readers is replaced by attitudes that only special educational experiences are likely to induce. Is this the case? I do not think so for several reasons. The whole pattern of reading development we have been considering has consistently been imagined as the product of the interaction of both maturing cognitive/affective capacities and specific sociocultural opportunities and demands. Furthermore, the readiest way to see the move toward studying and interpreting texts is as a version of Piaget's formal-operational thinking, not essentially different from the typical adolescent's (and adult's) ability to think in terms of hypothetical explanations and to evaluate the implications of these imaginable alternatives (I shall emend this view slightly in the next chapter, but it can serve for now). We may need to remind ourselves that in a sense all reading even at the simplest level involves making and testing hypotheses in a constant feedback between reader and text (Holland 1988, 85–9). Interpreting and criticizing are only more explicit and self-conscious methods of analysis that we turn to because our unself-conscious ways of processing a text fail to yield adequate results. They are as natural as any other way of reading, especially in a cultural situation where readers' experiences differ and their values conflict and society esteems the kind of analyses that explain these differences. Readers' experiences differ because of their social identities, but also because they develop different interests and skills. Piaget (1972) says that although formal-operational thinking is the basis of all adult logic, individuals will apply it to different areas and that the best place to see it at work will therefore be in areas relevant to a person's career interests and special aptitudes. So it should not be surprising that the study of literature produces both a higher degree of need to interpret works of literature theoretically and a higher degree of complexity of interpretation.

It is tempting to consider the conscious student role less as a distinct way of reading than as a detour on the way to more open and inclusive adult responses to stories, which readers can arrive at whether they have been English majors or have never gone to college at all. But that would undervalue the experience of studying literature merely to emphasize the continuity of adolescent and adult modes of reading. It is safer to say that there are alternative routes to adult reading styles and that studying how to interpret literature is one of them.

TWO STUDENTS READING

Dan

Dan is a nineteen-year-old college freshman, a biology major who plans to go to medical school. He is not, he says, a great reader. In high school, sports and school work took all his time; if his brother had not introduced him to science fiction, he might not have read anything at all outside of class work. He still reads science fiction "just for enjoyment," but he adds that now he notices one difference; when he read it in the tenth grade he did not "get anything out of it, just the story, but now I read it and I see what the author's points are, say, on war or utopia or something." He has enjoyed reading most of the novels required for his freshman English course (he mentions Hardy's *The Mayor of Casterbridge* and Lawrence's *Sons and Lovers*), but he says that he never would have read them if they had not been assigned. When asked why they were enjoyable, Dan gives two explanations that we have seen are characteristically linked in early adolescents' responses to fiction. The first is involvement in the experience of reading the book: "Maybe because I got absorbed into it . . . I couldn't put the book down." The second is identification with the characters or themes of the book: "It related to something that meant something to me. Like, for instance, I just got done reading, two weeks ago, *Sons and Lovers,* and although I didn't particularly like the book, I mean a lot of things are related to me in it. That's why I liked it . . . some of the relationships to the people . . . the characters in the book."

But Dan has made another discovery about reading and it turns up not so much in the discussion of his freshman English course as in some remarks he makes about being a biology major. He had just come from taking a biology quiz, which he thought he did well on until he talked to some of the other students in the course after the exam: "I got real upset. I'd studied so long . . . I thought I knew everything." Then he utters something of a paradox: "I think I'm getting much better at understanding the fundamentals [of biology], and when they give me an example I can see how it's related to the overall schemes and stuff, and I'm getting much better at it, but it seems my grades have gone down since eleventh grade... although I seem to know so much more. The book on biology... I feel like I know it inside out. Although I got an A − last time, this time it will be maybe a B. It seems that my test grades just don't seem to show it." Has he any idea why this is happening? "I think I'm too close to the book maybe. There'll be two answers, and one's a little better than the other, and I'll just sit there and debate between two multiple-choice answers for so long that I usually pick the wrong one, as it turns out." He laughs a bit ruefully: "It's pretty much one answer but they are all so closely related that it's sometimes hard to make a distinction between which one is the right one, but there's definitely a right answer."

In Dan's mind "there's definitely a right answer" to questions about biology. "Everything's based on theories and proof... and fact," he says later. English class, though, seems disconcertingly a matter of subjective opinion and individual ability. One instance is an essay from Joan Didion's book about California culture in the 1960s, *Slouching Towards Bethlehem*: "Well, she said that other than the fundamental social values, there's no way of knowing what's right and wrong... I mean, that's absurd. ... In biology, there's opinions, but a lot of things are based on fact. I mean, you can't deny things that happen, whereas in English it seems that some of them [i.e., writers] go as far as saying that murder is okay, although it's absurd. But there's no facts which you can prove ... whether it's right or wrong."

There are differences too in the way people in his class read the short stories and novels that are assigned: "There's a few [students] that I've picked out that seem to go home and they read the stuff and sometimes they seem to go a bit overboard in digging out meanings." But the results are not necessarily bad: "For the most part they do a pretty good job in what they think is going on in the story." He can even compare it to the way he interprets data in his own subject: "Just like a biology major. When I read the text on how the muscle works... in a sense, you have to relate that to why does it work that way... just as if one character kills another, you're going to say 'Well, why did he do this?' ... in the overall picture, to find a theme." But it puzzles him that some people are better at it then others: "I can't understand how someone could be good at math and not be good at, say, English or something. It seems to be systematic... something like chemistry. How some people can be good in chemistry and not in biology, and it seems to me they both seem to be equally learnable, but something doesn't click that in biology an English major can do it."

Dan has two ways of making sense out of his experiences in English and biology. One is to assume that people have different individual tastes and abilities: "My friend across the hall . . . he does much better than I in chemistry, and I do much better than him in biology, and it seems when talking with him that we know all the same things. . . . It seems strange. . . . Are people's abilities in different fields different?" The other way is to distinguish between subjects where fact and proof count (biology, for example) and those that belong to the realm of opinion (such as English). This strategy is not entirely successful, however, because Dan can see that the English major who is digging out the meaning is relating pieces of evidence to achieve an overall interpretation of the theme, much as he himself does in studying a text on how the muscle works. Worse yet, his recent experience with the biology test has made it clear that not even biology is unambiguously a matter of fact and that to some degree interpretation is required to make sense of biology quizzes as well as of English texts. To Dan, though, interpretation is uncomfortably close to opinion. Until his epistemological framework allows him to see that it is the way all complex understanding works, he will be stuck on the shrinking solid ground of the factual, with the waters of subjectivity and opinion encroaching around him.

Michael

Michael, age 25, is a graduate student in English. His world differs from Dan's in a number of ways. Not surprisingly, he lives in an atmosphere of books and academic talk about them. He is preparing for an exam in comical and satirical literature, reading for a seminar in literary theory, and teaching a section of freshman English. His voluntary reading is wide ranging: jazz writers, a biography of Wittgenstein, a collection of Susan Sontag's essays, detective fiction by Dashiell Hammett, Raymond Chandler, and Ross MacDonald, and the *Weekly World News* (a supermarket tabloid that he says makes the *National Enquirer* look like the *New York Review of Books*.) Many of these he reads from a student's point of view: the detective stories for their voice and dialogue, editorials in the *Weekly World News* because they offer interesting examples of a theoretical problem dealing with intentionality and interpretation.

Michael can be articulate about some issues that baffle Dan. He has been studying literature long enough to have acquired an extensive vocabulary for analyzing it. He can even see that he has gone through different changes in the way he reads books since he was a high school student or a college freshman. One measure of the difference, he says, is how he marks up books. In high school, it would just be a matter of occasionally underlining plot details and characters' names; now he cannot read anything without a pen in his hand to note his responses, to check the meanings of words, and especially to observe structural details. (This may be one of the symbols of apprenticeship as a literary professional. A professor of English says that she began marking her books in college and has never stopped; it was "a way of making tracks through things that were mine." Another colleague says: "It's as if every book that you read might be something that you might potentially teach. I've heard people say they can't avoid doing it even with detective stories.")

Structure is a key term for Michael. He jokes about the search for deeper meaning that was typical of his high school study of literature. He was also interested then in the influences on a given text, influences from other writers or from the historical zeitgeist – for example, he says, reading a poem by Donne against the background of the seventeenth-century English social structure. Now he finds himself more interested in the texts themselves and the structures that relate them to one another. He gives as an example the exam he is preparing for, on Rabelais, Thomas Nash, and William Burroughs, three writers related by genre, technique, and point of view, rather than by historical influence. "I think more about narrators or speakers and things like that," he says. "I guess I'm more prone to look for connections between things that I've already read and what I'm reading now."

Perhaps the most striking way in which Michael differs from Dan as a reader is that he has a highly flexible approach to what he reads and that he is comfortable with a complex response to the text and with conclusions that are provisional and clearly subject to revision. Part of the discussion is about Faulkner's short story, "Barn Burning." Michael has read a great deal of Faulkner and likes him. He can read this story as a participant in the action, but for the most part his stance is that of the literary critic. He comments on the boy's narrative voice in the story and on the peculiar way Faulkner occasionally uses it to comment on the action from points in time much later in the boy's life. Does this make the story artificial? "Oh, yes, but I'm not sure if that's good or bad. Maybe this is too much Faulkner coming in. In a story like this it seems to throw me a bit."

Michael often tests his own reactions like this, as he talks about the story. We discuss the ending of the story and the boy's decisions to warn the landowner that his father intends to burn down his barn and then to run away from his family. Michael formulates the issue facing the boy clearly: Which is more important, right and wrong or the family tie of blood relationship? He can see the resolution from a number of points of view: "I suppose his decision is a good thing. It's also a comic thing in a way, because what can this boy do out in the woods if he runs away? It's kind of a pathetic gesture as well as being a heroic gesture." He resists easy conclusions about the story. Does he think Faulkner wants us to see the boy's decision as a turning point in his life? "I don't know. I think I'd have to read it again. I get the impression that it's too . . . not funny . . . but too ridiculous maybe to take it completely that way. . . . I find it hard not to laugh, except, well, I guess it's a sort of an uncomfortable laugh. It's not just pastoral comedy."

In a sense we can say that both Michael and Dan are indecisive about what they are reading. Opinion seems to rule in both cases. The differences, though, are more significant. Whereas Dan cannot imagine any basis for deciding about a book other than his involvement with it and his identification with the characters, Michael can analyze the evidence in the text from a number of points of view. Dan's epistemology requires a definite answer and so he assigns any tentative conclusions to the realm of opinion. Michael grants *only* provisional conclusions because more careful readings might show him something further about the story. The really notable difference is in the very possibility of analysis. Dan is baffled by how others in his class do it. Michael swims in this water like a fish. How does someone get from Dan's need for hard facts and his suspicion that he will not find any in his English class to Michael's confidence in the evidential value of his own responses as clues to the meaning of the story and to his confidence that the story can be tested against different hypotheses and that it eventually will yield a firm meaning? In short, how does one get from Dan's distrust of interpretation to Michael's confidence in it? That is the general question this chapter proposes to deal with.

THE TRANSPARENT TEXT

It will be useful to break this transition down into a sequence of positions that readers occupy as they enter into the role of interpreters of literature. The starting point is the way they read at the end of high school or the beginning of college. It is a version of the picture already given in the previous chapter of how adolescents read. One way of describing readers at this level of development is to say that they do not see the text. Of course they read the words on the page, but they do not focus any attention on them as the place where a problem of interpretation is to be encountered. Instead they look through them, at the characters and at the actions the characters are engaged in, at the world depicted in the story. The text – the words and their arrangement on the page – has the transparency of a window; it is not what these readers are looking at when they read a story.

In a sense every writer aims at a transparent text, and from childhood through high school and into college and beyond we normally read many books as though the text were a perfectly lucid medium for telling a story or communicating an idea. This is what Scholes calls simply "reading." Even when at a certain level a reader questions the details of the text, this does not mean that the text itself is any less transparent. Young children, for example, will ask what particular words and phrases mean. Or they will ask why the author describes a character or a place in such a way, or why the author makes such and such a generalization about the events. These interpretive strategies draw attention to the words on the page and thus in a sense to the text. But even these do not treat the text as a focus of the reading activity. Rather, the text in these cases is a momentary obstacle to constructing an objective understanding of the work as a whole, an objective understanding whose reference point is outside the text – for example, accurate information about the definitions of words (as in a dictionary, say), or the knowledge of the world and the way things are that adults possess. Even older children's questions about what authors mean when they say something may not be queries about authorial intention so much as requests to be told what adults generally mean by these words. This kind of reference beyond the text to the world pictured in the story or to an objective order of authoritative truth is typical of readers for whom the text is transparent.

A good example of text transparency is the reader who talks about the characters in a story – and to a lesser extent the settings and events – as though they really exist or have happened. Very young children, as we have seen, might actually believe this to be the case. Older boys and girls certainly know that fictional characters do not exist in the world outside the imagination of author and reader, yet they talk about them as though they actually do. I am not referring to the impression all readers sometimes have of the lifelikeness of a character that is drawn in an exceptionally vivid way, but rather to the unself-conscious and normal way readers at a certain level discuss the characters in a story as though they are real people.

Some college students, for example, will write an essay about a character such as Maria in Joyce's story "Clay" without mentioning Joyce as author or the actual words on the page, but summarizing qualities that Joyce only implied, speculating about Maria's motives and feelings where Joyce does not tell us about them, and generally treating her as someone they have come to know. Identification with the character or situation may be a powerful stimulus to this way of reading. And characters do in a sense have extratextual lives, insofar as they may appear in sequels, for example, or in other stories by the same author (something that occasionally happens in Joyce). What may also be affecting the behavior of readers who talk about characters as though they really exist is the convention of using the present tense to summarize and discuss what happens in a story ("Maria works in a Dublin laundry . . . "). Oddly enough, though this convention seems intended to lessen the dependence of the story on a narrative time in the past and to make it easier to focus analytically on the text by treating both the story events and the writer's strategic choices as abstract facts in a timeless present ("Why does Joyce say that Maria has a pointed nose and chin? Is he suggesting that she is witchlike?"), for readers who have little awareness of the text as something constructed by a writer the convention may have the paradoxical effect of heightening the sense of a character's real existence.

This impulse to ignore the text is apparently a very profound instinct on the part of readers whose main responses to a story are to identify with the character and to become involved in the plot situations. For them the story is a given, and the text is simply the invisible medium of its transmission. In fact, however, even the youngest readers actively construct the story and its characters out of the material offered by a text as they read, though the realization that they do so is beyond their grasp. We can appreciate this by recalling that in the text the events we read about do not always appear in chronological order, the qualities of the characters are dispersed throughout the text, and all the details of the narrative content are filtered through some narrative prism or perspective. However, we abstract the narrated events from their disposition in the text, reconstruct them in their chronological order, and call this the story. We do the same thing with the characters, assembling the data of the text into stable entities that seem in our minds to have the reality of actual persons (Rimmon-Kenan 1983, 3). So text transparency is not really a more natural way to read than any other, but we have been trained by our early reading to accept the techniques of classical realism as the normal state of things and to process them unconsciously.

Awareness of this process comes slowly to the reader, if it comes at all. At first, the struggle to produce a self occupies the adolescent reader's attention, and books are judged by what they contribute to this struggle. The first step the reader takes away from this view is toward the insight that the text is something constructed by an author whose intentions for it can be imagined and deciphered. This decentering leads next to a parallel deconstructing of the idea of the author, so that the reader learns to look directly at the text itself as an object containing the full evidence about its meaning. Finally, though, problems of interpreting texts lead to the realization that the text is constructed not only by the writer but also by the reader and by all the codes and cultural contexts they both depend on. Then the full implications of the problem of interpretation face the student, who is forced to develop one, or more likely several, theoretical points of view to account for the complex activity that reading has become. The reader for whom the text is an invisible means of access to a story knows nothing of this process.

THE PROBLEMATIC TEXT

Readers stop regarding the text as transparent when they confront the fact that other readers find different things when they read the same text (discovering that one's own readings of a text differ from one time to another would have the same effect, but the ability to notice this probably comes much later). This experience of readers in conflict over the same text occurs typically in higher level high school courses or in freshman courses in college. Diversity of opinion about the meaning and value of a story creates a practical and theoretical problem for the student, especially when it is not only fellow students who disagree, but legitimate authorities such as teachers and critics as well. How does a reader deal with this kind of uncertainty? Generally, we can say that the very capacity to see alternative possibilities (a prime example of Piaget's formal-operational thinking) that in one sense gets the reader into trouble at this stage turns out to be the solution for the difficulty; the student is ready to envision and test out new forms of understanding the experience of reading.

A helpful framework for understanding readers' responses in this situation is the description William Perry gives of how students' beliefs about what constitutes truth and falsity and right and wrong change during the college years (the best summary of his work is Perry 1970, 28–40). Perry got interested in trying to understand the attitudes of Harvard undergraduates who came to the counseling center for advice about studying, writing papers, and taking exams. He found that the real issues underlying these problems had to do with the overall interpretive frameworks the students used to give meaning to their experience. He and his colleagues eventually devised a schema to describe the changes college students undergo in their cognitive and ethical development. In Perry's view, the principal developmental task of students is to come to terms with the multiplicity of truths and values that college presents to them.

Freshmen are apt to leave high school with a world view structured in terms of a single frame of reference, with clear distinctions between what is true and false, right and wrong, good and bad – in short, with a simple dualism, taken for granted, unexamined – and with a strong predilection to rely for their certainties on *authority,* whether it be that of parents, church, teachers, or peers. In college they encounter *multiplicity*: opinions, values, styles of behavior different from and in conflict with their own and often in conflict among themselves – the cognitive disequilibrium identified by Piaget. Students' first reaction is to consider the multiplicity as an illegitimate exception ("they're wrong" or "they're confused") or as a matter of mere appearance ("the instructor is giving us different points of view because we're supposed to figure out for ourselves which one is the right one"). A further step is to recognize some of the implications of multiplicity and to accept it as temporary because the authorities have not yet found the answer. When pressed by more and more incongruent experiences, however, students are apt to respond by consigning all multiplicity to the realm of opinion, that inaccessible territory where everyone has a right to private judgment. This maneuver preserves some area of fact and objectivity from the corrupting influence of multiplicity, though it is a rapidly shrinking one.

The pivotal position is arrived at when students discover that relativism is not just a special case, but an aspect of the nature of all knowledge, and that we are always going to be making up our minds in situations where we are the only ones with a firsthand view of the relevant data. The issue at this point is responsibility, and it shifts from outside to inside, from authorities to the authority of the student's own experience of what evidence counts in saying that something is true and false or right or wrong. These discoveries in a way constitute commitments, and Perry says that in the content and style of their commitments students come to a sense of identity. What they know and believe now may even be what the authorities of their youth taught them, but the style and the particular equilibrium they achieve are their own, because they have worked them out for themselves.

Perry's research focused on students in college in the early 1960s. His experience with freshmen ten years later suggested that the developmental shift he describes was already underway among high school students (1981, 98). At the other end of the scale, most subsequent studies have called into doubt whether college students generally reach the final stages of Perry's schema before they graduate or whether they reach it in all areas or only in the ones they specialize in (Kurfiss 1983). It seems likely, therefore, that the work of adjusting to the consequences of a relativistic view of knowledge goes on into the adult years. Nonetheless, the schema is an extremely suggestive model of a key transition in the thinking of college students whose overall validity has been empirically confirmed in a number of studies (Kurfiss 1983; Kitchener and King 1981). It also makes clear that the shift in the way students read is only one part of a larger epistemological transition that students experience in their moral and religious lives, as well as in their cognitive development.

The starting point of this transition is the dualist position that any given answer is either right or wrong. This point of view is implicit among readers who treat the text as transparent, because they do not even see anything to disagree about. It becomes explicit as a response to conflicting interpretations of the meaning of a story; only one reading can be correct, and the student's job is to figure it out or to learn what it is from an authoritative teacher or critic. Readers who say this are not necessarily unaware of the need to support their conclusions with evidence, but their responses are strongly influenced by how they conceive of the meaning of a story and by what they think appropriate evidence for the meaning is. Like Dan, the freshman biology major above, they think that the meaning is some sort of definite fact that knowledgeable readers can arrive at. "That was an easy one," a freshman says about a story she has read. "I got that one right away."

When the attitude that meaning is self-evident becomes no longer serviceable (because readers need help in discovering it or disagree about it when they do), the meaning has to be located somewhere where it can be discussed in an evidential way. The recourse that most students seem to take at this point is to think of the meaning as a function of the author's intention. It is what the author is "trying to say." This is a natural enough epistemological strategy, because the problem for a reader who confronts multiple interpretations for the first time is to preserve whatever definite facts he or she can against a confusing relativism, and the author looks like the obvious source of stable meaning. A story after all is self-evidently the product of a writer who on the face of it would seem to be the proprietor of its meaning, especially if meaning is taken to be what a person intends to say when he or she utters or writes down words.

This line of thought leads the dualist thinker to link story and author in a variety of concrete ways. If textual details are to be interpreted in light of what the author meant them to signify, a great deal of value may be attached to letters, journals, and commentaries that disclose the author's intentions. A common assumption related to this attitude is that a work of literature expresses the feelings and thoughts of an especially sensitive person whose state of mind the student therefore attempts to detect from the evidence in the story. (Note that this view of the creative imagination as an acute inner sensibility matches the self-image of adolescent readers in high school and college particularly well.) Readers with a moralistic bent may focus on the opinions of the writer and judge the work in terms of the acceptability or unacceptability of the author's attitudes. Another common version of this author-story focus is to interpret the details of the text autobiographically, as manifestations of the author's personal history, which can lead of course to psychoanalyzing the writer. A wider view of this biographical link can lead to the study of the historical period in which the author wrote, so that the work becomes meaningful as an index of the attitudes and ideas of an age.

All these author-focused points of view are common in high school and college literature classes. And allowing for changes in literary fashion, we have to say that they have also been pursued on extremely high levels of critical sophistication by eminent scholars. But dualist thinkers focus on the author because they cannot imagine any other approach to the problem of finding the right answer that will solve discrepancies of interpretation. How does a dualist thinker get beyond this way of reading?

For one thing, the assumption that a story has an evident meaning fades in the face of continuing argument about what the evidence means. The author's intentions for the work, for example, prove difficult to assess or to agree on. Or not enough is known about the author's life (Shakespeare's, say), to allow any useful inferences about the work in question. Or too much is known about the author (James Joyce, for example, or Virginia Woolf), so that biography and commentary become a barrier to easy access to the work. The history of ideas, of course, turns out to be an extremely complex subject. And critical opinion on all these points abounds and much of it is in disagreement. The result is that the validity of any interpretation becomes an explicit issue, and the student is forced to look for more reliable evidence to defend any position he or she takes. If the biographical and historical evidence do not yield sufficient certitude, then the clearest source of factual evidence may be the text itself.

This is a striking shift in the student's focus, but it does not happen all at once. In fact, the student has probably all along been becoming a more and more skilled handler of textual evidence, even while engaged in various author-focused strategies of interpretation, because disagreement about the results of these strategies pushes the reader to gather data more and more carefully to support conclusions.

Teachers clearly have a great deal to do with this shift. Every high school and college student has had the experience of being challenged by an instructor who asks, "Where do you find any evidence for this in the text?" The teacher may only be interested in forcing the student to support arguments with evidence, but the more carefully the student has to look for this evidence, the closer the student comes to the actual text, to the words, their denotations and connotations, their placement in relation to one another, the structured patterns in which they are arranged, and the total coherent organization they constitute.

This is not necessarily the end of dualistic thinking on the part of the reader, who may simply transfer the need for a single factual answer from the author to the text and guess at any bit of concrete evidence that looks like it might possibly lead to the right answer. This becomes harder to do, however, as the reader looks more closely at the text, because a text is inherently a multiple thing whose parts can be understood only by relating them to one another. Words are significantly affected by their position. Images grow by repetition and addition, and they can change in relation to other details of the story. Characters develop. Meaning is more and more a matter of relating the parts of a complex whole.

In Perry's terms, what is happening is that the reader is reluctantly abandoning the conviction that the meaning of a story is part of a one-dimensional, objective, absolute system of truth. Faced with conflicting versions of that truth, the student tries to hang on to whatever objectivity is possible, while simultaneously being forced to deal more and more with the relativistic aspects of interpreting textual evidence – that is, with the fact that the words of a text are not simple facts, but can be understood only in relation to each other, and that conclusions about their meaning are related to assumptions the reader makes about how they are put together.

The student may resist the relativistic implications of disagreement by a variety of stratagems – for instance, by putting faith blindly in the authority of the teacher because the teacher is thought to be a surer guide to the absolute truth and attempting to support guesses and intuitions about the work in question by imitating the teacher's style of discussing or writing about literature. Further down this slippery slope, the student may decide, like Dan, that although there are many gray areas of knowledge that are contaminated by an apparently unresolvable multiplicity of interpretations, there are at least some black-and-white areas where facts and absolutes and authoritative truths prevail. Usually, the natural sciences are thought of as the domain of fact and the humanities are thought of as governed by opinion. Students at this point will fall back on the position that everyone has a right to his or her own opinion about a story. When this uncertainty spreads to all the other areas, however, and becomes a doubt about the possibility of knowing anything absolutely, the individual reaches the crisis that is the turning point in Perry's view of college students' development.

What leads out of the crisis is the discovery that even though the gray areas are the rule rather than the exception, there are meaningful patterns and regularities in the evidence, that data can be related to the context in which they occur, that interpretations can be compared and evaluated, and that it is possible to arrive at plausible and defensible conclusions. Teachers and other authorities are seen to be fellow seekers of understanding, "different primarily in that they are experienced at making sense of the profusion of knowledge in their fields" (Kurfiss 1983, 17). Students do not discover this all at once. They may realize it at first only in one area of knowledge, and some time may pass before they are confident enough to extend it to other areas.

They may even develop the skills of relativistic thinking inadvertently, as a by-product of trying to hang on to dualist attitudes. In lectures, Perry often tells a story about a student who gets a poor grade on a paper, which the instructor says is full of unsupported generalizations and lacks factual evidence. The student, determined to give the instructor what he wants, fills the next paper with facts about the subject. The paper gets an equally poor grade, this time on the grounds that it is a collection of unrelated data. The student, more than ever determined to satisfy the instructor, decides that if it is connections the instructor wants, that is what he will give him, so he organizes the material into a plausible argument. He gets a good grade, but is not aware that he has done anything more than satisfy the demands of this authority who has some temporary power over his life (the basis for this story, if not the actual anecdote, can be found in Perry 1965).

Students can also refuse the encounter with multiplicity altogether. Every teacher knows students who seem stuck in a pattern of relying on vague intuitions about what they read, grasping at unrelated bits of evidence to support their conclusions, repeating the instructor's opinions in formulaic fashion when questioned, following instructions rigidly when writing and rewriting papers, and generally seeming unable to relate any of the parts of the material confidently. Sometimes this attitude will extend well beyond English courses, because it can be a symptom of a general pause in the development of the student's ability to think and judge critically. Perry calls it "temporizing." Other ways of refusing to face the implications of relativistic thinking may be variants of what Perry calls "retreat": withdrawal into a reactionary dogmatism that is certain that it already possesses absolute truth, or a rebellious identification with whatever cause opposes the position of authority, or simply a passive resistance to the influence of authority in any form. An insidious and not uncommon way a smart and cynical student may escape the developmental process altogether for a while is by learning to play the intellectual game of mastering enough of the vocabulary and techniques of a subject to be able to manipulate the instructor's reward system. This kind of student can often perform at a fairly high level, but may have no real intellectual commitment to the process and no belief in the conclusions he or she comes to.

Except for this last attitude, which is likely to have its roots in a much more pervasive set of attitudes than reading alone would explain, these styles of dealing with the challenge of interpretation are probably self-limiting, at least for students who continue to study literature, because these students will be more and more forced to confront the multiplicity of the text and therefore to become aware of the processes by which they assemble its parts into experiential wholes. As they become better at doing this concretely, they will find that they have gotten beyond the crisis that once seemed so threatening.

THE INTELLIGIBLE TEXT

Every year at least one freshman or sophomore is bound to ask what others are probably thinking: "Why do we have to analyze these stories? Why can't we just read them and enjoy them?" There certainly are profound issues wrapped up in these questions, but what these students are concerned about is only partly related to the debate about interpretation that literary critics might conduct around this point. They are, rather, testing the question of whether they want to continue to *study* literature.

Why someone decides to major in literature or any other subject is inevitably a mysterious matter. Love of reading, the influence of a particular teacher, the thought of being a writer, or maybe just doing well in this one subject – these and other motives might lead someone to this choice. College forces a decision to some extent and, though many students delay it or make only a provisional one or even sustain two or three majors at once, most students by sophomore or junior year have passed a fork in their academic development, which divides the serious study of literature from the pursuit of another discipline and perhaps the occasional literature course for nonmajors. An interesting aspect of this choice is the sense students often have that in some real sense it gives them an identity. "My roommate is an English major, so she really has to take apart the stories she reads and look for the symbols and that sort of thing," one college junior says. "I'm not, so I can just read for the fun of it." A senior math and economics major (22) describes the differences between himself and his friend, who is an English major. She reads a novel analytically, looking for metaphors and implications; he reads for enjoyment and goes by his gut reaction. On the other hand, when it comes to a newspaper, she reads just for the story, whereas he analyzes it: "That's my economics background . . . don't believe everything you read . . . test it against a theory you know."

At some point students seem to discover that they like a subject, that they are good at it, that their performance gets the approval and encouragement of teachers, that it fits them somehow, and that they feel at home in it. No doubt sometimes the choice is premature, tentative, or initially made for the wrong reasons, but when it finally clicks into place the sense of identity is partly a consequence of discovering that studying literature makes it intelligible in an increasingly satisfying way.

A junior-year English major (20) describes how he discovered this identity and what the process of exploring it feels like:

> I didn't read much as a kid... I played football, basketball, baseball; I'd bowl, go fishing. Anything I did read was something I could read through real fast, like *Jaws*. Once high school came around, I started working every afternoon, and I was doing homework or going out at night. The moderator of the high school paper suggested I go into journalism... but I think teaching was something I always thought about. My uncle is a professor and my dad was before he started working for the state. I think all I needed to do was latch onto a subject I enjoyed.... The core courses [in college] gave me the opportunity to at least touch on some things, and English was the one that I really enjoyed.... Freshman year I had the tendency more to read over the things quickly and just know what the general story line was... the plot... what happened to the characters. Now I'm looking up every word that I don't understand... looking up references in texts... outside sources. I used to just enjoy the story, but I feel now, for some reason, just being an English major, that I should be picking out the symbols [he laughs]. I'm taking a Milton class right now, where I have a friend who is in the School of Management... and when we go into a test or the midterm and we'll be talking about it, it seems that she has down what I just said... what happens and the characters. And I know that too, but I want to know how it relates to the classics... the Bible. I wouldn't have had that ability when I was a freshman, just because I didn't have the knowledge then. A lot of things are just starting to tie themselves together.... You can almost see a pattern.... I took a course on the Romantics and the Victorian period, and now I'm going over Milton and I can pick out whole lines I've read somewhere else ... how authors take from authors that have gone before them.... It makes it more fun to read.... I realize how little I know, but... I want to go on to grad school and possibly for a Ph.D. and teach some day. ... I want to know everything... it's as simple as that... everything about history, about philosophy, about English.

This is not necessarily a sudden or dramatic change and it does not guarantee a trouble-free existence as an English major, but by and large what characterizes the student of literature (indeed of any subject) in the upper years of college and into graduate school is growing confidence and competence in handling the analytic and organizational skills that make the subject more intelligible and coherent and that increase the student's involvement in it and the sense of identity it confers.

Concretely, what these skills are depends on who one's teachers are and on prevailing fashions in how literature is taught. When I was an undergraduate in the early 1950s, the dominant critical attitude I was exposed to might have been called "expressive realism" (Belsey 1980, 7): the theory that literature expresses the reality of experience filtered through the sensibility of a particular writer. We tended, therefore, to study literature in terms of writers' lives and ideas and in terms of the age in which they wrote and the point of view and sensibility expressed in their works. The text was important semantically and rhetorically as evidence for our conclusions (and formally, especially for its metrics and tropes, if it was a poem), but the real intellectual activity of interpretation centered on historical background and on the history of ideas, on the psychological realism of the characters and situations portrayed, and on the moral evaluation of the writer's vision. Some instructors added New Critical attitudes to these approaches, but as one more tool for doing the basic work of interpreting the text's vision of the world. Other approaches were pointed out to us – psychoanalytic and Marxist readings of literature, for example – but these were considered the slightly suspect enthusiasms of specialists.

Ten years later an undergraduate might have found teachers still employing all these approaches to literature in the average college English department, but the influence of the New Criticism would have been much more pervasive by then. Younger instructors would be more likely to focus on the close reading of the language and form of the text, to admit historical background and the ideas of the age and the psychology of the writer only through the gate of the words on the page, and even to replace the history of writers and ideas with the history of texts and their structures and relationships to one another. In the late 1960s and early 1970s, political and social readings of literature became commonplace in the form of moral evaluations of writers' attitudes toward their subjects or in the more text-oriented form of semiotic analyses of cultural values disclosed in language and literary structures themselves. Recently, poststructuralist theory and deconstructive criticism have led students to focus their attention on the complex relationships between language, thought, and consciousness. In this view any text is a problematic embodiment of cultural motifs that transcend the author's employment of them and that subvert both the author's intention for the text and the reader's impulse to interpret it as a coherent whole. What is missing or repressed or unspoken becomes more significant than what is said, and the task of criticism is to anatomize all the ways in which a text signifies something less or more than it was intended to – to rewrite the text so as to disclose how thought is captive to language and ideology.

Any or all of these points of view might be found in the classrooms of U.S. colleges today. The older and more conservative perspectives still flourish in even the most progressive departments, I suspect, partly because they correspond to ways of reading that everyone goes through in adolescence and partly because more sophisticated ways of analyzing a text add to, but do not necessarily supplant, the earlier responses of involvement, identification, and reflection on the meaning of a story. More students will probably be exposed to the critical attitudes associated with mimetic and expressive views of literature than those exemplified by pure New Critical methods of text analysis, and of those taught primarily the close reading of texts fewer still are likely to be converts to a pure deconstructive point of view. Still, the terminology and the techniques will doubtless spread, and it is not unimaginable that college freshmen somewhere talk about the indeterminacy of texts and learn to discover gaps and absent others in whatever they read.

Though critical fashions and the specific intellectual issues of the day may play a role in the first steps students of literature learn to take, it is probably truer to say that students begin by imitating the techniques and attitudes of their teachers. If the instructor demands close analysis of the meanings of words, that will be the student's guide to interpreting literature. If the instructor inclines to discussing the history of ideas or the writer's psyche, the beginning student will do the same. The student's motive is partly survival, but students are also looking for workable techniques of interpretation, and the instructor is presumed to be a source of authoritative guidance. Fastening onto the techniques taught by an early and influential teacher is especially likely if students still cling to the view that there is one way of reading literature that will produce the objective meaning of a text.

Exposure to different teachers and different emphases, however, gradually gives them an eclectic set of analytic techniques that they get used to applying to particular texts as particular questions arise. The narrative strategies can be looked at closely, the writer's political attitudes discussed, the archetypal structure of the work analyzed, its semantic ambiguities traced. As students go from freshman year toward doctorates in English, they become more and more successful syncretists, which is what most teachers of literature are. They may confess allegiance to one critical attitude over another in principle (a graduate school attitude, for the most part), but in practice they are almost certainly pragmatic practitioners of a variety of techniques of literary analysis.

Three things deserve notice about this overall process. One is that the student gradually internalizes techniques that in the beginning were mainly imitated from teachers; there is a gain in confidence, in a sense of identity, that comes from being able to do by oneself what one could do only by following the methods of respected authorities when one was just a beginner. Another is that the student more and more skillfully synthesizes the techniques being learned and applies them to the problems posed by concrete works of literature and the particular points of view from which they need to be examined. A third is that this practice of criticism becomes more and more a way of seeing alternative interpretations that open up the issue of meaning in a text to encompass on the one hand the breadth of readings that past critics have offered and on the other the growing life experience of the student and the uses to which he or she can now put the skill of reading. Something of the complexity of how individuals employ this process can be seen in studies based on detailed responses of actual readers to specific literary works (such as Squire, 1964; Holland, 1975; Bleich, 1978; and Steig, 1989).

The student thus confronts something like what Carol Gilligan and John Michael Murphy, in a study of intellectual and moral development (Gilligan and Murphy 1979), call the "dilemma of the fact" – namely that formal strategies or reasoning prove inadequate for judging the moral demands of actual experience and that individuals move away from the logical rigidity of adolescent thought about moral principles toward a dialectical or contextual application of principles (perhaps competing ones now) to concrete experiences. Particular works of literature pose the same kind of problem for the experienced student. They resist reductive analysis by any one supposedly authoritative technique; their intelligibility is most accessible when techniques are proportioned to the demands of each particular work. If they continue to study literature, undergraduates become increasingly adept at this flexible kind of performance; graduate students often become very good at it. It is also the practical strategy of most teachers, though their explicit theoretical commitments may affect the emphasis they give to particular analytic techniques.

Most students do not go beyond the undergraduate study of literature, and when they arrive at graduation they are by no means uniform products of a consistent pedagogy, even if they are English majors who have gone through the same college. Here are four senior majors who went through the same program, yet the different ways they have constructed their attitudes toward literature are as striking as the similarity of the issues they are dealing with.

Charlie

Charlie has been an avid reader all his life (Agatha Christie novels and *Harriet The Spy* in the third grade, Tolkien in the sixth, Faulkner and F. Scott Fitzgerald and Shakespeare in high school). Ever since high school, he says, his goal has been to comprehend T. S. Eliot's *The Waste Land*: "I've read it a zillion times." He talks knowledgeably about Eliot's sources, Ezra Pound's editing of the text, the new edition, the relationship of *The Waste Land* to Joyce's *Ulysses*. It is clear that this is real enthusiasm, not just parroting what he has heard in class. He also talks about his enthusiasm for Faulkner since high school. What is it about Faulkner that he likes so much? "When you read . . . it's an act of comprehension. You're given an experience and in order to comprehend it you have to do what it tells you to do. . . . I like being taken out on these . . . I don't know the term . . . what I like in Faulkner is the kind of wise, ponderous prose that takes these events out of being just events and brings them into some kind of universe of meaning. I like that . . . the challenge. It's like running a race or something . . . doing physical exercise or any kind of work . . . except this is a bit harder." The challenge is to comprehend the story patterns or structures, he says – Milton's, Shakespeare's ("his structures are all so similar you can draw outlines"). Would he be more interested in structures than, say, the psychological situation of a character? "I never think of that," he answers. "You can't afford to." The key terms for him are plot, style, imagery, narrative voice, patterns. At one point he calls this his objective theory, and of all the undergraduates interviewed his is the strongest avowal of this attitude.

Peter

Peter, another senior English major, talks with the same firmness about the objectivity of aesthetic judgment: "I believe there is an objective level to art, obviously. There is good literature and not-so-good literature." However, he immediately adds a qualification: "But it comes down to taste eventually." How can these two judgments be reconciled? Peter very confidently explains: "No one is going around saying, 'Shakespeare is great. Why? Because I like him.' You can point to all sorts of density of language and structure in the plays . . . the way they hold up even now . . . the characterizations . . . and you can talk about each of these components in objective terms . . . you can back them up with reasons." But after doing all these things, could your taste lead you to end up saying, "Yes but I just don't happen to like him?" "Sure, because I feel there is a certain level of irrationality to artistic taste. The transcendental experience . . . that's putting it a little bit too strongly . . . I don't think it is a rational experience . . . it's something no one has succeeded in explaining." He repeats this remark about the subjective, irrational element in art several times, but he will not abandon his confidence in objectivity either: "You can be basically sure, but you can never be really sure. . . . No one's free from their own mind. Everyone's operating from their internal conflicts, and that's life, I guess." Still, "art is like anything else: The more versatility and the more experience you have in the field, the more likely your judgment is to be correct."

Lisa

Lisa describes herself as a lifelong voracious reader. She used to write to her favorite authors when she was a kid; now she collects children's books and is thinking of going into publishing. Her way of talking about the books she likes is quite distinctive. Once she mentions a title – *Pride and Prejudice,* Herman Hesse's *Demian,* a book from her childhood called *The Saturday Club,* by Elizabeth Enright – she plunges into an enthusiastic synopsis of the story, descriptions of the characters, an evaluation of the book as a whole, and extended commentary on the effect it had on her when she read it. She talks in long paragraphs about the books that have meant something to her.

Like Peter, she balances the competing claims of objective judgment and personal response: "I realize you have to say something beyond 'I like it.' Professor D. [in a current course in critical theory] keeps stressing the 'because' clause. I'm getting good at that. It helps if you've read a lot because you can compare it to something else that either you like or you feel is well written. But I really think, in the end, it comes down to pure response. D. H. Lawrence hated Jane Austen, didn't he? I love her. Who's right? It's more a matter of taste." This ambivalence is a lively issue for her. She says that as a student doing the reading for a course she leaves her taste out of it, because "it's been decided that this is worth reading. And it probably is. I mean, some of the most horrible things are good for you . . . like medicine. And as an English major I'm supposed to read all these things whether I like them or not." Still, she does not entirely abandon her own judgment or her reliance on her own responses. She confesses that she never read beyond page 200 of *Ulysses* (for an advanced level freshman course): "Who decides that's great writing? I keep hearing 'He changed the novel.' I don't know. He's a big guy I'm supposed to know about, but from my experience with *Ulysses,* he's interesting but he's not anybody I would pursue with a vengeance. . . . I'll give it a second try some time, because I feel I should."

Lisa readily acknowledges the claims of the canonical tradition on her attention, but her strongest convictions are about the books she can get involved in personally: "When I look at all the books that made an impression on me when I was a kid, the kids in the stories weren't Goody Two-Shoes, but they were always doing interesting things. In one story they lived in a house with cupolas and discovered an island in the woods and they built this little stone house there. . . . When you live in suburbia it's like . . . gee, you wish that you could do those kind of cool things."

Now the style of her appreciation has changed, but the degree of enjoyment is still a touchstone of a good book: "I've read *Pride and Prejudice* at least twenty times; I'm sure of that. Why? Because I feel so good every time I read it. . . . I get a lot of enjoyment . . . she is so funny . . . so formal . . . so ironic . . . though she writes about the blandest things . . . I laugh out loud."

Anthony

Finally, there is Anthony, also a senior. He talks as confidently as Charlie and Peter about careful reading (he calls it self-conscious reading), attention to language, narrative point of view, and other matters that a model English major presumably ought to be conversant with at the end of his undergraduate education. But he adds a dimension that the others do not mention explicitly: the moral evaluation of what he reads. "I think books should have a purpose. . . . There are some things which are useless to spend time on . . . a trashy novel, for example . . . insincere . . . cliché ridden . . . there's a lot of films and music like that today too . . . very empty." For Anthony this is much more than just a conventional bow to quality; his reflections on his own responses to what he reads are quite nuanced. He talks about how much he likes *Life* magazine, its combination of scientific curiosity, human and aesthetic elements, the quality of its pictures. But "sometimes they have sensationalistic pictures and I feel guilty about why I'm looking at them." There was, for instance, a story about a burn clinic: "I think the photographs of some of the actual burn victims were valuable in a way . . . like demystifying the idea of what's happened to these people and just presenting the reality of it. But some of the pictures, I felt, were stylized in a way that seemed disrespectful to the solemnity or privacy of what was happening. There was a photo of the peeling away of the damaged skin of a victim. . . . I just felt like something had been stolen or defiled."

Anthony's judgments about books, music, and films (he is a dedicated reader of film criticism) emphasize the quality of their effect on him. He uses a curiously old-fashioned term, "I like to be edified," and then laughs. "I think content matters. Yet the ideas and the perspective of what a person has written matter to me whether I agree with that person or not. I think I need . . . I think reading should challenge me . . . it should exercise my imagination, stretch it, take it places, ask it to do things, to image things. . . . I think it's good when it leaves you with questions about why you reacted the way you did, what happened, why it happened the way it did." This moral attitude is an interestingly open and tolerant one.

It is striking that all four of these senior English majors from the same college program wrestle with the issue of objectivity in interpretation and that they resolve it in four different ways. Charlie's is the purest defense of a formalist approach to literary meaning. The other three balance the competing claims of interpretation that can be justified by objective evidence from the text with subjective responses that are also important to them: Lisa's test of whether a story can involve her enthusiasm (and her concomitant scepticism about the literary authority of important books that do not produce this effect), Peter's irrational or transcendental universe of meaning that a poem or novel discloses, and Anthony's finely tuned perception of the edifying effect of the work on himself as audience.

These students all passed through a program that taught them the kind of close reading of the text that has been the mainstream doctrine of college English departments for the past thirty years, yet they emerged with distinctive stamps on their common respect for the text and its imperatives. Are these simply variations due to personal style, or are they instead partial appropriations of what is involved in an ideally complete reading of a text? From another point of view, do the efforts of Peter, Lisa, and Anthony to balance the authority of the text with some other concern of their own represent an *advance* beyond what the idea of "the poem as poem" stands for? Or are they rather attempts to *preserve* something of what made their own engagement with books so important to them before they began to study literature formally?

Recall Jerome Bruner's remark, quoted in the Introduction: "It requires the most expensive education to shake a reader's faith in the incarnateness of meaning in a novel or poem" (1986a, 155). These four students have not yet, perhaps, faced the full implications of meaning's elusiveness. The issue for them is not the possibility of discovering meaning. They do not doubt it can be done, and they are comfortable talking about different ways of doing it. But they know too that their own readings are unfinished, still refinable. It is interesting that three of them at least want to reconcile ways they have been taught to read in the classroom with values they have brought along from some other part of their reading experience: enthusiastic involvement, deeper meaning, the effect of the work on one's moral sensibility. The destiny of these aspirations in their adult lives as readers remains to be seen.

Tim

It might be useful to compare the responses of these four English majors with those of another senior who has gone a different route. Tim is a finance major, a decision he says he made after reading Dreiser's *The*

Titan and then *The Financier* in high school. His high school team was called the Titans so he took the book off the library shelf out of curiosity. He decided after he had finished the two books that he would be a finance major, long before he ever took a course in the subject. Tim has been an omnivorous reader since childhood. He grew up in a family where books were common: "In my house, if you come home on any given day, the TV won't be on. My mother and father will be on the couch reading. My grandfather will be in his rocking chair reading. When my parents go to bed they'll take books up with them. It's constant." As a child he read indiscriminately – the Hardy Boys, Sherlock Holmes, James Bond, biographies – but he thinks he skipped most of the classic children's books: "By the time I was eleven I was reading adult books . . . big books. The first one was *Day of the Jackal*; I think I was in the fourth grade. *Gorky Park,* Ludlum's books, *Trinity* . . . I read that three or four times in high school."

What was the appeal of these books? "Intrigue . . . escape . . . plot twists. I like guessing what's going to happen, and it's almost more fun not to be right than to be right. I like tying the ends together, but not knowing until the very end, because that means you can keep guessing." But why would he read *Trinity* three or four times, then, if he liked guessing the outcome? "Probably for the adventure . . . and the characterizations. In all of Uris's books there's one strong male lead figure, who is a superhero almost. So it's like a hero wish." In high school too he "got hooked on a kind of science-fantasy series about the Alter Earth or something like that. This person got time-warped into the Alter Earth, which was a barbaric place where things were very much different. Something like the Conan books." He thinks kids like these books because of "the lack of discipline or law of any kind. They're also very male oriented . . . females are slaves and there's lots of one-on-one clashes with bad guys and swinging swords and riding across open plains and adventure after adventure . . . never-a-dull-moment sort of thing. Anything goes and you can accept anything because you say 'it might happen.'"

In a curious way Tim's view of his finance major is a bit like his view of the world of this kind of fiction: "I think it's a good way to get into the power structure [of business]. If you go into a corporate office you notice that the V.P. for finance is usually a lot closer [to the CEO] than the V.P. for Marketing, and a lot of it has to do with the fact that they have to work more closely together, on budgets, projections, and the whole bit. So I look on it as a means. I hope to get into general management." He thinks finance is more interesting, less mechanical, and more creative than other branches of business – "figuring out solutions . . . where there are no strict rules . . . especially in this volatile economy."

A distinct ambivalence runs through many of Tim's comments. He is a finance major who says that other business students sometimes drive him crazy: "In this policy class the professor asked what magazines we read, and someone said *People* and somebody else said *Sports Illustrated.* I said *The New Republic,* and no one knew what it was. Out of thirty-two seniors no one had heard of *The New Republic!*" He knows that his tastes have changed. "I reread *Trinity* and to me now it's very mindless and . . . flat. It's a fairy tale about things that never happened. . . . A lot more of the reading I'm impressed with now is sad . . . not necessarily sad but realistic . . . like the Holden Caulfields of the world . . . there's a lot more of them than the Conor Larkins of *Trinity.*" He still reads whatever he finds around the house when he goes home on vacation, and in the summer he may get in ten out of ten novels on the *New York Times* best-seller list. But when asked about what kinds of books he sees himself reading in the future, he talks wistfully about the difference between escapist books that demand no energy ("Most of the stuff I read I don't think is good, but . . . it kept me interested . . . I turned the pages.") and something more substantive that might distract him if he ended up in "a mindless job." The whole conversation with Tim communicates, in the middle of his excitement about his future as a financier, a distinct sense of a road not taken. He says a couple of times: "I'm a frustrated English major."

THE TEXT THEORIZED

It is remarkable how uninterested in theory many professional students and teachers are. Most of us are syncretists. We rely on intuitive responses to texts, shaped by our training, our interests, and our tastes. We test these responses by whatever analytic strategies we have come to rely on, pragmatically suiting them to the particular work and to the questions we need to answer. Like the Boston ladies and their hats, we have our approaches to literature. Most of us are not very interested in explicating the theories behind what we read. Revisionist theories especially seem reductive in comparison with the rich eclecticism of our usual practice.

Is this a bad situation? The case can be made that a skillful eclecticism is the mark of a mature practitioner of reading and criticism. This is the commonsense view, but even theories of intellectual development beyond the formal-operational stage can be read this way (see the discussion in Chapter 5). On the other hand, one can argue that critical practice without an explicit theoretical foundation simply perpetuates unexamined ideologies that may victimize student and teacher alike. It is difficult to say which side of this argument we should take, because we are at a level where the particulars of performance matter so much; theoretical analyses can be sterile and reductive or powerfully suggestive, and eclectic analyses can seem misguided and quirky or full of brilliant insights. But some students of literature are content with mastering a variety of reading strategies and applying them pragmatically to the works at hand, and others are willing to face the issues involved in analysis and interpretation with much more theoretical rigor. Is this a matter of personal style, an accident of training or of particular experiences, or is it an inevitable step if one pursues the systematic study of literature far enough?

I am inclined to a cautious conclusion favoring the notion that one is driven to theory sooner or later. M. H. Abrams's handy and well-known schema of the central relationships involved in interpreting a work of literature may help explain why (1953, 6). His diagram looks like this:

Abrams proposes that the historical development of literary criticism has more or less moved around the three outside terms in this diagram and then focused on the work itself at the center. That is, the oldest criteria for evaluating literature mainly had to do with its mimetic validity as a picture of the world. The next phase of literary criticism, broadly speaking, was concerned with pragmatic, reader-oriented theories that judged literature rhetorically, in terms of its capacity to entertain or to instruct its audience. The romantic view of literature as expressive of a specialized sensibility shifted the focus to the author. Only in this century, and especially under the influence of the New Criticism, has the study of literature centered more and more on the formal study of the work itself, independently of these other relationships.

These shifts in the historical development of criticism seem to be reproduced in the way an individual reader theorizes about literature. Once a reader gets beyond the spontaneous childhood response of involvement and identification and explicit criteria begin to come into play (in early adolescence), the first yardstick seems to be the mimetic validity of the story as a representation of the world of actual experience or of a world one could possibly experience. When the reader goes beyond this view of what a story is and begins to see that the representation demands interpretation, he or she focuses on the author as the originator of the story's meaning and apparent point of view. When author-oriented explications prove inadequate, the reader shifts attention to the text and to various analytic techniques that accumulate the evidence required for as objective an interpretation as is consistent with the nature of the material. The student who is an apprentice literary critic thus reproduces Abrams's phases of historical criticism.

But Abrams's history is unfinished. Contemporary criticism has shifted its attention beyond the text itself – to structures of meaning common to all sign systems, to the conditions under which texts are read, to the ideologies manifested or concealed in texts and their readings, and to the possibility and limits of communicating in language at all. In short, contemporary criticism makes the very possibility and conditions of interpretation its principal focus. The study of literature, having moved from part to part of Abrams's diagram, now stands back as it were and ponders the problematic nature of all the relationships the diagram represents. Because reading a text at this stage is indistinguishable from studying a text, this is inevitably the point of view a reader is likely to take after going through the earlier phases Abrams describes.

Is this impulse to face the problem of interpretation a normal development in postadolescent readers or is it an artifact of the history of literary study and especially of the influence of the New Criticism in the early twentieth century, as Jane Tompkins has argued (1980, 222)? Perhaps a distinction can help. Interpretation conceived as a response to a work of literature in the sense valorized by New Critical theory and practice, which entails explicating the formal and semiotic structures of a literary work, demonstrating its coherence, and establishing the ontological uniqueness of its meaning, is certainly a consequence of the special history of Anglo-American literary criticism in this century. But the impulse to explain failures in reading, to figure out the themes of literary works, to study systematically how texts and their codes create meaning-for-the-reader, and to construct a critique of these themes and codes by measuring them against values derived from other commitments in our lives (in short, to engage in what Scholes calls "interpretation" and "criticism") seems to be a much more general, if not a universal, phenomenon, at least among readers who read enough and at a high enough level to experience conflicting responses to what they read and to feel the need to resolve these conflicts intelligibly. This kind of reading (which is much broader than the New Criticism's conception of interpretation and potentially includes quite a range of different critical methods) seems to be implicit in the most fundamental experience of reading, if we trust Harding's insistence that when we read we are always both participant and spectator. If the youngest child is in some sense capable of playing an evaluative role in the process of reading (even if it is only to evaluate at a minimal level the difference between the invented world and the world of pragmatic consequences), then the potential for other discriminations that are more distanced from simple reading (in Scholes's sense) is right there from the beginning.

But it is not only the deeper experience of reading that confronts a student of literature with the problem of interpretation. In almost every field of study – physics, history, social studies, ethics, religion – contemporary debates about concrete problems lead to foundational questions about the possibility of knowing. The distinctive late-twentieth-century preoccupation of intellectuals thus seems to be hermeneutics, the theory of interpretation. This situation has many roots, including attitudes taken over from biblical criticism, comparative anthropology, history, natural science, linguistics, and so forth, not to mention the fact that all these studies have been, like literature, institutionalized within the university, packaged for consumption by the general population of students, and therefore have become the professional concern of many specialized researchers and teachers. The study of literature has been particularly responsive to this debate about the determinacy or indeterminacy of meaning, because in all these fields it appears more and more to be a debate about language. Compared with this broad development, the influence of New Criticism on students of literature, although real, is modest and by no means the only reason why a reader moves toward interpreting as a response to a poem or story.

Most readers and students of literature, though led by their own need for intelligibility to the ordinary varieties of interpretation and criticism, probably do not have the temperament or the motive to pursue questions about meaning into the philosophical thickets where contemporary literary theory flourishes. Literature teachers, and perhaps practicing critics and librarians, are likely to do so, because explanations are demanded of them and the business of lecturing and writing inevitably involves systematizing one's ideas. The closer one looks at the gaps and inconsistencies implied by the various eclectic interpretive strategies one brings to literature, the more one ought to want an overarching theory to make practice coherent.

The solution to this need might be sought on different levels of theoretical explicitness. The simplest attempt at theoretical coherence is the pragmatic one most literature teachers are familiar with: rereading classroom texts from year to year, adding new ones or reaching back to books long forgotten to see how they work and how they do or do not fit into one's current theories, connecting books into provisional networks of meaning, rethinking how to teach them to one's students. A more explicit theoretical formulation of what happens when one reads and interprets a text might lead to a phenomenological account, such as I. A. Richards offered in the 1920s, Louise Rosenblatt did a decade later, and contemporary critics such as Wolfgang Iser and Georges Poulet do today. This kind of account easily turns into epistemological and even ontological claims about the status of texts and the activity of reading, as it did under the New Critics earlier in this century. When these kinds of claims seem unsatisfactory one might deliberately borrow insights that have worked in other fields, for example, structuralist categories from linguistics and anthropology or the psychoanalytic account of mental operations, and use them as guiding ideas in working out an explanation of what occurs when we read. Or one might systematically ground one's reading in an ideological point of view, Marxism, for example, or feminism or religious doctrine, that one accepts as prior to and more fundamental than one's literary theory. There is a kind of gamut here – though I have greatly simplified the various positions – running from practical descriptions of reading to the point where the experience of reading becomes interesting mainly as an instance of a larger theoretical perspective at work. One might call it a movement from implicit theory to explicit theory to metatheory. The plausibility of contemporary deconstructionist approaches may have much to do with a scepticism about the adequacy of any theoretical claims, induced by the increasing speed with which each has succeeded the other. But, of course, the deconstructionist view implies theoretical claims of its own.

Contemporary styles of reading that combine deconstructionist methods with prior ideological perspectives (prior in terms of value or commitment) pose especially acute questions because they operate at margins where literary analysis is apt to be subsumed into some other kind of activity. An influential and exemplary contemporary case is the feminist proposal for readings that "re-vision" a text or "resist" its apparent intentions or its conventional meaning. Thus, Adrienne Rich speaks about the necessity "of looking back, or seeing with fresh eyes, of entering an old text from a new critical direction" (1972, 18). But this reading is more than a chapter in cultural history, Rich says, it is "an act of survival" or, in Judith Fetterley's words, "a political act whose aim is not simply to interpret the world but to change it by changing the consciousness of those who read and their relation to what they read" (1978, viii).

Feminist criticism has moved steadily toward this radical critical program as it has evolved, according to Elaine Showalter (1985, 3–10). At first it focused mainly on exposing the misogyny of male writers, the stereotyped images of women in literature, the connections between the literary and social mistreatment of women, and the exclusion of women writers from the canon of literary history. Its second phase was the recovery for readers of an extensive but neglected female literary tradition coexisting alongside the male-dominated one. In the 1970s and 1980s, however, feminist criticism has gone beyond the recognition of women's writing and tried to define a specifically female aesthetic that attempts to rethink the very nature of what it views as male-dominated ideas about writing and reading. The starkest formulation of this recent phase is Fetterley's assertion that a male-dominated literary establishment controls the reading of texts and that to learn to read, even for a woman, is to learn to read as a man (1986, 149–53). For women to read this way, though, is "psychic suicide" (1986, 159). They have to learn to read against these influences, to submit the practice and even the theory of reading to criticism from their own perspective.

Feminists have discovered what Marxists discovered before them, that all reading is political and that every critical practice implies an ideology, a Marxist concept inserted into the vocabulary of cultural discussion by Louis Althusser (1971, 1977) and elaborated in the writings of Raymond Williams (1977), Frederic Jameson (1981), and Terry Eagleton (1976, 1983). Most recently Lennard J. Davis has reviewed the history of the term's use and offered an important qualification of its value as a critical category (Davis 1987, 24–51). The concept of ideology, he says, has grown so global and general – referring now to the system of beliefs of a particular group or class, now to false ideas or false consciousness, now to the general cultural system that creates signs and meanings – that it has itself become an object of mystification. On the other hand "the individual has gotten lost in the social fabric (1987, 50). What is needed, Davis thinks, is to "combine our vast knowledge of the human psyche with our vast knowledge of the social conditions that shape its development," to ask "how does the individual accept and rely on the group" (50).

Davis's proposal illuminates the risk at the margins where ideological interest is furthest from the practice of individual readers. Indeed, the implicit risk in all theoretical criticism is that one will yield to the temptation of reading from one perspective exclusively and lose the corrective balance of other equally relevant points of view that concern themselves with the variety of responses readers actually have when they read. Reading at the service of a theory can be a powerful analytic tool for disclosing implications concealed in familiar texts, as, for example, Jameson's Marxist rereading of Lord Jim does in The Political Unconscious (1981), or for questioning prejudices latent in conventional critical practice, as Nina Baym does in her dissection of the canon of texts taught in U.S. literature courses (1985). In less skilled hands, though, texts can be reduced to ammunition for supporting particular theories and theories to weapons for waging political struggles; theory then does seem to be a dead end as far as its usefulness for productive reading is concerned.

Readers who feel the need to resolve the crisis of interpretation probably begin by using critical ideas the way new English majors use analytic techniques; one point of view serves to marshal all the diverse phenomena into a coherent order. This book, of course, is itself a sample of the impulse to find a systematic point of view that explains what seems like a mass of confusing evidence culled from the experience of reading and teaching. And it aspires to a goal analogous to Davis's: to resolve some of the issues in contemporary theorizing about reading by setting them within the framework of the reader's psychological development.

But with theories as with analytic techniques, reductive points of view prove inadequate. The inadequacy may be practical, because a given text or the experience of a given reading seldom yields completely to one critical approach, or theoretical, as the impossibility of discovering a theory of theories becomes evident. Or a reader may tire of depending on the ingenuity of what Jacques Leenhardt calls "privileged intermediaries," the critics or theorists who become indispensable guides through the labyrinth of the text (1980, 208). The reader thus comes face to face with the full extent of the problem that the determinacy or indeterminacy of literary works is not only built into the nature of language, but is also a function of the choices we make about how we read and indeed how we live. With this discovery, the project of studying literature seems to have gone as far as it can on its own terms. It either ceases or falls back on pragmatic and eclectic strategies of reading or turns into something else – a kind of reading whose object is the reconstruction of a self and a vision of the world adequate to the totality of one's lived experience.

IRONY

The attitude often most congenial to college students is irony. Irony and its militant version, satire, form the third of Northrop Frye's generic plots, but it is as an intellectual habit, rather than as an explicit fondness for satirical and ironic literary forms, that we are first apt to encounter irony in the maturing adolescent. The reason for its appeal, I suspect, is that irony is a powerful defense against the embarrassment of having one's cognitive disequilibrium come to light. Confusion about knowledge or ideals is not easy to admit in classroom or dormitory discussion. Irony – the technique, Frye says, citing Aristotle, of appearing to be less than one is, of self-deprecation, is a way of making oneself invulnerable (1957, 40). Students quickly learn to disavow their own expertise and their ideals and to play the game of deflecting substantive arguments into issues of language: "It all depends on what you mean. . . . "

Now the interesting thing about this attitude is that it corresponds to a genuine discovery that students must eventually make about language:

that it almost always means more than it says, especially when the words have been carefully put together to create an effect, and therefore that they ought to be sceptical about overt significance and covert rhetorical intentions. So it is not unexpected that students should talk about levels of meaning in what they read and disparities between surface and depth. New Critical employment of categories like ambiguity, paradox, tension, and of course irony itself has focused attention on the complex ways that the meaning of a literary text transcends any simple reading of the linguistic surface. As students learn these attitudes, they start finding hidden meanings in what was previously taken for granted, like the college junior who mentions that she can now hear Betty Smith's ironic voice in a book she took as an unequivocal romance in her childhood, *A Tree Grows in Brooklyn,* or like the student who in high school got angry at the characters in John Cheever's moralistic short stories but now finds them funny. It is only one step further (though perhaps a long one) to discover meanings where no one hid them – writers' unintended self-disclosures, for example, or values that they implicitly or inadvertently endorse. This way of reading might be called irony as a habit of mind.

Note that readers of this turn of mind tend to apply it to much more than just the literary voice or genre which Wayne Booth calls "stable irony" – works like Jonathan Swift's *A Modest Proposal* or Orwell's *Animal Farm,* where the author's intention to say one thing and mean another is patent and the reader cannot read the work successfully without reconstructing the finite and limited meaning intended by the author (1974, 3–8). Readers, to be sure, need to reach a certain level of sophistication and experience in language use to appreciate the "double exposure," as Douglas Muecke calls it (1969, 29), in works like these and in the more commonplace passages in which narrators or characters speak in ironic voices. But the ability to recognize this kind of intended irony is not the same as the habitual state of mind that searches all language for hidden meanings, intended or not, and applies to all books the scepticism that maintains that nothing is reliable, either the voice of the author or the naive experience of the reader as the center of meaning. This kind of irony is learned and depends as much on the reader's self-chosen stance as it does on the possibilities offered by the author's management of the text. Rabinowitz points out that judgments about genre are partly influenced by what the author has created and are partly a construct of the reader's habitual response. Thus, *Jane Eyre* is a romance to someone focusing on the love story of Rochester and Jane, but is ironic to someone focusing on the way they both contribute to the misfortunes of the hapless Bertha. Similarly, Natasha in *War and Peace* can be a romantic heroine or a victim of the oppressiveness of Russian society, depending on the point of view one brings to the reading (Rabinowitz 1987, 31–2).

What Frye means by irony as a generic plot, however, is a different thing still. He defines irony as this habit of mind translated into a scenario of how the world works. Irony, Frye observes, is a parody of romance; the hero is all too human, subject to the ills of the world, rather than linked by magical power to a transcendent one, his quests remain unfulfilled or they are wrongheaded or aimless, and he grows old and dies. Unlike romance where wishes come true or tragedy where greatness may be undone by a flaw or by fate, irony reflects the permanent discrepancy between what is and what ought to be. In its typical settings – the city, the prison, the hospital, the madhouse, hells of various kinds – the good and the innocent are the victims of the unscrupulous and love is more often thwarted than conquering. Frye says that this generic plot attempts to give form to the shifting ambiguities and complexities of unidealized existence (1957, 223). When it becomes a way of imaging life as hopeless and the world as meaningless, we have the point of view (which Booth calls "unstable" and even "infinite" irony and Muecke "general" irony) common in the works of, say, Samuel Beckett.

I do not think this world view is typical of college students (though they may suspect that it is of their instructors!). But ironic fiction forms a considerable part of the modernist canon that a student of literature will encounter, and theories of interpretation founded on the undecideability of meaning or the detection of meanings that subvert a work's apparent intention are the reigning orthodoxies at the moment. It is easy to imagine a sequence of steps that would illustrate the continuity between a habit of mind that uses language in self-defense or hunts for latent meanings and a vision of the world that reduces all ideals to ambiguous quests and meaningless conclusions. Moreover, irony is the dominant tone of much of the serious contemporary fiction that educated adults will be exposed to if they continue to read beyond college. The dispassionate and objective gaze that takes life as it finds it and suppresses all moral judgment about it (Frye 1957, 40–1) often suits, if not the college student exactly, then the middle-aged realist who is lurking in the wings.

5

Adulthood: The Pragmatic Reader

According to the 1983 Book Industry Study Group report half of the adults in this country read books regularly, but fiction of course competes for the reader's attention with biography, cookbooks, self-help psychology, religion, and, especially, job-oriented books. Among leisure activities reading comes after television, radio, time spent with family, and listening to music. What fiction is read by adults does not appear to be of high quality; the most favored categories are action and adventure novels, historical novels, mystery and detective novels, a category called "modern dramatic novels," and romances. The amount of reading an individual does is likely to stay the same from age sixteen to fifty, then drop off, especially among readers older than sixty-five. Not surprisingly, the amount correlates positively with education, income, and early reading habits. Adult readers of fiction are likely to be women, especially those who consider themselves heavy readers.

However, fiction accounts for somewhere between 15 and 25 percent of the world book production, which as recently as 1983 amounted to some 11.9 billion books, and over three-quarters of public library loans and about 70 percent of mass market paperbacks are fiction. As a conservative estimate, fiction reading occupies nearly an hour a day of the time of one-third of the adult population, so it is not a negligible phenomenon (Nell 1988, 18–25).

The evidence of how adults' reading habits change is rather sketchy; children and student populations are much more available to researchers. Purves and Beach in 1972 summarized the studies of changes among readers from childhood to adulthood, so far as reading content was concerned. They discerned general developmental shifts from fiction to nonfiction, from plot-dominated works to character-dominated works, and from evident fantasy (fairy tales and animal tales and the like) to implicit fantasy (adventure, mystery, and romance) (1972, 75). Clearly, adults as a group occupy one end of this spectrum of changes, but what does this mean and how do they get there?

Studying literature is one obvious way adults develop as readers, which can continue well into middle age if one becomes a teacher or practicing critic. But what happens to adult readers who do not go through this stage or who go only partway through it, those who never study literature systematically beyond high school or college, but who continue to read fiction throughout their lives? And what kind of books do students and literary professionals read in their off-duty hours? Apparently there must be alternative routes in the development of adult readers. To locate these questions in a concrete setting, let us consider in some detail the experience of one adult reader.

ELIZABETH

Elizabeth (as I shall call her) is a reference librarian in the public library of a suburb of a large Northeastern city. She studied Russian history as an undergraduate, has a graduate degree in library science, and is married and the mother of two grown children. Her work involves some selecting of current fiction for the library collection, but when she talks about books it is mostly about her own voluntary reading: "I like to read and it's a very big part of my life. I'm one of those people who gets nervous if I don't have a shelf of books ready. I'm pretty eclectic . . . politics, history, contemporary fiction."

She talks carefully and knowledgeably about books she has read. Her comments about fiction focus equally on the content of a story – the characters and the world they live in – and on the questions the story leads her to think about. She sometimes talks about aspects of a writer's craft or technique, but most of her responses to stories center around two themes. One is that fiction draws her into new worlds of experience: "Even when I was quite young I used to read about things that really were alien to my experience, but accessible. I loved to find out interesting things, you know, for information and for illumination of feelings." She mentions Bobby Ann Mason's stories in *Shiloh*:

> A whole world is evoked by these stories. It's a world of people with not too much education but who feel in a sense entitled to be part of the American dream, as we think of it – that is, that they should get ahead and should have good experiences and interesting relationships with other people. They're people of considerable feeling with very little really in the way of resources to express it. And she shows this in a way that really captures your imagination and makes you . . . understand a little more about this person and this background and what it means in their lives. I like to be drawn into a story. I like to feel

somehow or other that I am seeing a piece of life I might otherwise never know . . . I mean, that's why I read. I read because I can't afford to travel [she laughs].

So one aspect of reading for her is to have "a whole dimension of experience that I would not otherwise have." But the motive for this is anything but escape, and here the second theme in her comments emerges: "What I enjoy is the opportunity to enter another life and to consider the questions that occupy that life and that person." She hesitates to claim that these are her own questions: "I haven't had these experiences and I'm not likely to . . . although one doesn't know." But the characters in a book can become very real, "friends of yours in a sense," and reading Jane Austen's *Pride and Prejudice,* for example, is "like being able to sum up an experience of your own life." Finally she makes explicit the link between her own life and the enlarging experience of reading: "I guess I'm searching for my own world and this is one way to find it."

Indeed, one of the striking qualities of her comments about her reading is how explicitly they refer to her own sense of her role in the reading process. For instance, she confesses that the kind of books she really enjoys seem harder and harder to find nowadays, and that she does not feel guilty anymore about not sticking to the end with a book once she has started it: "I'm getting too old to do that now." She knows that she reads for different motives now that she is older: "When I was raising young children I craved adult minds to come into contact with, and so my reading was a real source of intellectual stimulation. But I don't have as much energy now. Here [at the library] I'm involved with talking about books and making judgments about them all day long, and as a result when I go home at night I'm perhaps more inclined to pick less demanding things."

She generalizes along these lines. Reading gives different kinds of satisfactions. Sometimes as a reader you want to be "challenged and to be kept slightly off-base. Where are we? Who's talking? What's going on here?" Joyce's *Dubliners* stories might do this or the work of Donald Barthelme. But "sometimes you just want to be told and led by the hand from beginning to end." Reading mysteries before going to bed is this kind of experience: "I'm in a familiar place . . . the formula is set . . . very little is demanded of me in terms of imaginative sympathy or empathy or any of those things." She classifies books in her own mind along this scale: much contemporary fiction that is "incredibly predictable" – family sagas, the recent spate of books "about women finding themselves"; then middlebrow books like Alison Lurie's *The Nowhere City* or *The War Between the Tates* that have "considerable wit . . . but [are] too easily accessible to spend one's best time on"; and finally the demanding kind of books that challenge your expectations and stretch your capacity for empathy (she mentions Tobias Wolff's *In the Garden of the North American Martyrs* and Raymond Carver's *What We Talk about When We Talk about Love*).

She has mixed feelings about this kind of classification of hard and easy books:

> It does depend a lot on how much I feel that I have to give in terms of energy and time. . . . From the time I was a small child and did a great deal of reading until today, I've always had the sense when I'm reading that I really should be doing something more constructive like cleaning out the closets or writing letters to friends. . . . I was amused to read in Russell Baker's autobiography that his mother would say when he was reading: "What's the matter, haven't you got any gumption? You sit around all day doing nothing."

This confession may betray a kind of puritanism about indulging in easy reading, but it may also indicate a maturing discrimination about the value of what she reads and a sense that she is responsible to herself for what she reads.

This picture of a reader for whom life's changes have made indiscriminate reading no longer a reasonable option is reinforced by remarks she makes about the fragility of one's wisdom at this age and about how much rethinking of her life might be occurring. At one point she says: "The more I read, the less I know about what I read. Every time I think that I've come to a conclusion, I read something new that forces me into other conclusions." She contrasts her experience with her children's:

> One is twenty-one and one is eighteen, and they're both heavy readers, but they read to . . . not only to widen their experiences, as I've always been accustomed to do, but to confirm or tell them what to think about so many of life's puzzles. I mean, you know, they read Camus and they read other philosophers with a tremendous need to have something . . . some philosophy that they can . . . perhaps only temporarily . . . hold onto . . . until the next kind of phase. And they're very much interested in playing with ideas and I certainly went through that at their age. . . . There's a particular time in life when one is particularly open to that, when one is going through adolescence . . . when everything is so important, you know, and everything is so on the surface and everything has a larger meaning and life is lived at a pitch, perhaps, that would be impossible to sustain once you've made certain choices about what you're going to do in life and are to some extent committed to effecting them. Then you don't reach out in the same way anymore. I certainly don't think I do. It's probably sort of sad, but I'm not likely to respond in that way anymore, although I certainly remember doing it. . . . I don't necessarily mean that one's mind closes or that it gets shut off from experience. But that perhaps you examine the experience . . . your own

experience . . . in a different way, and you let some larger questions rest because you have gone as far as you feel you can reasonably go with them at this. . . . I mean, you may pick some of them up again, depending on where your life experiences take you, but you can't perhaps sustain that constant changing of one's moral standards or one's political beliefs or whatever. . . . But you may look with considerably more acuteness and care at the ordinary activities of life and what they mean and your relationships with the people around you and the . . . I think one becomes much . . . as you get older, you perhaps get more attuned to what other people are thinking, and you realize that it's important to take care in certain ways.

Here is a clear statement of how different the middle of life feels from the energetic quest for new ideas and experiences that marked adolescence. Now it is not the larger questions that absorb one's attention; indeed, they may seem more clouded than ever: "The more I read, the less I know." Rather it is the ordinary activities of life, looked at with acuteness and care, that now seem important, especially relationships with people – "taking care," in Elizabeth's nice phrase. From this point of view, many books seem trivial and unchallenging. Formula fiction can still be enjoyable – the mystery in bed at night – but one also wants to make time for stories that enlarge one's empathy for other people and their lives. At this point in Elizabeth's search for her own world, this is one way reading can help her.

ADULTHOOD

Elizabeth's attitude toward reading resembles in some respects the points of view we have examined so far, but it is significantly different from them in other ways. Like juvenile readers, she expects books to enlarge her experience of other people and the worlds they live in, and like adolescents she is self-conscious about searching for a significant truth for herself in what she reads. Like students of literature, she can talk analytically about a writer's technique and how a story is put together. Yet her approach is much more personal than a student's. Analysis and the problem of interpretation are not really central issues. In a sense, for her a text is as transparent a medium for studying the characters and their situations as it is for any precritical reader. What really distinguishes her attitude toward reading from anything we have seen so far is her willingness to acknowledge the uncertainty she feels about the larger questions of life, her complacency in turning away from these questions for the time being, her sympathy for the young who still need to wrestle with such matters (and the distance she sees between their concerns and hers), and her conviction that the truth that matters to her now has more to do with the ordinary particulars of people's lives. We might sum up this point of view by saying that she knows much more about how she reads than younger readers we have seen and that she accepts herself, for now at least, as the kind of reader she is.

What accounts for this set of attitudes? Talking about books all day long as a librarian may explain in part why she is so observant and articulate about her experience as a reader. But why does her experience have the particular qualities it does? A common sense generalization might be to say that the joys and pains of adult life – work, marriage, bringing up children, caring for aged parents, retirement, serious illness, aging, and the proximity of death – are all supposed to make one a more reflective, tolerant, and self-aware person, and that these changes ought to show up in how one reads. But quite aside from the abundant evidence that adults do not always exemplify these virtues, this is too general an answer to be satisfactory. To understand the changes underlying adult ways of reading, we need a more detailed description of what midlife development means.

Jung was the first psychologist to propose that significant growth of personality continued into the later years of life. Objecting to Freud's emphasis on sexuality, he thought that there were other sources of development, particularly after adolescence. In adulthood, he suggested, we have the choice of whether to deal with our problems by clinging to the rigid ideas and achievement orientation of our youthful personalities or to allow the horizon of life to widen and the repressed side of the self to emerge by recognizing the *also-I*, the other masculine or feminine side of our personalities that hitherto had been buried. In the final stage of old age, life contracts physically, but a keener integration or *individuation* of the self becomes possible, as we detach ourselves from the outer world, turn inward, and immerse ourselves in the primordial symbols inherited from the past, which make up the groundwork of the human psyche (Jung 1969).

Erikson, starting from a similar critique of Freud's emphasis on sexuality and from Freud's remark that the tasks of normal adult life are to love and to work, built the detailed description of the life cycle and its potential successes and failures that we have already seen in part. In this schema, once the adolescent task of achieving a stable sense of identity has been accomplished, the issues of adult development involve whether a person can share this self with others in friendship and genuine intimacy, then whether he or she will invest in the establishing and guiding of the next generation that Erikson calls generativity, and finally whether the aging person will accept the triumphs and disappointments of his or her life and the significant people in it and achieve the ripeness, coherence, and wholeness that Erikson calls integrity. These are the positive outcomes, matched at each stage by equally possible negative outcomes. Thus, the failure of intimacy brings a deep sense of isolation and stereotyped interpersonal relations that keep at a distance the forces that threaten one's fragile self-possession; the failure of generativity means boredom, self-absorption, and stagnation; the failure of integrity results in disgust and despair at the meaninglessness of one's life, and the conviction that the time is too short to try out alternative roads to wholeness. For Erikson, then, adult development follows an uncertain scenario. The last stage may bring despair or it may bring the gift of wisdom, the acceptance of a life bounded by death, and the perspective that finally transcends the limitations of one's own identity and one's tragicomic engagements in the life cycle (1968, 135–41; 1982, 61–72).

As studies of adult psychology have multiplied, the predictability of any pattern of adult development has become a controversial notion. Some would argue that personality changes little during adulthood and that modifications in behavior, attitudes, social roles, interpersonal relationships, and so forth are really the result of environmental circumstance interacting with stable and enduring personality traits (e.g., McCrae and Costa 1984). Others make the opposite argument, that there are fixed, age-related stages of adult development, but they describe these stages and their timing differently and the most famous of them, the midlife transition, is in some versions a tumultuous crisis and in others one of several relatively undramatic transitions adults go through (Levinson 1978; Gould 1978; Vaillant 1977). Neugarten and her colleagues concluded that at best only some of the changes of adult development can be related reliably to chronological age (1964, 188–200).

A more promising line of thought accepts the unpredictability and complexity of adult development. Klaus Riegel has suggested that development consists of a ceaseless flux involving four major dimensions (inner-biological, individual-psychological, cultural-sociological, and outer-physical) along which an individual moves simultaneously. Only the biological determinants, for example, bodily growth, the birth of children, and aging, seem to follow a predictable order. Cultural and physical factors, such as being fired from a job, an economic depression, serious illness, a war, a flood, or a fire, are typically arbitrary in their timing. All these dimensions constantly interact with each other, and because changes in one of them affects but will not necessarily be synchronized with changes in the others, psychological growth is a complex process. The study of development, then, should focus not only on the synchronies and equilibriums, but also on the conflicts among the dimensional changes and on the different circumstances in which these conflicts work themselves out over time in one's life (Riegel 1975, 1976).

This point of view, which is not incompatible with Erikson's schema of stages, gives a more panoramic view of the factors involved in an individual's traversal of the developmental trajectory and suggests more reasons why growth might be uniquely inhibited or skewed, rather than predictable. Indeed, Riegel proposed that dialectical thinking, which comprehends its objects in the multitude of their contradictory relations, is the distinctive mode of adult cognition, rather than the formal operations of Piaget. The interplay of ambiguities, contradictions, and intuitive models, he argued, is more distinctive of adult thought than the logic of formal-operational thinking (Riegel 1973).

Riegel has not been the only one to try to describe adult thinking in terms different from Piaget's (the arguments are surveyed in Broughton 1984, especially 396–401). One line of speculation argues that what is most typical of adult thinking is the realization that concepts, ideas, and facts exist in dialectical relationship to other concepts, ideas, and facts and in relationship to the lives of the knowers who employ them (Basseches 1980). Another suggestion is that though formal-operational thinking is useful for problem solving once a problem has been formulated, the messy, often slow, creative thinking that can be called problem finding may represent a higher stage of adult thinking (Arlin 1975). Still another proposal is that the formal-operational model does not take into account the pragmatic, contextualized kind of thinking that people use to deal with concrete problems; for this kind of thinking, accumulated life experience may be more useful than abstract reasoning ability (Labouvie-Vief 1980, 1982; Gilligan and Murphy 1979; Fowler 1984).

Does all this disagreement mean that the psychological picture of adulthood is so cloudy that it is useless for someone to try to understand how adults read fiction? By no means. Disagreement underscores the complexity of the processes being described; doubtless it also says something about methodological differences among studies and about ideological preferences among researchers and theorists. But the main lines of a useful picture of adult development emerge from overviews of the research (such as those of Offer and Sabshin 1984; Cytrynbaum 1980; Merriam 1979; and Kimmel 1980). The overarching theory that holds this picture together, for those who take at least some kind of developmental perspective, can be described as *Erikson amplified*. Thus, these composite views of adult development usually take into account individual personality differences, social systems, and historical and cultural contexts. They envision developmental change as being triggered by significant life crises, such as parenthood, a job change, or a serious illness. The issues and tasks of midlife are virtually the same in all theories – to reassess the meaning of one's work, to deepen primary relationships, to guide the next generation, to come to terms with biological limits and aging. Accomplishing these tasks results in changes (in personality or ego identity, at least in role and style) that fundamentally alter one's relationship to the world, and these changes are described as stages that constitute a predictable pattern in the life trajectory.

Thus, what seem like the distinctive characteristics of Elizabeth's point of view at age forty-six – her sense of how different her own search for the truth of her life is from her children's, her complacency about having answers for the larger questions of life, her interest instead in finding meaning in the ordinary things of daily life, her empathy for people quite different from herself, her emphasis on caring for people and things – would, in the view of these general developmental theories, be attitudes that one would expect to find in someone dealing with the issues of midlife development.

THE USES OF READING

How then do adults read? It can only be partly satisfactory to classify readers from such a large age group and such different levels of life experience into one category and call it adulthood. If doing so is justifiable at all, it is because research about adult development is scanty and conjecture has to fill in a lot of the blank spaces, so it is better to assert too little than too much. If psychological studies of infant and adolescent development could easily overflow a boxcar, those on adults would fit handily into a small trunk. Research specifically relevant to adult reading is even scarcer. Intuition suggests that there ought to be differences between the responses of younger and older adults, but the interviews I have done do not suggest any obvious subdivisions relating to age.

So I do not intend to suggest specific age-related categories among adults nor to try to pinpoint one way of responding that is characteristic of all adult readers. Instead, I suggest that we think in terms of several variables in the adult experience of reading. First of all, there are different motives for reading or different uses that all adults make of fiction – to escape from the intractable problems of everyday life, to enlarge their consciousness of the world, to discover images that have power and meaning for their lives. Furthermore, most adults seem to combine these different uses of reading in different proportions, and most adults probably exemplify one of them more than the others at any given moment in their reading history or with particular books. I also suspect that each use of reading may vary considerably along a trajectory from early to late adulthood. Thus, some adult readers may change considerably as they mature, whereas others, perhaps most of them, may not advance much beyond the responses they had when their formal education as readers ended.

An important point to be made about adult reading is that it combines and reconstellates all the ways of reading that have mattered to an individual across a lifetime of responding to stories. The child is here as well as the juvenile and adolescent and student of literature, their special experiences available for recycling and refiguring as part of the complex responses adults have to what they read. C. S. Lewis remarks that as an adult he likes hock, which he is sure he would not have liked as a child. That he also still likes lemon squash he calls growth or development. Where he formerly had one pleasure, he now has two. But it is not simply a matter of addition: "I now enjoy the fairy tales better than I did in childhood: being now able to put more in, of course I get more out" (Lewis 1963, 234).

Perhaps the most important point is that adult readers choose to read and are very much aware of how voluntary their reading is. They choose reading over other activities that claim their time: "You have to make time to read." They choose the kinds of books they read and are often quite articulate about their choices: "I never read that kind of stuff." "My tastes have changed." "I don't finish a lot of books I start; when I was young I would never have done that." And more than readers at other ages, they even seem to choose how they read and the kinds of responses they want to have. Adults are in this sense the most pragmatic readers of all. Consciousness of their own motives and responses may be the one truly distinctive mark of adult readers, whatever their age.

The rest of this chapter describes what seem to me the three most significant uses adults make of reading. They can best be understood as different strategies for dealing with the complex experience of adult development sketched above. That there are three is somewhat arbitrary. The evidence could probably be divided differently and the uses given other names, but granted the quality of the evidence available now, these three seem to be a useful way of surveying the ground.

ESCAPING

Readers, especially adults, frequently say that they read to escape. "When I'm tired the books I read before I go to sleep are light mysteries or something like that," a woman in her fifties says. "It's my escape." The common use of this word to talk about reading seems to belie the dramatic connotations – feeling threatened, getting out of danger, reaching a safe place – that the underlying image might suggest in other contexts. What do readers mean when they describe their experience so vividly? Critics for their part routinely condemn escapist fiction as trivial and trashy, an attitude even readers may share, because they often talk apologetically about this kind of book: "I know it's junk but. . . . " Why should books that provide such a significant experience be dismissed so readily? Clearly the idea of escaping through reading embraces some contradictions that need exploring.

The term describes a motive or payoff of reading. But it is a particular kind of experience, not the more general feeling of being absorbed, involved, or even lost in a book. Readers do not commonly apologize for getting absorbed in Proust or Saul Bellow. They associate a certain kind of book – mysteries, Westerns, Harlequin romances, best-sellers, and the like – with escape.

We might understand the experience better if we ask what readers are escaping *from*? The most general answer seems to be the boredom and frustration that accompany the intractable problems of everyday adult life – or, we might say, by precisely the challenges described by Erikson and other developmentalists as characteristic of middle age. "As I get older I read more junk," a thirty-five-year-old woman who teaches literature full-time says. "I get less patient. I need stuff that's easier and faster. . . . I'm more tired at the end of the day. I also watch more TV than I would have before. I think there's just more demands on me, maybe, since having a child . . . more sort of emotional demands during the course of the day." Reading at the very least seems to provide distraction. "I can sit and read Dick Francis for three hours," she says.

An interesting version of this motive is the claim that reading provides escape not only from problems, but also from the problematic treatment of problems: "[At night or on vacation] I don't like to read literary stuff that's hard work, you know; I like stuff that just goes fast . . . that does not demand much intellectual work." Virtually all readers offer some version of this distinction when they are asked about their reading. Juvenile and adolescent and college-age readers distinguish between school reading and voluntary reading, but adults distinguish between escape reading and books that are challenging or demanding. So it may be not only their own problems that adult readers want to turn away from, but also the kind of fiction that, with its complicated narrative methodology, ironic perspective, and lack of clear resolution, makes the problems it deals with seem as intractable as those of readers' own real lives. We have the paradox, then, that the very qualities that make these books adult fiction, the perspectives and formal strategies that match an adult's complex experience, are the ones readers want to escape from. The accessibility of escape fiction thus seems to be an important part of its appeal. Intellectually it makes relatively few demands on readers. Even where there is a rich descriptive surface and abundant incident, storytelling techniques are usually uncomplicated, narrators omniscient, characters simple, and plots suspenseful but readily intelligible (these are, of course, the ingredients of the mimetic illusion established by the kind of novel we have learned to read most easily, the classic realistic nineteenth-century novel).

In some kinds of fiction, such as adult series novels (detective stories around one central character or historical sagas would be prime examples, but writers in other genres such as espionage or comedy of manners produce a kind of series even with changing characters), predictability or at least variation on a predictable theme is even a prime virtue from the reader's point of view. "To repeat with variation is the ultimate security," one literature teacher said about her own enthusiasm for a series of historical novels. "To walk with a familiar person in an unfamiliar but still manageable territory is very solacing." This remark suggests that emotionally, too, escape literature has to be undemanding; the manageability of the territory it leads a reader into is a key ingredient of its appeal. Readers do not expect it to deal with the really complex issues of actual life in ways that would be perplexing or disturbing. Yet another paradox is that they do want to find their own problems in these books; adults do not after all turn to juvenile and adolescent fiction for escape. Harlequin and blockbuster romances as well as family sagas are full of the ordinary and extraordinary crises of adult life, and detective stories and espionage novels and Westerns do not avoid crime and human suffering. Indeed, we could say that most of these kinds of books focus on the problems of human life, but they deal with them in special ways.

One clue to how romances appear to deal with real problems yet offer escape from them is the *utopian* character of this kind of reading, the fact that it embodies both a vision of an ideal state that would satisfy our longings and an implicit criticism of the structures that prevent our achieving them (Jameson 1979). It gratifies us by describing characters who lead more interesting lives than we do, who suffer more extremely, who are punished more drastically for their faults and rewarded more decisively for their virtues than we ever are. These characters appear to be *complete* individuals, Davis says, and thus offer the hope of overcoming the alienation inherent in modern life (1987, 131). The characteristic form of the classic novel and of much escape fiction – the realistic illusion and the explanatory role of the omniscient narrator – contributes to the utopian element, too; the lives and motivations of these characters are intelligible in ways that our own lives are not. But of course we really are looking at our idealized selves in these fictions, just as the troubled but finally ordered and virtuous community that prevails in them is a wish-fulfillment version of the world we live in.

An important mechanism at work in these fictions is the easy exercise of repressed desires and fears. Of course, all literature allows readers to

project feelings onto characters and to identify with conflict and its resolution, but the escapist motive seems to require the kind of fiction that
provides this payoff at little risk to the reader. Lesser points out that
popular fiction "exploits the satisfaction we secure from dealing with
anxiety under controlled conditions which assure its eventual liquida-
tion." But the anxiety is not generated naturally, as a by-product of
examining painful aspects of the human predicament: "It is blown up
artificially so that we may have the pleasure of seeing it deflated" (Lesser
1957, 261). Unacceptable desires can be gratified by seeing them enacted
in the most villainous ways; deep anxieties can be aroused and safely
exorcised in the spectacular predicaments of the fictional characters. But
escapist fiction does not probe the really painful troubles of our lives; it
offers us metonymic substitutes for them. The dramatic crimes, diseases,
accidents, and catastrophes of popular fiction do not mirror the realities
of our own lives any more than the vivid ecstasies and triumphs do; they
stand in for them, but at some distance from their problematic actuality.
They constitute "an imaginary world in which the audience can encounter
a maximum of excitement without being confronted with an over-
powering sense of the insecurity and danger that accompany such forms
of excitement in reality" (Cawelti 1976, 16). In fact, their very shorthand
quality enables them to represent what we unconsciously wish for and
fear, and their predictability keeps them comfortably in control. We play
in fantasy all the roles, now as spectators now as participants, Lesser
says, and the formula guarantees that we can do this safely, knowing
that the proportion of good and evil will come out right at the end (1957,
251-9).

It should be clear by now that escapist reading lies squarely within the
generic mode that Frye calls *romance*, whose central premise is that anxieties can be confronted and allayed and that wishes can be fulfilled. Adult
popular fiction may differ from juvenile adventure in the kind of subjects
it deals with (marriage, career, family, warfare, international intrigue,
violent crime) and in the relative complexity of its treatment of character,
plot, and setting, but there are no unreliable narrators, for example, or
multiple perspectives; characters are representative types and suspenseful
action moves the plot forward. The quality that really places escape
reading in the genre of romance, however, is the psychological rewards
it offers. As we have seen, it appears to confront intractable problems
of good and evil, reduces them to manageable shapes, and provides the
assurance of a happy ending. It offers the image of a central character
who can ultimately control threatening circumstances and achieve a glorious destiny.

The romance mentality in adult escape reading is sometimes overlaid
with tragic sensibility insofar as the central characters may suffer serious

illness, extreme anguish, and even death, but these sufferings are not the deeply explored crises of genuine tragedy that remind us of our all too insistent mortality and fallibility; they represent just enough of the serious evils of life to enable adult readers to feel that real problems are being addressed, but they are enclosed within the heroic adventure and happy ending of romance. The genre of tragedy, standing as it does between romance and irony, can blend into either one. Serious tragedy is likely to be suffused with the ironic sensibility which sees the complexity and ambiguity of human striving. Tragic romance is, at very least, an escape from irony.

The satisfactions of romance and tragic romance would seem, therefore, to be suited to the psychology of the developing juvenile and adolescent reader. If these genres reward the escapist motive, how well do they serve adult readers? Well enough, perhaps, if one supposes that the goal of reading is simply entertainment. But as we have seen Lesser point out, popular fiction falsifies the issues of adult life to render them susceptible of happy resolution; the relief it offers from the anxieties of living is ephemeral and brief (1957, 260–1). So escape reading embodies a peculiar contradiction; it readily offers the illusion that it faces and deals with serious problems, yet it simultaneously assures the reader that its treatment and resolution of them, no matter what entertaining variations on the formula intervene, will be conventional and predictable, in other words ultimately unsatisfying, as soon as one has learned the formula. When the book is finished, the reader is returned to the unresolved anxieties and desires of actual life. The result would either seem to induce a craving for repeating the experience, so that the genre turns into a narcotic, or to intensify the reader's dissatisfaction with the false comfort induced and to bring about an eventual revolt against this kind of reading altogether. Sales figures suggest that addiction is the more common reaction.

Adult addiction to romance is a fascinating phenomenon. Series like the Harlequin and Silhouette books are turned out, in the same fashion as the Nancy Drew and Hardy Boys books, by syndicates of writers following a rigidly prescribed formula. Some writers are industries all by themselves. Bantam distributes more than 10 million copies a year of Louis L'Amour's Westerns, which included 101 titles as of 1987, and there are an estimated 182 million copies of his books currently in print worldwide (Jackson 1987). Crime fiction and suspense is another enormous category of addictive reading. Like some juveniles with comic books, readers of detective novels often cannot remember the titles and plots of the stories they have just finished. One study uncovered a group of fans who marked lending-library books with a code so they could tell which ones they had already read. Titles, authors' names, and covers apparently were not enough to remind them (Ennis 1965). Why should this kind of reading be so pervasive among adults?

Nell distinguishes between readers who want to dull consciousness and readers who want to heighten it. Readers in the first group fear the kind of negatively toned fantasy that reminds them of their own anxieties; for them, reading can be a way of keeping busy, a distraction, literally an escape from self-consciousness. Usually formulaic fiction with its familiar exercises satisfies them, and they often read it at great speed – so as, in one case Nell cites, to forget it quickly and be able to enjoy it again. On the other hand, readers who want to heighten consciousness experience positive fantasies; they want to be involved with the characters and the situations in the books they read, and they find reading a vehicle for self-exploration and the enlargement of their experience. Interestingly, the more complete escape is available to these readers, Nell thinks, because their lack of self-preoccupation enables them to achieve the kind of total involvement in a book that he calls "entrancement," and they can do this even with demanding and complex books, whereas the involvement of the first group is a shallower degree of absorption in books whose qualities are necessarily predictable. Although both kinds of readers can therefore be said to escape, the first group seems to be the genuine addicts and are presumably the ones we think of when we label escape reading pejoratively (Nell 1988, 227–34).

Janice Radway studied a group of middle-class women in a small Midwestern city who would seem to be addicts of escape, according to Nell's categories (Radway 1984). They were intensive readers of mass-market romances. A third of them read five to nine romances a week *along with other books,* and some even claimed they read fifteen to twenty-five a week (1984, 60). Some felt guilty about the time and money they spent on books and about the implication that the romances were close to pornography, and many reported hiding the books from their husbands and families (1984, 103–6); but they also defended their private time away from family responsibilities, and they offered the interesting rationale that their reading not only provided pleasure but was also instructive in that it expanded their knowledge of other times and cultures, built up their vocabularies, and gave them useful information about the world (1984, 107–14).

These readers were not undiscriminating in the kind of romance they read or in their favorite authors. The main thing they were looking for, Radway found, was a "compensatory" escape from the psychologically demanding and physically draining task of caring for the needs of their families (1984, 92). "We read books so we won't cry," one woman said (1984, 98), and another described reading as a safer outlet than pills and alcohol (1984, 87). A romance that provides this escape in an acceptable form has two main features, Radway found; it offers the reader a chance to identify with a heroine who gains the attention and recognition of a male (and thereby the culture's highest approval), and in the tender and protective love of this idealized male the reader can also relive her childhood experience of being the exclusive object of her mother's profoundly nurturing love (1984, 84). This idealized fantasy explains why these women objected to sexually explicit writing, to violence, and to intractable problems such as illness, handicaps, and aging; these problems are emotionally threatening, too close to the fears readers want to escape from, too difficult to transform plausibly by a happy ending.

Radway argues that women read (and reread) these romances in such quantity because they satisfy a deep-seated need arising out of the limited roles a repressive patriarchal culture allows to women. But might we also see in this behavior a more general form of needs and satisfactions that both men and women feel when they turn to the generic mode of romance? In other words, does romance reading have any positive developmental functions for adults?

One plausible hypothesis, as Radway's thesis partly implies, is that escapist reading represents a necessary therapeutic regression, temporary or habitual, to childhood forms of pleasure. After we have left the dream vision of early childhood, romance is the first form of story that we become conscious of as a paradigm of our lives. Our earliest visions of ourselves confronting danger and emerging successfully are packaged in the conventions of romance. No wonder that it is a desirable experience to recover. One student pointed out to me that reading in bed not only continues a common childhood habit, but comes close to reproducing as an adult the experience of being held in someone's lap. Reverting regularly to romance from the midst of our adult problems may be something we do compulsively, a distorted "ritualization" of experience (to use Erikson's term) that we cannot do without, but it may also be a temporary, expedient retreat from the complexities of more demanding reading or from the exigencies of adult life.

A different explanation is that many adults may be stuck in their reading development at the level of romance. Cognitively, they cannot handle narrative forms more complex than romance, and affectively they want the satisfaction of identifying with characters who graphically embody their anxieties and their desires and of immersing themselves in a plot whose dramatic crises will end happily. Repetitive reading of series novels or particular genres is typically a phenomenon of juvenile development, where it is an aspect of a young person's struggle to come to a sense of competence in a world represented as intelligible and predictable. That many of us habitually read the same way as adults may mean that we are still dealing with the unfinished tasks of early youth.

Is this addiction self-curing? Some juvenile readers digest dozens of series novels and then tire of the conventions and turn to more realistic reading. Perhaps for adults the escapist addiction is not merely the frivolous pastime that critics and teachers often assume it to be, but is in some sense a temporary but necessary corrective to the emptiness in much of daily life. Peter Brooks argues that melodrama is an attempt to confer on everyday material existence the kind of significance and meaning that we see in higher drama (1976, 219). Does escape reading then ultimately lead to growth? Tanya Modleski argues that women read Harlequin romances and gothics with a double vision; they see their real problems mirrored in the stories and believe at least temporarily in the possibility of transcending them (1982, 37). Romance reading can therefore be interpreted as a determination to adapt utopian ideals to existing circumstances. One would like to think that addiction to romance leads to political awareness, but the evidence for it seems slender, and Modleski concedes that the conventional resolutions only reinforce the oppressive features of the social roles that created these problems in the first place (1982, 58). Radway certainly thinks that romance reading is psychologically therapeutic, but she stops short of the conclusion that it changes the lives of its readers in any positive way, though some of the women she interviewed argued that it did (1984, 101–2).

It seems more likely that many adults simply do not, without the intervention of some other kind of developmental stimulus, progress beyond the level of romance or tragic romance in their habitual reading, either because they cannot imagine a more adequate view of the world or their education has not led them further or their psychological development does not dispose them to demand more complex kinds of satisfaction from reading. If addictive romance reading is developmentally useful at all, it may be as a plateau where the reader can rest from the exigencies of more challenging kinds of reading. Perhaps, too, habitually repeating the conventions of romance does not always wear them out, but deepens the archtypal grip of the fears and desires they embody and the desirable solution they represent, and this experience in some way prepares a reader for changes that will happen later.

SEARCHING FOR TRUTH

If escape is one motive for reading fiction and the principal motive for some readers of fiction, another reason adults read is that they see themselves as searchers for wisdom of some sort and look to fiction to provide them with insight into the world or into their own lives. These readers, Nell says, want to heighten their consciousness rather than dull it. I interviewed one sixty-three-year-old woman who said:

"Somebody said to me the other day, 'Reading fills the time,' and I thought: It doesn't fill my time, it adds to my time. . . . I'm going out of myself in some way and sharing life with the author or the people in the book. . . . I like getting beyond my own life, not leaving it but getting beyond it." We have already seen Elizabeth say about books that let her enter the lives of people different from herself: "I guess I'm searching for my own world and this is one way to find it." Another woman, age 46, who has brought up three children and is now finishing a graduate degree in social work, explains her sense of identification with characters in the fiction she reads: "I think I get into more stories about women . . . women are very interesting people right now . . . they're searching for their identity and where they belong." She mentions recently reading Gail Godwin's *A Mother and Two Daughters*: "The relationships between mothers and daughters . . . interest me professionally too. That's probably one of the reasons why I read fiction about women." "Learning to read books," Scholes writes, "– or pictures, or films – is not just a matter of acquiring information from texts, it is a matter of learning to read and write the texts of our lives" (1989, 19).

On the other hand, a fifty-year-old man, a teacher of literature, appears to disavow this motive. "I don't read literature for wisdom, as I once did. I think a lot of undergraduates become English majors because they have this feeling that novels and poems can teach them about life or change the quality of their moral experience better than other things can. And I find that to be less and less true."

When pressed to say what the appeal of reading is at this point in his life, he says: "Records of human experience. There's some way that I think that . . . I feel that . . . I've really become much more . . . conscious of the fallibility of an author. So that I wouldn't take any novelist seriously as a moralist, or as somebody from whom I was going to learn anything important about how to live. And yet, at the same time, there's some way that that's more moving. I think I read, particularly fiction, more autobiographically than I ever did. I'm more conscious of what sort of imaginative expression it is of the person writing, and I think of that person as a person."

He contrasts his own experience with his students' responses when he was teaching *The Charterhouse of Parma* the previous year: "Undergraduates don't want to hear about Stendahl. They're not very interested in how that novel connects with his life. They want to respond to it for itself, much more than I do. I'm fascinated by its connections with his life . . . by what it meant to him in some sort of intimate way." He struggles to articulate what this means to him, falling back on the phrase "a record of human experience": "It's the saying of certain kinds of things, qualified by all the particular circumstances of that saying . . .

certain kinds of things that nobody else could say in quite that way or nobody has said." But there's a personal sense in which these records matter to him too: "I would connect the story with [the author's] life, but I would also enjoy it . . . in a way that I don't think people can do very well, if they haven't had [a similar] experience, or if they haven't set up some kind of sensibility that would respond to it. . . . There's some reason teachers and older students, you know, respond to novels in a different way than younger ones, because they're much more apt to connect them with experiences in their own lives." So, though the author of a work of fiction may be no source of wisdom about the world for this reader, the work itself is a record of human experience that moves him because he can recognize himself, even his fallibility, in it.

The search for truth can take different forms; these readers' remarks indicate something of the range of possibilities. Jung, Erikson, and others have pointed out that the need for intellectual clarity and certainty is often a mark of young adulthood. This attitude can turn into ideological rigidity and fanaticism; there is *a* truth, and it must be discovered, and the claims of competing truths must be shown to be false. But its positive side is the determined quest to understand, to solve problems and construct theories, to get to the bottom of things. The idea that stories offer readers insight into the truth of things fits naturally into this epistemology of the young adult.

Is this approach to a story what Rosenblatt calls "efferent" reading – focusing attention "on what the words refer to, on what is to be taken away from the transaction" (1985, 38)? Perhaps it often is, especially in the minds of self-absorbed readers. Efferent reading is interested in acquiring information, reaching conclusions, following instructions. The adult search for truth in fiction, however, seems closer to what Rosenblatt calls "aesthetic" reading. It focuses on what the reader "is living through during the reading-event" (1985, 38). Even when a reader chooses to sum up his or her experience of a work of literature in a formula, this kind of reading has to do with the unique way the reader selects and synthesizes the ideas, feelings, and images aroused by the work. Scholes (1989, 18) says:

> We humans are the animals who know that we shall die. We know that our lives are shaped like stories, with a beginning, a middle, and an end, and that the end is inevitable. Reading, I am contending, consists, among other things, in recognizing and facing the signs of this pattern, too. We read life as well as books, and the activity of reading is really a matter of working through signs and texts in order to comprehend more fully and powerfully not only whatever may be presented therein but also our own situations, both in their particularity and historicity and in their more durable and inevitable dimensions.

The understanding we come to in our maturity lies in recognizing the alignment of the wisdom in texts with the pattern of our own lives.

A naive or uncritical assumption about this truth is that it is something objective that will be found outside somewhere, in some experience one has not yet had or in a particular idea or perspective that wiser people know but that one has not yet discovered for oneself. The undergraduate students of the professor just quoted expect literature to teach them about life: "They come to it looking for wisdom, but the wisdom they want is something very exalted and outside themselves. It's a kind of hero worship. They see this great work of art at an immense distance from themselves and it's very moving to them." The image of searching for a hidden or elusive prize conveys very well the subjective experience of the person in this frame of mind.

It is easy to think this way because the structure of narrative mimics the quest for meaning. Even the simplest story seems to propose a journey somewhere, to move toward some decisive equilibrium that resolves the disequilibrium set in motion and elaborated by the events of the plot. More to the point, the resolution of almost any narrative other than the simplest schematic plot appears to consist of some disclosure about the truth of the events: What really happened? Why did it happen? What is the meaning of what happened? In Barthes's terms, we want the "enigma" that was "marked" at the outset of the tale to be resolved by explanation (1975b, 17, 75–6). The detective story is one of the purest embodiments of this theme, acknowledged by its nickname, a whodunit. Perhaps it is a popular form of adult recreational reading because it reinforces so directly this archetype of the quest for significant explanation.

Even the complex narratives that define modernist style do not avoid this theme of a search for the secret that will give meaning to otherwise inexplicable events. Virginia Woolf's *To the Lighthouse* ends with Lily putting the last stroke of paint onto the canvas that she has been struggling to finish all through the novel; with the dab of color that finally manages to get Mrs. Ramsay into the scene she says, "I have had my vision." Joseph Conrad's *Lord Jim* depicts a double search: by Jim for the means to expiate his cowardice, and by Marlowe, the narrator, for the meaning of Jim's search. In Henry James, the obsessive search for a secret truth is virtually a trademark. "The Jamesian narrative," Todorov says, "is always based on the quest for an absolute and absent cause" (1977, 145). The paradigmatic instance is the story "The Figure in the Carpet," in which a young literary critic searches fanatically and vainly for the secret that will explain the meaning of the works of an older author he admires. But he is only one among many James protagonists who spend their energies trying to understand mysterious secrets. Typically, the quest is

for insight into others' lives (for instance, Strethers's attempt to understand Chad Newsome's Europeanization in *The Ambassadors*) or for understanding their own experience (Stransom's exploration of his
fascination with the cult of death in "The Altar of the Dead"). But
sometimes James problematizes the quest itself. In *The Turn of the Screw*
the tale-within-a-tale narrative deflects attention from the question of
what the events at Bligh mean onto the question of what actually happened at Bligh; the secret shifts, in effect, from what the events meant
to the governess to what they mean to the reader. And in stories like
"The Figure in the Carpet," James turns the work of art itself into a
secret that perplexingly points only to itself, is enigmatic to the characters, and is doubly enigmatic to the reader because this tale about tales
says in effect that the reader's quest for an authoritative insight will never
be satisfied.

This is the distinctively modern note, of course, that the quest for
disclosure is finally unresolved. If James's characters discover anything,
it is rarely the secret they were searching for. The gesture of finishing
her painting has a symbolic definiteness for Lily Briscoe but whatever
she means by her vision, the reader is not spared the complex task of
interpreting and deciphering it. And when he has finished telling Jim's
tale, Marlowe and the reader have more questions than answers about
its meaning. This is storytelling for an age of uncertainty.

Or perhaps it is just a more mature storytelling than the kind that
offers the reader the satisfaction of neatly discovering what really happened. The truth that adult readers seek may have more to do with
questions and contradictions and fruitful puzzles than with clear conclusions and it may have more to do with particular images of experience
that provoke and disturb and force the reader to confront his or her own
choices than with larger-than-life fantasies that end happily.

I have mentioned the argument going on among developmental psychologists about the adequacy of Piaget's view that structural changes in
cognitive development end with the attainment of formal-operational
thinking (the onset of which occurs in adolescence), when thought becomes logical, hypothetical, and abstract. Revisions of this account, such
as those of Riegel, Basseches, and others, argue that what is most characteristic about mature adult thinking is that it is grounded in polarities
of experience, that it juggles contingencies and partial truths, that it deals
in fragile and provisional certainties, and that it therefore has a dialectical
character rather than the logical clarity of formal-operational thinking.
These emendations of Piaget appear to mirror the view of adult experience and of the confidence (or lack thereof) we can have in our certainties that modern novels do. Insight into life's problems might be
imagined as a search, but there is no simple discovery at the end and the

journey is more likely to be a painful, inward one rather than one that goes along the high road of adventure to a satisfying goal.

When she was thirty-eight, the poet Louise Bogan wrote to Theodore Roethke: "I must say, I get terribly sick of novels that go along, riding a hidden or ostensible I, in a straight line, with some bumps, from start to finish" (1973, 117). John Muller cites this remark in an essay about the experience of aging that Bogan records in her poetry. It compels her to a painful scrutiny of her inner life, a process that is full of darkness as well as light, and it moves in anything but a straight line. Muller, following Jacques Lacan's psychoanalytic view of the subject, is interested in the illusory images of ourselves that we form out of mirrored others and that we use language and social organization to give a structure to as though they were true (1986, 83–4). Discerning the lures of this deceptive other, stripping away the distorted reflections, and locating the symbols that are still valid is the chief task of the aging person. Muller (1986, 84) cites an entry from one of Bogan's notebooks: "First [we require that life] be romantic, exciting; then, that it should be bearable; and, at last, that it should be understandable!" But the struggle to understand ourselves does not issue in clear conclusions. "Perhaps we touch the truth," he says, "rather than see it or become seen by its light. We grope. We establish contiguous relations. Or perhaps it is better to say we are touched by the truth. In any case, the truth is always for us humans metonymic, partial, inevitably a process of displacement and unfinished movement, not an ego-directed pursuit to a conclusion" (1986, 93).

W. B. Yeats was much influenced by a related idea that he found in Nietzsche and Jung, that of the *shadow,* the darker self that is hidden, often even from ourselves, by the mask we present to the world. Jung thought that our early lives are spent constructing a persona through which, like actors, we play our social roles and that the work of the second half of life is to probe beneath this mask and confront the darker other that is "also-I" in order to integrate the self (1969, especially 396ff.). Yeats in midlife became obsessed with exploring his "antithetical" self, the "hollow image of fulfilled desire" that he was all too afraid he had constructed in his poetry (1959, 329). This image, like Lacan's mirrored reflection, gives a familiar and acceptable shape to "the infinite pain of self-realization," but for that very reason it cannot be trusted (1959, 334). He imagined that another kind of opposite, his "daemon" or "double," would come to his aid and "disclose all" that he sought by helping him trace his life back to its start (Yeats 1983, 160). These notions helped an aging Yeats carry out a struggle to reexamine and reorganize the imagery on which his psychic life was built. He carried the effort through in the astonishing poems of the last years of his life. But none of his symbols satisfied him completely, or perhaps it is better to say that he found them at best partial realizations of an ever-elusive truth. Three weeks before he died he wrote: "I am happy, and I think full of an energy, of an energy I had despaired of. It seems to me that I have found what I wanted. When I try to put all into a phrase I say, 'Man can embody truth but he cannot know it'" (Yeats 1954, 922).

The force of this paradox shows up in the adult realization that we have to judge, act, choose, and embody truth in spite of the limitations of our knowledge of the truth. The way we read confronts us with one of these choices, it seems. Gadamer (1975) compares the problem of interpreting a text with Aristotle's analysis of making an ethical decision. The reader needs, Gadamer says, not what Aristotle calls *episteme* or scientific knowledge of the kind that can be known beforehand and can be taught, but something more like *tekne,* the craftsman's skill in applying his habitual knowledge to a particular situation. More precisely, this person needs *phronesis,* the virtue of reflection that we bring to bear when we make a moral judgment in a concrete situation. This virtue is a kind of experience, developed through education and practice and over time. It yields reliable knowledge only when it is brought to bear in the immediacy of concrete action. This kind of moral decision making, Gadamer argues, should be our model for interpreting a text. A text contains no universal truths that readers extract and apply to themselves. Rather, its meaning and significance can only be known by the interpreters if they start by relating it to their own particular situation. Text, experience, and meaning combine only in a concrete act of interpretation (Gadamer 1975, 278–89).

Here is one illustration of text and life experience influencing a particular interpretive attitude in a concrete set of circumstances. Mary is a sixty-three-year-old woman who did clerical work in an office and then brought up six children. Although her education did not go beyond high school, she has been a constant reader all her life. She talks about a group she belongs to at the local library that reads and discusses books. She is the oldest woman in it by ten or fifteen years. Their most recent book is *McKay's Bees,* a 1979 novel by Thomas McMahon about the social and sexual relationships among a group of settlers in Kansas during the nineteenth century. She enjoyed it, but others in the group had different reactions: "One woman just couldn't make head or tails out of the characters . . . the way they lived, their attitudes towards one another." How to explain this puzzles Mary:

> Maybe this is an odd thing to say, but I think she was coming out of her generation and it just didn't hit her. Whereas I have six children and, you know, the oldest is forty and the youngest is twenty-four. . . . I think I can relate more to the way they lived. . . . I think she's

married, the woman I'm talking about. She's had a good job and a stable life. I think I'm more accustomed to all the different attitudes that young people have today that we didn't have and weren't exposed to.... I wouldn't say, "Well, I don't see how people could live like that and think like that," when you know from what you're hearing and seeing that people do live in certain ways. You can't just discount it as not happening if it does happen.

This tolerance does not mean that she has no firm opinions about what she reads. Their group has talked a lot about censorship:

I was brought up with the idea of protecting yourself against bad influences... but now that I'm older I can read a lot of things... and be critical of them.... I can judge them.... I found a book in the house ... one of my daughters brought it back from California, *The Sensuous Woman,* I think it was called. And when I looked through it, as a mother and a married woman I thought: A lot of it is just baloney that these kids are going to be taken in by. I couldn't censor that book, but I would say, "Hey, forget it!"... I guess the older you get you know there are limits to everything.

One test of our maturity as readers is to have our responses be adequate to the wisdom we have accrued from our experiences. Tolerance, openness to others' experience, knowing the edges of one's own certainties, but still taking responsibility for one's own convictions – these are attitudes one does not learn quickly or without considerable accumulated experience of the changes of life. Adult readers like Mary are less confident about the absoluteness of the truths they have learned, more conscious of being instructed by views different from their own, more aware of being responsible to sources of meaning that they are only imperfectly in touch with. Their experience seems to be enlarged from within and from without.

That we choose and act in the midst of all these motives that encourage us to accept life's complexities passively is a puzzle, yet it is one of the marks of adulthood that we take responsibility for much in our lives even when the truths and consequences of our acts are only partly within our control. Is this the case in reading too? When a woman in her forties, a writer, a mother of two children who has seen one of them slowly die of cancer, says "I'm too old to waste time on junk," some standard is operating to discriminate what is worth reading from what is not in her eyes. But many adults, even the wisest, read little fiction or read it with motives that have nothing to do with discovering these kinds of truths about themselves. The kind of reading that looks beyond the whodunit satisfactions of popular fiction and expects a story to hold up more than a mirror that reflects our own fantasies requires more courage than many of us want to invest in reading. It can be emotionally risky to look at unflattering pictures of ourselves through a lens that has more irony than romance in it. Real mirrors are no friends to aging people. Despair, after all, is as equally possible an outcome as integrity in Erikson's final stage of the life cycle. The attitude toward truth that grows out of hard-won knowledge of one's own limits, that embraces contradictions, and that is content with a wisdom that comes in fragmentary images may describe the lives of many adults, but it is not necessarily a wisdom we want to see reflected in what we read.

This kind of reading may be uncommon not just because of the courage it takes, but because it also is intellectually demanding. Literature that is emotionally complex typically makes formal demands on its readers as well (we saw the reverse in escape reading). Following the James sentence to its carefully balanced conclusion takes patience. The intellectual playfulness of Nabokov, the political, probing mind of Nadine Gordimer, and the flat surfaces and unresolved encounters of Raymond Carver's stories demand the kind of commitment that not every adult reader will make without some conscious choice. Readers who have no tolerance for forms and authorial voices different from the ones they learned in their youth may be expressing simply a deficit of their aesthetic education, an incapacity to bring to this kind of literature the response it demands intellectually.

Nonetheless, if we take reading seriously and if we take seriously the values we are committed to in other parts of our lives, we will find that the personal implications of what and how we read cannot be avoided. I am thinking of the evaluative aspect of reading that Scholes calls "criticism" – judging the world views and their consequences in the books we read, in the light of interests we have because we are members of specific social communities. For Scholes, this is not an option we may or may not choose to exercise for personal reasons, but the inevitable and indispensable consequence of reading and interpreting a text. Something will be missing in our response, if we do not relate the literary text to the social text in which we live (Scholes 1985, 18–38). Booth has also recently argued at length for restoring ethical criticism to the center of our engagement with literature (1988). The instructive examples for his thinking, he acknowledges, are the feminist and black critics and the neo-Marxists and religious critics who have offered explicit reassessments of the values implied in mainstream criticism. But he demonstrates with wit and verve that disguised moral judgments have been the staple of even those critics whose theories strove for the purest formal responses to literature. Booth proposes instead that we acknowledge frankly that reading is an encounter of the ethos or character of the storyteller with that of the reader and acknowledge that we continually evaluate the quality of life we experience in this encounter. To be sure, Booth is less interested in judging a book good or bad than in a pluralistic conversation about the variety of personal and social consequences it might have for a reader's life, but he does not shirk from the conclusion that what and how we read matters to us ethically. Holland too has recently argued that we need the opportunity to "hear ourselves think" about what is going on in the reading process and therefore how we respond to what we read (Holland 1988, 154–81). And Lennard Davis's thesis in his study of the role of ideology in fiction is that a self-conscious reader should actively "resist" the tendency of novels to involve us in wish-fulfillment fantasies and to distance us from our real feelings and from the realities of the world around us (Davis 1987, especially 15–23).

The ethical truths that mature readers search for in fiction seem increasingly to require a turning inward and personal gaze, and to have to do with the "ordinary activities of life" and the "relationships with the people around you" that Elizabeth mentions. Like the older students and colleagues the teacher of Stendhal noticed, adults tend to connect what they read "with experiences in their own lives." Readers from early adolescence onward say that they like books whose characters they can identify with. I have suggested that acknowledging that the world of good and evil is more complex than childhood literature makes it out to be and demanding that the characters and issues of fiction embody the rough edges and obscurities of the reader's deepening experience are the first steps in qualifying the idea of romance. The history of anyone's life as a reader can be thought of as a search for images adequate enough to identify with personally. But as an adult reads, the process by which "something happens to the reader," according to Iser's theory (1978, 152), occurs more fully. We comprehend the meaning in a text, but in absorbing the meaning into our own existence we also "formulate ourselves and thus discover an inner world of which we had hitherto not been conscious" (1978, 158). One might say, using the terms Hirsch developed for these two aspects of the reading act, that for adults the "significance" of the work for the reader is at least as important as the "meaning" of the work to its author (1976, 1–13, 79–81).

This is why the search for an absolute truth in fiction ultimately fails. The more we explore the implications of the discovery that we experience truths rather than a truth and that fiction captures them only in fragile and time-bound images and that the significance we read in them is constructed out of our own earned wisdom as much as it is out of author's, the less we demand that fiction will teach us anything. This chastening experience makes us humble about even our own hard-won truths and willing to allow others to find their own. A retired professor of literature says:

I don't want my students to like my interpretation of the story better than the story. I think that years ago that was almost my aim. I can remember feeling once that I had done a very good job with [Milton's] "Lycidas" . . . by talking about the elegy . . . and applying the form to the piece, and everybody seemed very interested in it. But I think in the end I had a class which really never got to read "Lycidas" but was quite taken by my appreciation of it, and that seemed to be not what I wanted. . . . I guess I have enough faith now that if they read the story then interpretation takes care of itself. . . . It seems that if I've ever discovered anything through the years, it's been . . . to feel that in teaching a story there is a kind of communal experience that's involved in it and that can kind of arise out of a free discussion of the story. You may find that somebody will go this way or somebody will go that . . . and some of these departures can be shown to be misreadings, but some of them you just have to accept as possibilities. . . . I let them argue about it as much as possible, and sometimes arguments can't be settled. I say, well I don't think you're right but nevertheless I can't really show that you're wrong. I guess if I have any hopes about it, it's that maybe as you read it more and more you'll discover what I think is the truth.

The truths we do discover are no less precious to us because we are willing to let others discover their own. In fact, they may be all the more valuable because they are hard won and they are our own. But we will give up the illusion that if only we search more keenly through finer fictions, some final and objective truth will yet be disclosed to us.

The imaginal status of fictional truth may be one reason why some adults who were intensive readers in their younger years stop reading fiction altogether. It comes to seem merely recreational, to be an insufficient source of wisdom about life's important problems. "I got away from fiction," said a retired theology professor in his seventies who was a great reader in his boyhood and student days. "After I started to teach, life became very busy and there seemed to be so many other books I should read . . . not only theology, but sociology, history, cultural history especially. . . . I think you can lose the habit of reading fiction. You reproach yourself: 'I could be improving my mind, instead of just dawdling away time on this stuff.'" These lapsed fiction readers do not seem to have a need to experience their lives or their world imaged in stories. Or perhaps this need is satisfied in other ways, in popular fictional media such as films or television or in poetry (the theologian who stopped reading fiction in his thirties reads poetry in bed every night) or music or visual art.

Some people, of course, cannot not read. The imaginal status of the truth of fiction is no problem for them. If it is not addiction or escape or wisdom that fiction provides for these readers, what is it that rewards them?

DISCOVERING USABLE IMAGES

In speculating about how personal associations coalesce around particular images from the past, T. S. Eliot writes:

> Why, for all of us, out of all that we have heard, seen, felt, in a lifetime do certain images recur, charged with emotion, rather than others? The song of one bird, the leap of one fish, at a particular place and time, the scent of one flower, an old woman on a German mountain path, six ruffians seen through an open window playing cards at night at a small French railway junction where there was a water-mill: such memories may have symbolic value, but of what we cannot tell, for they come to represent the depth of feelings into which we cannot peer. (1933, 148)

I have no doubt that we could each make a list of images that would parallel Eliot's in its concreteness, its apparent randomness, and in the privacy of the associations each image carries with it for us. Readers of a psychoanalytic bent might not agree that peering into the depths of our feeling and discovering what our valued images symbolize is wholly impossible. The more interesting question Eliot's observation raises for our purpose, though, is what function this image-making activity has as we grow older. I suggest that it is a clue to something else we do as adults when we read: We accumulate and simplify a personal anthology of the images – books, characters, scenes, turns of phrase, metaphors, words – that have power and meaning for us.

This point is illuminated by an account in John Kotre's *Outliving the Self* that has nothing explicitly to do with reading but much to do with stories, not with the life stories of the eight men and women that Kotre records and interprets in his book, but with a parable and a fable that his last subject uses to explain the meaning of his life (1984, 227–47). Chris Vitullo, a man in his seventies, was born in a fishing village in Sicily, learned to be a barber, came to the United States as a boy, married, prospered as a barber and grocer, but then lost much of his money in land investments and returned to barbering in his old age. His business disappointments and the chronic ill health of his wife did not affect his generous temperament; he cared for family members, helped friends, and was active in church charities and in the neighborhood where his shop was. Eight years after his wife's death, at the age of seventy-four, he married a widow he met at the YMCA.

When Chris was narrating his life to Kotre, at one point he stopped and said that he wanted to tell a story (1984, 228). It was told to him when he was a child by his father and concerns a young man who comes to see his godfather after many years of separation and asks to borrow a hundred lire. The godfather tells him that the cup on the shelf has what he needs. The young man takes out a hundred lire and says that he will return the money as soon as he can. A year later he comes back and asks a second time for a hundred lire. The godfather points to the cup again and says it has what he needs. When the young man finds no money in the cup, he reminds the older man that he took it last time and so now there's nothing. The godfather then tells him: "You get back what you put in! I had a hundred lire, and I gave it to you, and you didn't bring it back. How can I give it to you again?"

The idea that you get back what you put in seems to have a special meaning for Chris. It sums up what he was taught by his father, what his own experience has taught him, and what he wants to pass on to others. Three times in the interviews with Kotre he refers to the story, and in their final conversation he says: "I gotta leave in the cup for those that are dear to me. . . . I tell them about the Commandments. 'Love thy neighbor.' They have to learn that if you love others like you love yourself, then it's good material in the cup. In the cup you put the respect for your friends, the love for your mother and father, the love for your relatives and for your friends. If you haven't got that and you think you can do without, I think you're wrong. . . . You don't expect nothing in return but the same thing you put in" (Kotre 1984, 245).

He subsequently tells another story, the first one he remembers hearing from his mother when he was a child. It is a version of the traditional fable of the country mouse who envies the easy life of the town mouse, until he sees the town mouse caught by the clever cat (Kotre 1984, 232): "What my mother was telling me [is] that it's not what you would like to have, it's what you actually have that counts. If you could be happy on the wild onions, good. If you're looking for beautiful cheeses, you could get in trouble. So why not live happy where you are at?"

These stories, Kotre suggests, function as scenarios into which Chris can condense the major themes and motifs of his long life as he recalls them. He reaches back into his boyhood culture for these tales, sums up with their help the meaning his life has for him now, and uses them to pass on the lessons he thinks those who come after him should know. In these stories his life takes on a mythic quality. It is, in Kotre's phrase, "a life made fabulous," not divorced from historical truth but "moved a few steps in the direction of myth" (1984, 252). The details of Chris's life become a bit more marvelous, a bit more exemplary, in the telling. His personal story seems now to be a retelling of a collective ancient one.

The reminiscing of older people may be much more than just the nostalgic retelling of better days. It seems to have the important psychic function of allowing a person to review past experiences, particularly unresolved conflicts, and to fit them into a perspective. This "life review," as Robert N. Butler calls it (1963), may have happy or unhappy outcomes: anxiety and depression, when feelings of the meaninglessness of one's life in the face of approaching death are overwhelming or candor, serenity, and wisdom, when one accepts one's life as meaningful and as one's own.

Erikson, it will be remembered, calls these two outcomes of the last stage of the life cycle "despair" and "integrity." He offers an analysis of a particularly vivid example of the life review in Ingmar Bergman's *Wild Strawberries* (1978, 1–31). The film dramatizes the reminiscences of a seventy-six-year-old professor as he journeys by car to the city where he is to receive an honorary doctorate. There are a number of vivid scenes and images. The professor recalls a dream of his own funeral procession. The auto trip is interrupted at the old summer house of his childhood where wild strawberries still grow. There is an auto accident along the road, a memory of a midsummer family celebration, a frightening dream of his final examination in medical school, then the doctoral ceremony at which he is honored for his life's work, and at the end a scene of reconciliation with his daughter-in-law and his son. These images embody the process through which the professor comes to terms with the achievements and failures of his life. They are images of Bergman's devising, of course, but if they render Dr. Borg's consciousness of his life plausibly, it must be because we recognize that psychically we work the same way, that the meaningfulness of our lives gathers around certain images, or as in Chris's case, stories, because these images have the power to unite mythic truths with personal experience and to sum up our deepest fears and hopes. The roots of these images are deep and hidden, as Eliot's remark makes clear, but I want to suggest that locating and shaping the images is one of the uses we put our reading to.

For Jung, the work of the second half of life is to integrate the personality. The resources for this work include not only our individual experiences of identity with the world around us, but also the inherited wisdom of the culture, the primordial images and symbols that give a structure to our collective psychological world: "It is only possible to live the fullest life when we are in harmony with these symbols; wisdom is a return to them" (1969, 402–3). We encounter these collective symbols in ancient myths, in folk culture, religion, and dreams, and of course in works of art. The integration that Jung assigns to the second half of life consists in merging this collective with the personal, in finding and deepening the connections between them that give a sense of the integrity of our lives. The literature and art that embody these collective symbols become a prime resource that help us articulate the personal symbols that express the wholeness of our lives.

Development aspires to integration, however frail our hold on the experience of completeness is while we are in the midst of the process. How much is involved is hinted at in the metaphors that convey what is important about the final stages in the various developmental theories we have been considering: formal thought, integrity, balance, harmony. A still more comprehensive view of development appears in the later work of philosopher and theologian Bernard Lonergan.[1]

After a lifetime spent working out a description of how humans appropriate themselves as knowers, in the many forms – practical, scientific, and artistic – that knowing takes, Lonergan realized that he had to supplement his cognitive account of the development involved in self-appropriation with an affective one. He proposed two inverse but complementary movements or vector forces at work in development. One operates from the bottom up in four steps. This movement begins in our *concrete experiences* of the world, advances to constructing the insightful generalizations that supply *understanding* of that experience, then moves to the kind of critical reflection that issues in *judgments* about what we have understood of our experience, and ends in concrete *decision making that expresses the values* we place on the judgments we have made about our understood experience. This movement has something of Piaget's *assimilation* in it, insofar as it experiences the world through the categories we bring to bear on it.

Yet however convincing this is as a conceptual model of some aspects of our cognitive growth, we know that it does not describe all that goes on, even cognitively, in human development, because throughout our lives (and especially when we are young) we frequently make decisions to act on behalf of particular values long before we have reflected critically about them, and we trust generalizations about our experience long before we have had enough experience to know whether our insights are valid. So this movement alone cannot account for all the ways in which we absorb the social context and the knowable world around us. Lonergan would say that we need to imagine another movement, which operates simultaneously from the top down. In this movement we are first *immersed in the values* of a community (for example, of our parents and families and the place we live) that we absorb affectively in an atmosphere of trust and belief, then we come to *recognize these values reflectively,* and only after this do we slowly grow in *understanding* of what these values and beliefs mean, and then finally we are able to arrive at a *mature experience* of all that they entail (Crowe 1985, 1–22).

These are not two different movements. Lonergan insists that consciousness is one and that there is two-way traffic between the two movements, a ceaseless dynamic interaction among the different steps along each vector, each one successively integrating and changing the previous ones, and between the two vectors themselves. When we are children we interpret the data of immediate experience according to the received values and beliefs of the community we live in, but these values and beliefs are also influenced by our attempts to understand things for ourselves. These understandings in turn are informed by explanations and judgments about the world that we have accepted on trust, which in their turn may be modified by the intellectual and ethical commitments we make, and so forth. In this constant interaction between vectors there is a forward movement, though, toward an equilibrium. In childhood, the influence of the outer-directed movement is greater. The inner-directed movement gains in force in adolescence and early adulthood. Only in maturity can the two forces be integrated in a balance (Crowe 1985, 25–6).

Most models of the reading process do not do justice to the complexity of the experience that this view of the dialectic of development includes, or to the reader's self-appropriating role at the heart of this process, or to its unfinished and ongoing nature. Norman Holland, starting from a quite different point than Lonergan in his most recent book, offers an unexpectedly similar picture of the way a reader's characteristic identity develops in the reading process (Holland 1988). Searching for a better metaphor for reading than the text-active model (a poem *contains* a meaning that it delivers or it *determines* the reader's response by its signs and codes), Holland offers a reader-active model drawn from brain physiology and cognitive psychology. In this model, reading is a dialectic of reader, text, and world that operates by continuous loops of hypothesis, testing, and feedback. These loops do not operate mechanistically. They are arranged hierarchically, so that one loop sets the standard for another, and at the center of the process is an organizing principle or governor – Holland calls it the reader's characteristic identity – that arranges feedback toward the ends that satisfy this identity (1988, 89).

Holland's description of the two main feedback loops in the reading process is similar to Lonergan's double-vector picture of the individual growing into experience of the world. One loop moves from the bottom up and from inside toward outside. It begins with the biophysical act of reading, engaging with eye and page-turning fingers the black marks on the page. By these acts we set the text against the linguistic codes we have learned and so hypothesize about its meanings. Finally we test the text against the canons of value and belief common in the cultural communities we belong to and make judgments about these meanings or revise our judgments about these canons. But this movement can also be described from the top down and from outside in. In this sense the loop starts with the internalized canons of our culture and time, which we use to organize the linguistic codes of the text, and with these codes make sense out of the black marks on the page (1988, 170–1). The small loops of these individual steps compose the two large loops that interact with one another in a hierarchy of loops that models the ongoing process.

Holland and Lonergan help us see that reading a text, reading the text that is the world, coming to understand how we appropriate our own knowledge of text and world, and appropriating ourselves by our choices are all related activities. They are related by the complexity of the input they make use of – stretching from childhood experience all the way to the canons of the culture; by the dialectical process of testing and feedback involved; and by the unfinished nature of the outcome. Governing this process, controlling but also being shaped by the continuous loops of hypothesis and feedback, is the identity we each have – our personal tastes, values, morality, style, or character, expressed in our choices (Holland 1988, 171). This identity is the product of a lifelong process of development. The "truth" about it, Holland says, is like the "truth" about literature: that it is "a process, a continuing discussion, something open, not closed" (1988, 152). In the interaction between the limbic system of the brain that enables or inhibits actions through emotions and the neocortex with its plans and abstractions arises this identity as well as our picture of the world, both the world of pragmatic consequences and the fictional world we create out of our hopes and fears. "At root, then, literature rests on a pre-verbal habit of constructing worlds, something visceral, emotional, and personal rather than an act of purely linguistic interpretation" (1988, 178).

I think this view of development helps us see what is at stake in our humanity – both the range of possibilities we can imagine for ourselves and yet the gap between what is imaginable and what we can grasp at any moment in our lived experience. The goal of development, one student of Lonergan says, is to appropriate ourselves fully, both as spiritual beings oriented by an unrestricted desire to know and at the same time as embodied spirits operating in and through sensory and imaginable experiences and in and through a cultural framework that centers our world in the mysterious unknown that orients and scales our lives. We appropriate ourselves not only by knowing, but by acting. Therefore, choosing how to live – in the existential tension between what we know and what we are capable of knowing, between the restraints our time-bound and culture-bound experience imposes and what we can imagine our destinies to be – is the challenge that defines us as human beings (Flanagan 1989).

Integration, balance, harmony – these are distant hopes. But we have to make choices and act here and now, conscious of this gap that yawns between what we are and what we want to be. The images we collect and count on to fill in our ignorance and to give us usable models are like ropes we throw across this gap to give us a start toward the other side. The incongruity of being caught thus between glittering possibility and sweaty reality may be pictured solemnly or comically. For as we move toward the inclusive, integrating perspective that sees the world and life whole, we move inevitably toward the point of view of comedy, and as we see ever more keenly the disparity between this vision and our lives as embodiments of it we ourselves become comic figures.

Joseph Epstein has a witty essay about his life as a "serious desultory reader" – rarely going out without a book tucked under his arm, reading at meals and in the bathroom and while watching television, counting some twenty-three books with place markers in them lying around his apartment one day (not including the ones he is reading for professional reasons nor all the magazines and newspapers), finding no pattern in all this behavior except that it represents all his whimsical interests that "exfoliate endlessly, like a magical rose." At the end of the essay he says:

> As one grows older, reading becomes an ever keener pleasure and an ever greater comedy. Part of the pleasure derives intrinsically from the activity itself; and part from its extrinsic rewards, not the least of which is knowing that there will always be plenty to read and so superannuation presents no real fear. (Great readers have this advantage over great lovers.) The comedy of reading is owing in part to one's memory, which in the natural course of things retains less and less of what one reads; and in part to that oldest joke of all, which Dostoyevsky insists comes to each of us afresh. I speak – hushed tones please – of death, which among other erasures rubs out all that one has read over a lifetime. (Epstein 1989, 336)

What, we might ask, is comic about the failure of memory, about death and its erasures? What is the point of desultory reading in the face of this joke?

One way to think about this is to see comedy as the completion of the cycle of generic stories that begins as romance, is transformed into tragedy, and reaches its dark nadir as irony and satire. The comic vision, Frye says, celebrates the power of imagination to raise human experience above the limits of time and space and to transform people and things into the desirable images we have of them (1964, 150–2). Its theme is integration and reconciliation of individuals with one another, but especially of as many characters as possible into a new social order (1957, 165). Comedy is typically about relationships and roles – familial, political, sexual – that get temporarily blocked, but the obstructing and unreasonable characters are transformed and the happy ending celebrates a new society, typically symbolized by a feast, a dance, or a marriage. The most comprehensive comic vision, although it faces and exposes to laughter – sometimes even bitter laughter – the limitations and follies of the world of experience, finally asserts faith in more powerful images of renewal or rebirth. Think of a gentle comedy, like *A Midsummer Night's Dream,* which begins with quarrels between the spirits, mistaken identities among the lovers, and the burlesque of the workmen and their play and ends in a final dance in celebration of love's reconciliations. Or of a harsh one, like *The Winter's Tale,* a story of jealousy and recrimination among the elders and frustrated love among the young, which ends in forgiveness and reunion and even the dead returned to life. "Shakespearean comedy illustrates," says Frye, "as clearly as any mythos we have, the archetypal function of literature in visualizing the world of desire, not as an escape from 'reality,' but as the genuine form of the world that human life tries to imitate" (1957, 184).

The comic vision is so compelling not because it imagines a world transformed into some merely abstract order, but because it imagines what we most desire: to recover the identity we seem to have had once and lost, to recognize ourselves, to be at home in a world entirely possessed and occupied by the human imagination (1964, 80). At the end of his capacious survey of theories of comedy, Holland says that when we laugh we suddenly and playfully recreate our identities and reconfirm who we are (1982, 174). Most of the explanations he discusses – that we laugh because we notice incongruity, or because we are enacting our archetypal victory of life over death, or because we are releasing pent-up psychic energy, or because we are expressing our self-satisfied superiority over others, or because the ego is slyly subverting the control of the superego, or because we are defending ourselves against something we fear, or because laughter is a socially adaptive form of communicating with each other, or because what is comic frees us to accept ourselves or restores our collective social norms or has a revolutionary force or is life affirming or enables us to transcend our impulse both to accept what we are and to reject what we are – begin by acknowledging some kind of incongruity, fracture, and contradiction in our experience and end by proposing our triumph over it, its catharsis. But the victories of comedy are temporary, at least on this side of the great joke Death; they are always trying to hold together in a fragile moment of vision the all but irreconcilable surmises that we have about ourselves. Perhaps that is why, as Holland says, we reconfirm our own identities in our laughter. Not only do we recognize that it is human to be caught between the splendid and the petty, but in the particulars of each comic moment we laugh because we recognize with a flash of discovery our own aspiring and ridiculous selves.

The identity that we recognize in the comic vision, however, is not simply an individual one, but a social one. Comedy is above all a view of a community transformed and redeemed from its limitations. Tragedy and irony, though never entirely divorced from social implications, none-

theless tend to focus on isolated individuals or depend on highly individualized narrative perspectives. Comedy is closer to romance because
in the end both envision ideal societies and focus on the integration of
individuals within the community. Romance does this in naive terms;
comedy through a more complete acknowledgment of the evil to be
transformed into good. Comedy is therefore the context out of which a
genuinely political criticism of literature can take place. Political criticism
is too limited when it takes for its context romance, which is too easily
seen as naive, or tragedy, which seems merely egocentric and privatized,
or irony, which is too evidently a product of alienation. A genuine
political criticism has to be grounded in the comic vision that completes
the cycle of the generic modes of storytelling by enclosing the others
within its horizon.

The comic perspective likewise forces the reader to confront the social
and political implications of reading. So much about the activity of reading, once we learn to do it on our own, reinforces the idea that it is a
private pastime whose benefits are entirely personal. The availability of
mass-market cheap editions, the consumer-oriented organization of book
distribution and selection, the socially acceptable practice of withdrawing
into private communion with a book – all these aspects of reading culture
readily emphasize that reading is primarily a means to personal education
or entertainment. Even the schema of development that this book proposes, which culminates in the pragmatic reader self-consciously choosing what suits best his or her personal needs, can be said to reinforce the
same view of reading. That is why the comic vision so usefully corrects
the imbalance involved in focusing so closely on the individual reader.
Comedy reminds us that reading begins as a social activity, as an initiation
into a community and into a communal vision of human life and of a
world that can be envisioned and reenvisioned by the human imagination,
and that a reader changes and develops through a dialectic of self and
culture. The comic view is a counterweight to our tendency as readers
to be content with sympathetic characters and private voices that we can
identify with our personal conflicts. It confronts us with the demand that
we include, in principle, everyone and everything in the horizon of what
is meaningful and valuable to us. Savater therefore distinguishes between
the unrepeatable time of the novel as a genre, which deals with private
experience and hence underscores finally the fact of death, and the cyclical
time of myth and communal experience that stories deal with, which
emphasizes, in contrast, "the full restitution of what we have possessed,
the restoration, intact, of the strength we have spent in combat lost or
won, the reconstruction of the world, the abolition of all that is irre-
mediable" (1982, 13).

If comedy is nearest to romance in its vision of a complete community, it is the opposite of tragedy insofar as it reverses all the typical motifs of that generic mode (just as, Frye says, irony is a parody of romance). Instead of isolation there is reintegration, wrong choices are absolved, enmities reconciled, destinies rendered benevolent, ideals vindicated. Indeed, the most complete comic visions include both the painful descent and the glorious triumph in one story. The title of Albert Cook's (1966) *The Dark Voyage and the Golden Mean* links both these notions. The journey of the hero toward a confrontation with good and evil that is likely to end with his defeat and death, Cook says, is in the realm of the "wonderful"; its literary form is tragedy. On the other hand, the celebration of the social norm of the reasonable belongs to the realm of the "probable," whose literary form is comedy. The serene, sublime comedies of the greatest writers (Cook has the Homer of the *Odyssey*, Dante, and the late Shakespeare in mind) encompass both tragic discord and comic rebirth in the point of view Cook ingeniously calls "the-wonderful-as-probable" (1966, 174). It is a perspective that comes only with the wisdom of maturity: "Age is concerned with the wonderful because it stands near death, and with the probable because it can look back personally on the course of life. With the prospect of eternity, life in time appears ephemeral and evanescent, like a mirror . . . or a dream" (1966, 177).

In terms of Frye's four generic modes of storytelling, we can consider the comic view from two different points in the full cycle. It may be looked at as the result of moving beyond the radical antinomies of irony. Thus, the painful discrepancy in the world of our experience between what is and what ideally ought to be is obliterated by a vision of a world once again golden. Alternatively, we can think of the comic view as resulting from retracing the path of our reading history from irony back through tragedy and romance to the childhood vision of an imaginary world in which we can safely play – recapitulating in Eriksonian fashion the gains of each stage of our development as readers into comedy's vision of the flawed but redeemable world. Moving in either direction completes the circle that these four generic plots form, because comedy is the link that like play starts the reader into the cycle of symbolic forms through which we experience the world and like an integrating vision brings it to a close.

This is why motifs of childhood imagination are often useful in describing what is positive in the psychic functioning of old age. Ricoeur (1967, 351), for example, thinks that symbols can only be fully apprehended by achieving a "second naiveté" akin to the innocence with which the precritical mind responds to fantasy. From this point of view

Barthes's (1975) final critical stance of playfully seeking out the pleasures provided by his idiosyncratic encounters with the text is less mystifying than his earlier structuralism would make it seem.

From this perspective too the broad significance that Huizinga (1950) attaches to play in *Homo Ludens* becomes intelligible, when it might not have if we had only childhood play to illustrate it. All culture arises in the form of play, he says, and the great archetypal activities through which we attempt to transform and reimagine the outer world – language, myth, and ritual – and the distinctive activities of human society – law, poetry, warfare, art, philosophy – are all permeated with play from the start. What is this play? It is a free activity, not something we have to do. It steps out of ordinary life and creates a pretend world, which exists disinterestedly beyond the satisfaction of wants and appe-'tites, a magical world with its own special space and time. Play with its rules creates order, indeed *is* order; into an imperfect world it brings a temporary, limited perfection, a beauty that we tend to describe in aesthetic terms: tension, balance, variation, resolution, and so forth. Play draws us into community with one another, where we share secrets and special identities, yet is marked off from the common world by disguises and other means. Above all, the function of play, especially in the form of ritual, is to imagine, to make actual, and to re-present an order of things that is more beautiful or more sublime or more sacred than our ordinary experience. In Huizinga's view a thread runs from the earliest pastimes of childhood to the most meaning-laden structures of adult society. It is the "ludic" function of imagination transforming the world we have into the world we hope for that play in all its forms makes present for us, temporarily, fragmentarily, in evanescent but beguiling shapes.

The persuasiveness of this idea of comedy depends perhaps on whether we can trust in the possibility of an integrating vision of existence that is not simply a projection of our needs and our cultural training, or whether we distrust any metaphysics that connects self and world in a human image. These are fundamental choices of ideology between which thoughtful men and women move uneasily. For all that the comic vision resembles the playful fantasies of childhood, we know that we are no longer children. Too many friends have died and we have betrayed too many of our ideals for us ever to believe in an innocent picture that we devise of ourselves. "Happy endings do not impress us as true, but as desirable," Frye says acutely, "and they are brought about by manipulation" (1957, 170). Can we concede the manipulation without losing confidence in the vision?

Italo Calvino (1986), long a student of folk tales, cautiously attempts a formulation. Literature is indeed a game of playing with language, and all the scepticism we have learned from contemporary linguistics pervades our realization of this. Still, literature continually attempts "to say something it cannot say, something it does not know and that no one could ever know." The game of word play suddenly reveals an unexpected meaning, "slipped in from another level," the level of myth, because "myth is the hidden part of every story, the buried part, the region that is still unexplored because there are as yet no words to enable us to get there" (1986, 18). The linguistic game, he says, can dissuade us from understanding the world, but it can also challenge us to further our understanding of it.

Wylie Sypher's (1956) analysis of Kierkegaard makes a similar point about an existentialist faith in the face of the absurd. The struggle of existence is both pathetic and comic in the same degree, Kierkegaard says, but "the more thoroughly and substantially a human being exists, the more he will discover the comical" (1956, 21). The comical exists in the contradictions of life, and the most profound contradiction is the chasm between the finite and the infinite. The highest form of comedy, therefore, is that "the infinite may move within a man, and no one, no one be able to discover it through anything appearing outwardly" (1956, 20). Once again the joke lies in the discrepancy between what we are and what we seem to be.

Yeats liked the phrase tragic joy as a statement about his feelings in old age. Erikson refers to the tragicomedy of aging, because there is no total victory of integrity over despair, only a balance (if we are lucky) in integrity's favor. He calls the point of view that holds the balance in place "faith," the adult version of the first and most basic human strength acquired in childhood, which he calls "hope." Hope is the enduring belief in the attainability of our primal wishes, in spite of the dark urges and rages that mark our existence and threaten us with estrangement. The images that contain this hope may be the ones we have held onto the longest or they may be the prizes of our old age. The possibility of discovering new ones is a motive that keeps us reading.

Notes

Introduction

1 See Jeanne S. Chall, *Stages of Reading Development*; Margaret Meek, *Learning to Read* and *Achieving Literacy: Longitudinal Studies of Adolescents Learning to Read.* Meek, Aidan Warlow, and Griselda Barton have also edited a wide-ranging collection of articles about children's literature, *The Cool Web: The Pattern of Children's Reading.*

2 Nigel Hall provides a good overview of the issues involved in this discussion and of recent research in *The Emergence of Literacy*. The importance of early experiences of literacy for later school success is argued by Gordon Wells in a chapter contributed to *Literacy, Language, and Learning: The Nature and Consequences of Reading and Writing*, ed. David R. Olson, Nancy Torrance, and Angela Hildyard. For a wide-ranging perspective on literacy, see the annotated bibliography by Ron Scollon in the same work.

3 Useful overviews of this topic can be found in Susan R. Suleiman and Inge Crosman, eds., *The Reader in the Text: Essays on Audience and Interpretation;* Jane P. Tompkins, ed., *Reader-Response Criticism: From Formalism to Post-Structuralism;* and Robert C. Holub, *Reception Theory: A Critical Introduction.*

4 See, for instance, the bibliographical overview of Alan C. Purves and Richard Beach, *Literature and the Reader: Research in Response to Literature, Reading Interests, and the Teaching of Literature;* Charles R. Cooper, ed., *Researching Response to Literature and the Teaching of Literature: Points of Departure;* and journals such as *Research in the Teaching of English* and *Reading Research Quarterly.*

5 See, for example, Wayne Booth, *The Rhetoric of Fiction;* Wolfgang Iser, *The Implied Reader: Patterns of Communication in Prose Fiction from Bunyan to Beckett;* and Seymour Chatman, *Story and Discourse.*

6 Among others, Roland Barthes, *S/Z;* Michael Riffaterre, *Semiotics of Poetry;* and Umberto Eco, *The Role of the Reader: Explorations in the Semiotics of Texts.* Jonathan Culler surveys the structuralist analysis of literature in *Structuralist Poetics: Structuralism, Linguistics, and the Study of Literature.*

7 Jonathan Culler again provides a useful overview in *On Deconstruction: Theory and Criticism after Structuralism*, but there are numerous other surveys.

8 Louise Rosenblatt, *The Reader, the Text, and the Poem: The Transactional Theory* *of Poetry;* Wolfgang Iser, *The Act of Reading: A Theory of Aesthetic Response;* Norman N. Holland, *The Brain of Robert Frost: A Cognitive Approach to Literature.* See also Georges Poulet, "The Phenomenology of Reading," and Michael Steig, *Stories of Reading: Subjectivity and Literary Understanding.*

9 For some of the key positions in positive hermeneutics, see Wayne C. Booth, *The Rhetoric of Fiction* and *A Rhetoric of Irony;* E. D. Hirsch, Jr., *Validity in Interpretation* and *The Aims of Interpretation;* Hans Georg Gadamer, *Truth and Method;* Paul Ricoeur, *The Conflict of Interpretations: Essays in Hermeneutics.* For the negative approach, see especially Jacques Derrida, *Of Grammatology* and Jonathan Culler's survey of deconstructionist theory, *On Deconstruction: Theory and Criticism after Structuralism.*

10 Norman Holland, *The Dynamics of Literary Response, Five Readers Reading,* and *Poems in Persons: An Introduction to the Psychoanalysis of Literature.* Cf. also David Bleich, *Subjective Criticism.*

11 For historical approaches, see R. D. Altick, *The English Common Reader: A Social History of the Mass Reading Public, 1800–1900;* Hans Robert Jauss, *Toward an Aesthetic of Reception;* Ian Watt, *The Rise of the Novel: Studies in Defoe, Richardson, and Fielding.* Theoretical studies of social influences on reading include Lucien Goldmann, *Towards a Sociology of the Novel* and Jacques Leenhardt, "Toward a Sociology of Reading," in Suleiman and Crosman, eds., *The Reader in the Text.* Other pertinent titles are mentioned in the discussion of gender, class, and politics later in this introduction.

12 For example, Stanley Fish, *Is There a Text in This Class? The Authority of Interpretive Communities;* Jonathan Culler, *Structuralist Poetics;* and Stephen J. Mailloux, *Interpretive Conventions: The Reader in the Study of American Fiction.*

13 D. W. Harding offered an early developmental sketch of reading responses in his 1966 Dartmouth Seminar paper, "Response to Reading." Anthony Petrosky has explored some issues that would be involved in a comprehensive study of readers' responses, and he sketched out plans for an investigation of adolescent responses from a stage-developmental point of view (Petrosky 1977, 1985), but so far as I know the studies have not been finished.

14 For example, Nicholas Tucker, *The Child and the Book: A Psychological and Literary Exploration,* and F. Andre Favat's study of the appeal of fairy tales for young children, entitled *Child and Tale: The Origins of Interest,* which combines insights from Freud, Piaget, Propp, and others.

15 Bibliographic references to Piaget and other theorists whose views are discussed in the subsequent chapters occur at the relevant places in the text.

16 For reviews of the discussion, see C. J. Brainerd, "The Stage Question in Cognitive-Development Theory"; R. Gelman and R. Baillargeon, "A Review of Some Piagetian Concepts"; and Susan Sugarman, *Piaget's Construction of the Child's Reality.*

17 For example, Marilyn Cochran-Smith, *The Making of a Reader;* Shirley Brice Heath, *Ways with Words: Language, Life, and Work in Communities and Classrooms;* Lillian S. Robinson, *Sex, Class, and Culture;* Scollon and Scollon, *Narrative, Literacy, and Face in Interethnic Communication;* and Denny Taylor and Catherine Dorsey-Gaines, *Growing up Literate: Learning from Inner-City Families.*

18 See Jean Baker Miller, *Toward a New Psychology of Women;* Nancy Chodorow, *The Reproduction of Mothering: Psychoanalysis and the Sociology of Gender;* Robert May, *Sex and Fantasy: Patterns of Male and Female Development;* and Carol Gilligan, *In a Different Voice: Psychological Theory and Women's Development.*

19 See especially the review of the discussion in Elizabeth A. Flynn and Patrocinio P. Schweickart, *Gender and Reading: Essays on Readers, Texts, and Contexts.*

20 See for example Bob Dixon, *Catching Them Young,* Volume 1: *Sex, Race, and Class in Children's Fiction,* and Volume 2: *Political Ideas in Children's Fiction;* Ariel Dorfman, *The Empire's Old Clothes: What the Lone Ranger, Babar, and Other Innocent Heroes Do to Our Minds;* Martin Green, *Dreams of Adventure, Deeds of Empire* and *The Great American Adventure;* Fred Inglis, *The Promise of Happiness: Value and Meaning in Children's Fiction;* and Fredric Jameson, *The Political Unconscious: Narrative as a Socially Symbolic Act.*

21 Lennard J. Davis, *Resisting Novels: Ideology and Fiction.* Davis also offers a useful history of the development of the concept of ideology in literary analysis.

22 Peter J. Rabinowitz, *Before Reading: Narrative Conventions and the Politics of Interpretation.*

23 Northrop Frye, *Anatomy of Criticism: Four Essays.*

Chapter 1

1 Margaret Meek describes the process of becoming literate before schooling begins in the first two chapters of *Learning to Read,* as does Nigel Hall in Chapters 2 and 3 of *The Emergence of Literacy.* A delightful account of what this development feels like from the child's point of view can be found in Leila Berg, *Reading and Loving* (1977, 18–50).

2 Wells (1985) argues that the kind of reflective, disembedded thinking that is crucial for later school success is developed not just by general preschool literacy activities, but precisely by listening to stories and by the child's interaction with a competent adult reader (a parent and later teachers) in the whole story-hearing situation.

3 Shirley Heath describes alternative routes to literacy and some of their consequences, as do Denny Taylor and Catherine Dorsey-Gaines. Their findings are discussed later in this chapter. Berg (1977, 51–76) gives a vivid picture of the development of children who are not encouraged to read.

4 The accounts of Carol and Rachel and Anna just ahead in this chapter bear out this conclusion, but for a really vivid demonstration of how books and the help of loving parents enabled one child to enter a world she might not otherwise have known, see Dorothy Butler, *Cushla and Her Books.* Cushla was born in New Zealand in 1971 with severe physical deficiencies, which doctors readily interpreted as implying mental retardation. Through the unremitting attention of her parents, and especially through her books, she became by age six, in spite of physical handicaps, a happy child of above-average intelligence and a fluent reader in an ordinary school with children of her own age.

5 First-person accounts of childhood reading experiences, such as writers often give in their memoirs, might seem to be a plausible source of information, but I have avoided using them because they seemed likely to reflect the attitudes of a specialized group of readers and to be filtered through the lens of memory and colored by mature attitudes toward writing and reading. G. Robert Carlsen and Anne Sherrill have recently assembled and analyzed a fascinating collection of "reading autobiographies" that Carlsen collected over a thirty-year period of teaching English teachers and librarians in *Voices of Readers: How We Come to Love Books*. I have not drawn on these accounts, but they could illustrate my hypotheses as well as any stories I have used, perhaps because these students are describing experiences that are still very vivid in their memories.

6 Piaget's work is most accessible in a short book he wrote with Barbel Inhelder, *The Psychology of the Child*, or through the work of his commentators, especially John H. Flavell, *The Developmental Psychology of Jean Piaget*, or John L. Phillips, Jr., *The Origins of Intellect: Piaget's Theory*.

7 Anyone who doubts the general assertion that nursery schools and kindergartens effectively teach culture-specific values to children should read Joseph J. Tobin, David Y. H. Wu, and Dana H. Davidson, *Preschool in Three Cultures: Japan, China and the United States*.

8 Not all children's home lives have prepared them for this. As we have seen, in the Athabascan Indian community in Canada where Rachel Scollon lived for part of her childhood, reading was associated with church and school, but not with the home (Scollon and Scollon 1981). In a mill town in the Carolina Piedmonts, Shirley Brice Heath studied two working-class communities, one black and one white. Both were in their own ways literate communities where reading and writing functioned significantly in the daily lives of the people. But where families did not read to children, ask them the names of things in picture books, use printed stories to help them make sense of their environment, encourage them to write, and so forth, children had difficulty in school and as adult readers they did not advance beyond magazines and newspapers, the Bible, and the literacy requirements of their work and social lives (Heath 1983, especially 230–5, 348–54). Heath's study suggests the conclusion that kinds and levels of literacy can be correlated with the social structure of the community, its history and traditions, the quality of its schools, and the economic opportunities of its people. Denny Taylor and Catherine Dorsey-Gaines make a contrasting claim in their study of literacy among black families in Newark (1988). Their striking conclusion that "sex, race, economic status, and setting cannot be used as significant correlates of literacy" (1988, 201–2) is borne out by the vivid stories they tell of the varied functions reading and writing play in the lives of the people they studied. But these are stories of accomplishment in the face of enormous difficulties, and the few accounts that even begin to resemble the book-oriented family lives of the children in the nursery school where Cochran-Smith did her research do little to discredit the notion that economic and social disadvantages play a largely negative role in the development of readers.

9 The bedtime story and the nursery school are not the only models of how young children encounter reading. For some children, *television* may be the primary medium for encountering the fictional world. Does television watching by very young children result in a different response to stories than reading provides? In spite of large and intuitively appealing claims for the distinctive "medium effects" of television (such as those of Marshall McLuhan in *Understanding Media*), the evidence so far is inconclusive, perhaps because these studies are still in their infancy.

Clearly, television and illustrated children's books overlap enormously in the way they present stories. Studies of how primary school children perceive plot complexity, understand causal relationships between events, and make inferences about characters' motives in television programs suggest that these abilities undergo an age-related development (Collins 1983) comparable to the kind readers go through. There is some evidence, however, that the heavily visual emphasis of television and the formal characteristics of its way of telling stories (camera techniques, cartoon styles, etc.) lead children to process story content in distinctive ways (Meringoff et al. 1983). The even more radical argument has been made, though tentatively, that television watching changes the cognitive performance of very young children, leading them to expect that other sources of information will be organized, like much children's television, in brief units that emphasize surface detail (Salomon 1983).

The most frequent charge against television, however, is that it induces a passive stance in the young viewer. The "plug-in drug," according to one popular analysis, produces a trancelike stupor of absorption in front of the TV screen that is the opposite of the mentally active processing that reading requires (Winn 1985). There is some scholarly support for this position in the work of Jerome and Dorothy Singer, who suggest that the "busyness" of commercial television in the United States (on whose formal characteristics the short unrelated units of *Sesame Street* were consciously modeled) minimizes self-awareness and reflective thought in young viewers, and that without adult mediation preschoolers are apt to be passive attenders rather than active learners as a result of watching TV (Singer and Singer 1983). However, the argument has also been made that television watching is a much more active than reactive processing of information and that there is little hard evidence for the intuitively popular notion that reading is a more cognitively demanding activity than viewing television (Anderson and Lorch 1983).

Doubtless this debate is going to go on for some time. One apparently common-sense conclusion about the effect of watching television on reading habits involves the "displacement" phenomenon; children who watch a lot of TV have little time for reading or being read to, and therefore less chance to practice and develop as readers (Zuckerman, Singer, and Singer 1980). And children do seem to spend a lot of time in front of the television. According to a 1983 Nielsen Report, children watch TV an average of twenty-five or thirty hours a week. In 1984, according to the National Assessment of Educational Progress report, 27 percent of nine-year-olds said they watched six hours of TV a day (Applebee, Langer, and Mullis 1985). But the significance of this phenomenon may be less obvious than it seems. One study of sixth-to-ninth graders surprisingly shows that heavy TV viewing correlates positively with heavy reading (Morgan 1980). However, the low-IQ students in this study watched the most television and these heavy viewers also had lower scores in reading comprehension. When we note further that the kind of reading favored by the heavy readers mirrors the common television fare (stories about love, teenagers, and TV and movie stars), then it seems that developmental level may really be the central issue here, and not simply the correlation between time spent watching television and reading. Another study suggests that although television viewing actively engages the child's cognitive and emotional responses, older children often watch television "automatically," with little investment of mental effort and little questioning of the expectations they bring to it (Salomon 1983). In this situation, television viewing in fact may be the passive and time-wasting activity its critics allege it is.

Light viewing of television (15 hours a week), however, did no harm to the reading ability of children in grades three to five in one school with a well-developed reading program; in fact, it seemed to be positively related to their enthusiasm for class and their capacity for imaginative play (Zuckerman, Singer, and Singer 1980). The 1984 NAEP report came to a similar conclusion. Because students who watch TV up to two hours a day have reading proficiency scores above average for their age group, it is unlikely that TV viewing in and of itself lowers reading proficiency. It may divert children's attention from reading and school work, but only when viewing is excessive (Applebee, Langer, and Mullis 1985). This would seem to underscore the soundness of assuming that television can reinforce as well as undercut a child's education in the strategies and conventions of story reading. One British study of preschoolers argues that TV can be either a child minder or a positive aid to development. It *can* widen knowledge of the natural and human world, encourage singing and movement to music, instruct about the family, teach stories, poems, and rhymes, stimulate fantasy and imaginative play, and suggest activities that develop basic skills and help the child to come to terms with the world. But preschoolers' use of TV reflects parents' attitudes; if they think of television, in Alistair Cooke's vivid phrase, as "audible wallpaper," their children will not look, listen, and learn from it either (Dunn 1977). Like reading, television at this age depends on the catalyst of adults' participation if it is to be productive developmentally.

10   Erikson's picture of development can be found in any of his major works, such as *Childhood and Society, Identity: Youth and Crisis,* and *The Life Cycle Completed: A Review.*

11   For helpful overviews of research on play, see Singer, *The Child's World of Make-Believe;* Bruner, Jolly, and Sylva, *Play: Its Role in Development and Evolution;* Millar, *The Psychology of Play;* Sutton-Smith, *Play and Learning;* Rubin, "Fantasy Play"; and Bretherton, *Symbolic Play.*

Chapter 2

1   All the characters named here (and more than sixty others) were the invention of the remarkable Edward Stratemeyer (1862 to 1930), who developed the idea of syndicating juvenile adventure stories and who created the largest and most successful of these publishing operations, responsible for over 1,300 books, with estimated sales of more than 200 million copies from 1898 to the present. See Carol Billman, *The Secret of the Stratemeyer Syndicate: Nancy Drew, The Hardy Boys, and the Million Dollar Fiction Factory,* and Peter A. Soderbergh, "The Stratemeyer Strain: Educators and the Juvenile Series Book, 1900–1980."

2   Eighty million Nancy Drew books have been sold since they were introduced

in 1930, 2½ million paperback copies from 1981 to 1984 alone, according to figures supplied by the Stratemeyer Syndicate (Billman 1986, 100). On average, one million Hardy Boys books are sold per year (Soderbergh 1980, 73).

Chapter 3

1   See, for example, the comprehensive review in Purves and Beach (1972), Petrosky's analysis of the 1979–1980 NAEP survey (in Petrosky 1982), Shores (1964), and the lengthy British study by Whitehead and coauthors (1977).
2   For case studies of individual adolescent readers that confirm this general picture, see Cramer (1984), Culp (1977), and Petrosky (1976).
3   Compare the successive patterns of identification between reader and hero suggested in Jauss (1982, 159).
4   A wise and useful guidebook for high school teachers of literature, one which suggests ways of integrating students' personal responses to texts with their thinking about both the meaning of these texts and how literature works, is Denise Palmer Wolf's *Reading Reconsidered: Literature and Literacy in High School*.

Chapter 5

1   Lonergan's two principal works are *Insight: A Study of Human Understanding* (1957) and *Method in Theology* (1972). The basis for this notion of a double development is implicit in *Method in Theology* (see Chapter 4, especially 115–18), but was worked out only in later essays, particularly in the ones reprinted as Chapters 6, 12, and 13 of *A Third Collection: Papers by Bernard Lonergan, S.J.* I have drawn especially from *Old Things and New: A Strategy for Education*, by Frederick E. Crowe, S.J., a study of Lonergan's views on development and education.

Bibliography

Abrams, M. H. *The Mirror and the Lamp: Romantic Theory and the Critical Tradition*. New York: Oxford University Press, 1953.

Althusser, Louis. *For Marx*. London: New Left Books, 1977.

Lenin and Philosophy. New York: Monthly Review Press, 1971.

Altick, R. D. *The English Common Reader: A Social History of the Mass Reading Public, 1800–1900*. Chicago: University of Chicago Press, 1957.

Altieri, Charles. "Plato's Performative Sublime and the Ends of Reading." *New Literary History* 16, 2 (1985): 251–73.

Ames, Louise Bates. "Children's Stories." *Genetic Psychology Monographs* 73 (1966): 337–96.

Anderson, Daniel R., and Elizabeth Pugzles Lorch. "Looking at Television: Action or Reaction?" In *Children's Understanding of Television: Research on Attention and Comprehension*, edited by Jennings Bryant and Daniel R. Anderson. New York: Academic Press, 1983.

Applebee, Arthur N. *The Child's Concept of Story: Ages Two to Seventeen*. Chicago: University of Chicago Press, 1978.

Judith Langer, and Ina V. Mullis. *The Reading Report Card: Progress toward Excellence in Our Schools. Trends in Reading over Four National Assessments, 1971–1984*. Princeton, N.J.: Educational Testing Service, 1985.

Arlin, P. K. "Cognitive Development in Adulthood: A Fifth Stage?" *Developmental Psychology* 11 (1975): 602–6.

Barthes, Roland. *The Pleasure of the Text*. Translated by Richard Miller. New York: Hill & Wang, 1975a.

S/Z. Translated by Richard Miller. New York: Hill & Wang, 1975b.

Basseches, Michael. "Dialectical Schemata: A Framework for the Empirical Study of the Development of Dialectical Thinking." *Human Development* 23 (1980): 400–21.

Baym, Nina. "Melodramas of Beset Manhood: How Theories of American Fiction Exclude Women Authors." In *The New Feminist Criticism: Essays on Women, Literature, and Theory*, edited by Elaine Showalter. New York: Pantheon, 1985.

Belsey, Catherine. *Critical Practice*. London and New York: Methuen, 1980.

Berg, Leila, *Reading and Loving*. London: Routledge & Kegan Paul, 1977.

Best, Raphael A. *We've All Got Scars: What Boys and Girls Learn in Elementary School*. Bloomington: Indiana University Press, 1983.

Bettelheim, Bruno. *The Uses of Enchantment: The Meaning and Importance of Fairy Tales*. New York: Knopf, 1976.

Billman, Carol. *The Secret of the Stratemeyer Syndicate: Nancy Drew, the Hardy Boys, and the Million Dollar Fiction Factory*. New York: Ungar, 1986.

Bissex, Glenda L. *Gnys at Wrk: A Child Learns to Write and Read*. Cambridge, Mass.: Harvard University Press, 1980.

Blasi, Augusto, and Emily C. Hoeffel. "Adolescence and Formal Operations." *Human Development* 17 (1974): 344–63.

Bleich, David. "Gender Interests in Reading and Language." In *Gender and Reading: Essays on Readers, Texts, and Contexts*, edited by Elizabeth A. Flynn and Patrocinio P. Schweickart. Baltimore: Johns Hopkins University Press, 1986.

Subjective Criticism. Baltimore: Johns Hopkins University Press, 1978.

Bogan, Louise. *What the Woman Lived: Selected Letters of Louise Bogan, 1920–1970*, edited by Ruth Limmer. New York: Harcourt Brace Jovanovich, 1973.

Book Industry Study Group. *1983 Consumer Research Study on Reading and Book Publishing*. New York: Book Industry Study Group, 1984.

Booth, Wayne C. *The Company We Keep: An Ethics of Fiction*. Berkeley: University of California Press, 1988.

The Rhetoric of Fiction. Chicago: University of Chicago Press, 1961.

A Rhetoric of Irony. Chicago: University of Chicago Press, 1974.

Botvin, Gilbert J., and Brian Sutton-Smith. "The Development of Structural Complexity in Children's Fantasy Narratives." *Developmental Psychology* 13, 4 (1977): 377–88.

Brainerd, C. J. "The Stage Question in Cognitive-Development Theory." *Behavioral and Brain Sciences* 2 (1978): 173–213.

Bretherton, Inge, editor. *Symbolic Play: The Development of Social Understanding*. New York: Academic Press, 1984.

Britton, James N. *Language and Learning*. London: Allen Lane-Penguin, 1970.

"Response to Literature." In *The Cool Web: The Pattern of Children's Reading*, edited by Margaret Meek. New York: Atheneum, 1978.

"The Role of Fantasy." *English in Education* 5 (1971): 39–44.

"Viewpoints: The Distinction between Participant and Spectator Role Language in Research and Practice." *Research in the Teaching of English* 18, 3 (1984): 320–31.

Brooks, Cleanth, and Robert Penn Warren. *Understanding Poetry: An Anthology for College Students*. New York: Holt, 1938.

Brooks, Peter. *The Melodramatic Imagination: Balzac, Henry James, Melodrama, and the Mode of Excess*. New Haven, Conn.: Yale University Press, 1976.

Broughton, John M. "Development of Concepts of Self, Mind, Reality, and Knowledge." In *Social Cognition*, edited by William Damon. New Directions for Child Development, 1. San Francisco: Jossey-Bass, 1978.

"The Divided Self in Adolescence." *Human Development* 24, 1 (1981): 13–32.

"Not beyond Formal Operations but beyond Piaget." In *Beyond Formal Operations,* edited by Michael L. Commons. New York: Praeger, 1984.

Bruner, Jerome. *Actual Minds, Possible Worlds.* Cambridge, Mass.: Harvard University Press, 1986a.

"Value Presuppositions of Developmental Theory." In *Value Presuppositions in Theories of Human Development,* edited by Leonard Cirillo and Seymour Wapner. Hillsdale, N.J.: Erlbaum, 1986b.

A. Jolly, and K. Sylva, editors. *Play: Its Role in Development and Evolution.* New York: Basic Books, 1976.

Butler, Dorothy. *Cushla and Her Books.* Boston: Horn Book Press, 1980.

Butler, Robert N. "The Life Review: An Interpretation of Reminiscence in the Aged." *Psychiatry* 26 (1963): 65–76.

Buxbaum, Edith. "The Role of Detective Stories in a Child Analysis." *Psychoanalytic Quarterly* 10 (1941): 373–81.

Calvino, Italo. *The Uses of Literature.* New York: Harcourt Brace Jovanovich, 1986.

Campbell, Joseph. *The Hero with a Thousand Faces.* Princeton, N.J.: Princeton University Press, 1968.

Carlsen, G. Robert, and Anne Sherrill. *Voices of Readers: How We Come to Love Books.* Urbana, Ill.: National Council of Teachers of English, 1988.

Cawelti, John G. *Adventure, Mystery, and Romance: Formula Stories as Art and Popular Culture.* Chicago: University of Chicago Press, 1976.

Chall, Jeanne S. *Stages of Reading Development.* New York: McGraw-Hill, 1983.

Chandler, Michael J. "Relativism and the Problem of Epistemological Loneliness." *Human Development* 18 (1975): 171–80.

Chatman, Seymour. *Story and Discourse: Narrative Structure in Fiction and Film.* Ithaca, N.Y.: Cornell University Press, 1978.

Chodorow, Nancy. *The Reproduction of Mothering: Psychoanalysis and the Sociology of Gender.* Berkeley: University of California Press, 1978.

Chukovsky, K. *From Two to Five.* Berkeley: University of California Press, 1968.

Clay, Marie M. *Reading: The Patterning of Complex Behavior.* London: Heinemann, 1972.

Cochran-Smith, Marilyn. *The Making of a Reader.* Norwood, N.J.: Ablex, 1984.

Coles, Robert. *The Call of Stories: Teaching and the Moral Imagination.* Boston: Houghton Mifflin, 1989.

Collins, W. Andrew. "Interpretation and Inference in Children's Television Viewing." In *Children's Understanding of Television: Research on Attention and Comprehension,* edited by Jennings Bryant and Daniel R. Anderson. New York: Academic Press, 1983.

Cook, Albert. *The Dark Voyage and the Golden Mean: A Philosophy of Comedy.* New York: Norton, 1966.

Cooper, Charles R., editor. *Researching Response to Literature and the Teaching of Literature: Points of Departure.* Norwood, N.J.: Ablex, 1985.

Crago, Maureen, and Hugh Crago. *Prelude to Literacy.* Carbondale: Southern Illinois University Press, 1983.

Cramer, Barbara B. "Bequest of Wings: Three Readers and Special Books." *Language Arts* 61, 3 (1984): 253–60.

Crawford, Mary, and Roger Chaffin. "The Reader's Construction of Meaning: Cognitive Research on Gender and Comprehension." In *Gender and Reading: Essays on Readers, Texts, and Contexts,* edited by Elizabeth A. Flynn and Patrocinio P. Schweickart. Baltimore: Johns Hopkins University Press, 1986.

Crowe, Frederick E., S.J. *Old Things and New: A Strategy for Education.* Atlanta, Ga.: Scholars Press, 1985.

Culler, Jonathan. *On Deconstruction: Theory and Criticism after Structuralism.* Ithaca, N.Y.: Cornell University Press, 1982.

  Structuralist Poetics: Structuralism, Linguistics, and the Study of Literature. Ithaca, N.Y.: Cornell University Press, 1975.

Culp, Mary Beth. "Case Studies of the Influence of Literature on the Attitudes, Values, and Behavior of Adolescents." *Research in the Teaching of English* 11, 3 (1977): 245–53.

Cytrynbaum, Solomon. "Midlife Development: A Personality and Social Systems Perspective." In *Aging in the 1980's: Psychological Issues,* edited by Leonard W. Poon. Washington: American Psychological Association, 1980.

Davis, Lennard J. *Resisting Novels: Ideology and Fiction.* New York: Methuen, 1987.

Derrida, Jacques. *Of Grammatology.* Translated by G. C. Spivak. Baltimore: Johns Hopkins University Press, 1976.

Dickinson, Peter. "A Defense of Rubbish." In *Children and Literature: Views and Reviews,* edited by Virginia Haviland. Glenview, Ill.: Scott, Foresman, 1973.

Dixon, Bob. *Catching Them Young.* Volume 1: *Sex, Race and Class in Children's Fiction.* Volume 2: *Political Ideas in Children's Fiction.* London: Pluto Press, 1977.

Donaldson, Margaret. *Children's Minds.* New York: Norton, 1978.

Dorfman, Ariel. *The Empire's Old Clothes: What the Lone Ranger, Babar, and Other Innocent Heroes Do to Our Minds.* New York: Pantheon, 1983.

Dunn, Gwen. *The Box in the Corner: Television and the Under-Fives.* London: Macmillan, 1977.

Eagleton, Terry. *Literary Theory: An Introduction.* Minneapolis: University of Minnesota Press, 1983.

  Marxism and Literary Criticism. Berkeley: University of California Press, 1976.

Eco, Umberto. *The Role of the Reader: Explorations in the Semiotics of Texts.* Bloomington: Indiana University Press, 1979.

Eliot, T. S. *The Use of Poetry and the Use of Criticism: Studies in the Relationship of Criticism to Poetry in England.* Cambridge Mass.: Harvard University Press, 1933.

Elkind, David. *Children and Adolescents: Interpretive Essays on Jean Piaget.* 3rd ed. New York: Oxford University Press, 1981a.

  The Hurried Child: Growing up Too Fast Too Soon. Reading, Mass.: Addison-Wesley, 1981b.

Ennis, Philip. *Adult Book Reading in the U.S.: A Preliminary Report.* Chicago: National Opinion Research Council, 1965.

Epstein, Joseph [Aristides, pseud.] "Waiter, There's a Paragraph in My Soup!"
  American Scholar 58, 3 (Summer 1989): 327–36.
Erikson, Erik H. *Adulthood.* New York: Norton, 1978.
  Childhood and Society. 2nd ed. New York: Norton, 1963.
  Identity: Youth and Crisis. New York: Norton, 1968.
  The Life Cycle Completed: A Review. New York: Norton, 1982.
  Toys and Reasons: Stages in the Ritualization of Experience. New York: Norton,
  1977.
Favat, F. Andre. *Child and Tale: The Origins of Interest.* NCTE Research Report,
  19. Urbana, Ill.: National Council of Teachers of English, 1977.
Fein, Greta. "Play and the Acquisition of Symbols." In *Current Topics in Early
  Childhood Education,* edited by Lilian G. Katz. New York: Ablex, 1979.
Fetterley, Judith. "Reading about Reading: 'A Jury of Her Peers,' 'The Murders
  in the Rue Morgue,' and 'The Yellow Wallpaper.'" In *Gender and
  Reading: Essays on Readers, Texts, and Contexts,* edited by Elizabeth A.
  Flynn and Patrocinio P. Schweickart. Baltimore: Johns Hopkins Uni-
  versity Press, 1986.
  The Resisting Reader: A Feminist Approach to American Fiction. Bloomington:
  Indiana University Press, 1978.
Fish, Stanley. *Is There a Text in This Class?: The Authority of Interpretive Com-
  munities.* Cambridge, Mass.: Harvard University Press, 1980.
Flanagan, Joseph S.J. "Origin and Destiny of Disembodied and Embodied Spir-
  its." Lonergan Workshop, Boston College, June 1989. Unpublished
  essay.
Flavell, John H. *The Developmental Psychology of Jean Piaget.* Princeton, N.J.:
  Van Nostrand, 1963.
Flynn, Elizabeth A. "Gender and Reading." In *Gender and Reading: Essays on
  Readers, Texts, and Contexts,* edited by Elizabeth A. Flynn and Patrocinio
  P. Schweickart. Baltimore: Johns Hopkins University Press, 1986.
  and Patrocinio P. Schweickart, editors. *Gender and Reading: Essays on Readers,
  Texts, and Contexts.* Baltimore: Johns Hopkins University Press, 1986.
Forster, E. M. *Aspects of the Novel.* New York: Harcourt Brace, 1927.
Fowler, James W. *Becoming Adult, Becoming Christian.* San Francisco: Harper &
  Row, 1984.
  Stages of Faith: The Psychology of Human Development and the Quest for Meaning.
  San Francisco: Harper & Row, 1981.
Freud, Sigmund. "The Creative Writer and Day-Dreaming." In *The Standard
  Edition of the Complete Psychological Works of Sigmund Freud, 9.* Translated
  by James Strachey. London: Hogarth Press, 1955.
  "Five Lectures on Psycho-Analysis." In *The Standard Edition of the Complete
  Psychological Works of Sigmund Freud, 11.* Translated by James Strachey.
  London: Hogarth, 1953a.
  "The Interpretation of Dreams." In *The Standard Edition of the Complete Psy-
  chological Works of Sigmund Freud, 4 and 5.* Translated by James Strachey.
  London: Hogarth Press, 1953b.
  "Introductory Lectures on Psycho-Analysis." In *The Standard Edition of the*

Complete Psychological Works of Sigmund Freud, 15 and 16. Translated by James Strachey. London: Hogarth Press, 1953c.

Frye, Northrop. *Anatomy of Criticism: Four Essays.* Princeton, N.J.: Princeton University Press, 1957.

The Educated Imagination. Bloomington: Indiana University Press, 1964.

Gadamer, Hans Georg. *Truth and Method.* New York: Seabury, 1975.

Gardner, Howard. "Brief on Behalf of Fairy Tales." *Semiotica* 21 (1977): 363–80.

M. Kircher, E. Winner, and D. Perkins. "Children's Metaphoric Productions and Preferences." *Journal of Child Language* 2 (1975): 125–41.

Ellen Winner, Robin Bechhofer, and Dennie Wolf. "The Development of Figurative Language." In *Children's Language,* edited by Keith E. Nelson. New York: Gardner, 1978.

Gelman, R., and R. Baillargeon. "A Review of Some Piagetian Concepts." In *Handbook of Child Psychology,* edited by J. H. Flavell and E. M. Markman. 4th ed. New York: Wiley, 1983.

Genette, Gerard. *Narrative Discourse: An Essay in Method.* Ithaca, N.Y.: Cornell University Press, 1980.

Gilligan, Carol. *In a Different Voice: Psychological Theory and Women's Development.* Cambridge, Mass.: Harvard University Press, 1982.

and John Michael Murphy. "Development from Adolescence to Adulthood: The Philosopher and the Dilemma of the Fact." In *Intellectual Development Beyond Childhood,* edited by Deanna Kuhn. New Directions for Child Development, 5. San Francisco: Jossey-Bass, 1979.

Girard, Rene. *Deceit, Desire, and the Novel: Self and Other in Literary Structure.* Translated by Yvonne Freccero. Baltimore: Johns Hopkins University Press, 1965.

Goldmann, Lucien. *Towards a Sociology of the Novel.* Translated by Alan Sheridan. London: Tavistock, 1975.

Goodman, Kenneth S. *Language and Literacy: The Selected Writings of Kenneth S. Goodman,* edited by Frederick V. Gollasch. London: Routledge & Kegan Paul, 1982.

Gould, Roger L. *Transformations: Growth and Change in Adult Life.* New York: Simon and Schuster, 1978.

Green, Martin. *Dreams of Adventure, Deeds of Empire.* New York: Basic Books, 1979.

The Great American Adventure. Boston: Beacon Press, 1984.

Hall, Nigel. *The Emergence of Literacy.* Portsmouth, N.H.: Heinemann, 1987.

Harding, D. W. "The Bond with the Author." In *The Cool Web: The Pattern of Children's Reading,* edited by Margaret Meek. New York: Atheneum, 1978.

"Psychological Processes in the Reading of Fiction." In *Aesthetics in the Modern World,* edited by Harold Osborne. London: Thames & Hudson, 1968a.

"Response to Literature: Dartmouth Seminar Report." In *Response to Literature,* edited by J. Squire. Champaign, Ill.: National Council of Teachers of English, 1968b.

Hawkins-Wendelin, Karla. "A Summary of Lewis Terman and Margaret Lima's Study: Children's Reading." In *Reading Research Revisited,* edited by Lance M. Gentile, Michael L. Kamil, and Jay S. Blanchard. Columbus, Oh.: Merrill, 1983.

Heath, Shirley Brice. *Ways with Words: Language, Life, and Work in Communities and Classroom.* Cambridge University Press, 1983.

Hepler, Susan I., and Janet Hickman. "'The Book Was Okay. I Love You' – Social Aspects of Response to Literature." *Theory into Practice* 21 (1982): 278–83.

Hickman, Janet. "A New Perspective on Response to Literature: Research in an Elementary School Setting." *Research in the Teaching of English* 15, 4 (1981): 343–54.

"Research Currents: Researching Children's Response to Literature." *Language Arts* 61, 3 (March 1984): 278–84.

Hilgard, J. R. *Personality and Hypnosis: A Study of Imaginative Involvement.* Chicago: University of Chicago Press, 1979.

Hirsch, E. D., Jr. *The Aims of Interpretation.* Chicago: University of Chicago Press, 1976.

Validity in Interpretation. New Haven, Conn.: Yale University Press, 1967.

Holland, Norman N. *The Brain of Robert Frost: A Cognitive Approach to Literature.* New York: Routledge, 1988.

The Dynamics of Literary Response. New York: Oxford University Press, 1968.

Five Readers Reading. New Haven, Conn.: Yale University Press, 1975.

Laughing: A Psychology of Humor. Ithaca, N.Y.: Cornell University Press, 1982.

Poems in Persons: An Introduction to the Psychoanalysis of Literature. New York: Norton, 1973.

"Reading Readers Reading." In *Researching Response to Literature and the Teaching of Literature: Points of Departure,* edited by Charles R. Cooper. Norwood, N.J.: Ablex, 1985.

Holub, Robert C. *Reception Theory: A Critical Introduction.* London: Methuen, 1984.

Huizinga, J. *Homo Ludens: A Study of the Play-Element in Culture.* New York: Roy, 1950.

Inglis, Fred. *The Promise of Happiness: Value and Meaning in Children's Fiction.* Cambridge University Press, 1981.

Inhelder, Barbel, and Jean Piaget. *The Growth of Logical Thinking from Childhood to Adolescence.* New York: Basic, 1958.

Iser, Wolfgang. *The Act of Reading: A Theory of Aesthetic Response.* Baltimore: Johns Hopkins University Press, 1978.

The Implied Reader: Patterns of Communication in Prose Fiction from Bunyan to Beckett. Baltimore: Johns Hopkins University Press, 1974.

Jackson, Donald Dale. "World's Fastest Literary Gun: Louis L'Amour." *Smithsonian* 18, 2 (May 1987): 154–70.

James, Henry. "The Art of Fiction." In *The Art of Criticism: Henry James on the Theory and Practice of Criticism,* edited by William Veeder and Susan M. Griffin. Chicago: University of Chicago Press, 1986.

Jameson, Fredric. *The Political Unconscious: Narrative as a Socially Symbolic Act.* Ithaca, N.Y.: Cornell University Press, 1981.

"Reification and Utopia in Mass Culture." *Social Text* 1 (1979): 130–48.

Jauss, Hans Robert. *Aesthetic Experience and Literary Hermeneutics.* Translated by Michael Shaw. Theory and History of Literature, 3. Minneapolis: University of Minnesota Press, 1982a.

Toward an Aesthetic of Reception. Translated by Timothy Bahti. Theory and History of Literature, 2. Minneapolis: University of Minnesota Press, 1982b.

Johnson, Dale M., Gary G. Peer, and R. Scott Baldwin. "Protagonist Preferences among Juvenile and Adolescent Readers." *Journal of Educational Research* 77 (1984): 147–50.

Jung, C. G. "On the Relation of Analytical Psychology to Poetry." In *The Spirit in Man, Art, and Literature.* Translated by R. F. C. Hull. *The Collected Works of C. G. Jung, 15.* New York: Pantheon, 1966a.

"The Phenomenology of the Spirit in Fairy Tales." In *The Archetypes and the Collective Unconscious.* Translated by R. F. C. Hull. 2nd ed. *The Collected Works of C. G. Jung, 9.* Princeton, N.J.: Princeton University Press, 1959.

"The Stages of Life." In *The Structure and Dynamics of the Psyche.* Translated by R. F. C. Hull. 2nd ed. *The Collected Works of C. G. Jung, 8.* Princeton, N.J.: Princeton University Press, 1969.

"Two Kinds of Thinking." In *Symbols of Transformation.* Translated by R. F. C. Hull, 2nd ed. *The Collected Works of C. G. Jung, 5.* Princeton, N.J.: Princeton University Press, 1966b.

Kearney, Richard. "Paul Ricoeur and the Hermeneutic Imagination." In *The Narrative Path: The Later Works of Paul Ricoeur,* edited by T. Peter Kemp and David Rasmussen. Cambridge, Mass.: MIT Press, 1989.

Kegan, Robert. *The Evolving Self: Problem and Process in Human Development.* Cambridge, Mass.: Harvard University Press, 1982.

Kelleher, John V. "The Perceptions of James Joyce." *Atlantic Monthly* 201 (March, 1958): 82–90.

Kimmel, Douglas C. *Adulthood and Aging: An Interdisciplinary Developmental View.* 2nd ed. New York: Wiley, 1980.

Kitchener, Karen S., and Patricia M. King. "Reflective Judgment: Concepts of Justification and Their Relationship to Age and Education." *Journal of Applied Developmental Psychology* 2 (1981): 89–116.

Kohlberg, Lawrence. *The Philosophy of Moral Development: Moral Stages and the Idea of Justice.* Essays on Moral Development, 1. San Francisco: Harper & Row, 1981.

Kohlberg, Lawrence, and Carol Gilligan. "The Adolescent as a Philosopher: The Discovery of the Self in a Postconventional World." *Daedalus* 100 (1971): 1051–86.

Kotre, John. *Outliving the Self: Generativity and the Interpretation of Lives.* Baltimore: Johns Hopkins University Press, 1984.

Kriss, Ernst. *Psychoanalytic Explorations in Art.* New York: International Universities Press, 1952.

Kurfiss, Joanne. *Intellectual, Psychological, and Moral Development in College: Four Major Theories. Manual for Project QUE (Quality Undergraduate Education)*. Washington, D.C.: Council for Independent Colleges, 1983.

Labouvie-Vief, Gisela. "Beyond Formal Operations: Uses and Limits of Pure Logic in Life-Span Development." *Human Development* 23, 3 (1980): 141–61.

"Dynamic Development and Mature Autonomy: A Theoretical Prologue." *Human Development* 25 (1982): 161–91.

Laing, R. D. *The Divided Self.* London: Tavistock, 1960.

Leenhardt, Jacques. "Toward a Sociology of Reading." In *The Reader in the Text: Essays on Audience and Interpretation,* edited by Susan R. Suleiman and Inge Crosman. Princeton, N.J.: Princeton University Press, 1980.

Lehrman, P. R. "The Fantasy of Not Belonging to One's Family." *Archives of Neurology and Psychiatry* 18 (1927): 1015–23.

Leondar, Barbara. "Hatching Plots: Genesis of Storymaking." In *The Arts and Cognition,* edited by David Perkins and Barbara Leondar. Baltimore: Johns Hopkins University Press, 1977.

Lesser, Simon O. *Fiction and the Unconscious.* Chicago: University of Chicago Press, 1957.

Levinson, Daniel J. *The Seasons of a Man's Life.* New York: Ballantine, 1978.

Lewis, C. S. "On Stories." In *Of Other Worlds: Essays and Stories.* New York: Harcourt Brace Jovanovich, 1966.

"On Three Ways of Writing for Children." *Horn Book Magazine* 38, (October 1963): 459–69.

Lonergan, Bernard F. *Insight: A Study of Human Understanding.* New York: Philosophical Library, 1957.

Method in Theology. New York: Herder and Herder, 1972.

A Third Collection: Papers by Bernard J. F. Lonergan, S.J., edited by Frederick E. Crowe, S.J. New York: Paulist Press, 1985.

Mailloux, Steven. *Interpretive Conventions: The Reader in the Study of American Fiction.* Ithaca, N.Y.: Cornell University Press, 1982.

Mandler, Jean Matter. *Stories, Scripts, and Scenes: Aspects of Schema Thinking.* Hillsdale, N.J.: Erlbaum, 1984.

Maranda, E. K., and P. Maranda. *Structural Models in Folklore and Transformational Essays.* The Hague: Mouton, 1971.

Martin, Wallace. *Recent Theories of Narrative.* Ithaca, N.Y.: Cornell University Press, 1986.

Mason, Bobbie Ann. *The Girl Sleuth: A Feminist Guide.* Old Westbury, N.Y.: Feminist Press, 1975.

May, Robert. *Sex and Fantasy: Patterns of Male and Female Development.* New York: Norton, 1980.

McConaughy, Stephanie H. "Developmental Changes in Story Comprehension and Levels of Questioning." *Language Arts* 59, 6 (1982): 580–9 and 600.

McCrae, Robert R., and Paul T. Costa, Jr. *Emerging Lives, Enduring Dispositions: Personality in Adulthood.* Boston: Little Brown, 1984.

McLuhan, Marshall. *Understanding Media: The Extensions of Man.* New York: McGraw-Hill, 1964.

Meek, Margaret. *Achieving Literacy: Longitudinal Studies of Adolescents Learning to Read.* London: Routledge and Kegan Paul, 1983.

Learning to Read. London: Bodley Head, 1982.

Aidan Warlow, and Griselda Barton, editors. *The Cool Web: The Pattern of Children's Reading.* New York: Atheneum, 1978.

Mellon, John C. *The National Assessment and the Teaching of English.* Urbana, Ill.: National Council of Teachers of English, 1975.

Menig-Peterson, Carole L., and Alyssa McCabe. "Children's Orientation of a Listener to the Context of Their Narratives." *Developmental Psychology* 14, 6 (1978): 582–92.

Meringoff, Laurene K., Martha M. Vibbert, Cyntha A. Char, David E. Fernie, Gail S. Banker, and Howard Gardner. "How Is Children's Learning from Television Distinctive? Exploiting the Medium Methodologically." In *Children's Understanding of Television: Research on Attention and Comprehension,* edited by Jennings Bryant and Daniel R. Anderson. New York: Academic Press, 1983.

Merriam, Sharon. "Middle Age: A Review of the Research." *New Directions for Continuing Education* 2 (1979): 7–15.

Mikkelsen, Nina. "Talking and Telling: The Child as Storymaker." *Language Arts* 61, 3 (1984): 229–39.

Millar, Susanna. *The Psychology of Play.* Baltimore: Penguin, 1968.

Miller, Jean Baker. *Toward a New Psychology of Women.* Boston: Beacon Press, 1976.

Modleski, Tania. *Loving with a Vengeance: Mass-Produced Fantasies for Women.* New York: Methuen, 1982.

Morgan, Michael. "Television Viewing and Reading: Does More Equal Better?" *Journal of Communication* 30 (1980): 159–65.

Moshman, David, and Edith Neimark. "Four Aspects of Adolescent Cognitive Development." In *Review of Human Development,* edited by Tiffany M. Field. New York: Wiley, 1982.

Muecke, Douglas C. *The Compass of Irony.* London: Methuen, 1969.

Muller, John. "Light and the Wisdom of the Dark: Aging and the Language of Desire in the Texts of Louise Bogan." In *Memory and Desire: Aging–Literature–Psychoanalysis,* edited by Kathleen Woodward and Murray M. Schwartz. Bloomington: Indiana University Press, 1986.

Nell, Victor. *Lost in a Book: The Psychology of Reading for Pleasure.* New Haven, Conn.: Yale University Press, 1988.

Nelson, Katherine. "How Children Represent Knowledge of Their World in and out of Language: A Preliminary Report." In *Children's Thinking: What Develops?,* edited by R. S. Siegler. Hillsdale, N.J.: Erlbaum, 1978.

Neugarten, B. L. *Personality in Middle and Late Life.* New York: Atherton, 1964.

A. C. Nielsen Company. *Nielsen Television Index: Report on Television Usage.* Hackensack, N.J.: A. C. Nielsen Co., November, 1983.

Offer, Daniel, and Melvin Sabshin, editors. *Normality and the Life Cycle: A Critical Integration.* New York: Basic Books, 1984.

Olson, David R., Nancy Torrance, and Angela Hildyard, editors. *Literacy, Lan-*

guage and Learning: The Nature and Consequences of Reading and Writing. New York: Cambridge University Press, 1985.

Ong, Walter J. *Orality and Literacy: The Technologizing of the Word.* New York: Methuen, 1982.

Orwell, George. *Shooting an Elephant.* New York: Harcourt Brace, 1950.

Paley, Vivian Gussin. *Boys and Girls: Superheroes in the Doll Corner.* Chicago: University of Chicago Press, 1984.

Wally's Stories. Cambridge, Mass.: Harvard University Press, 1981.

Perry, William G., Jr. "Cognitive and Ethical Growth: The Making of Meaning." In *The Modern American College: Responding to the New Realities of Diverse Students and a Changing Society,* edited by Arthur Chickering. San Francisco: Jossey-Bass, 1981.

"Examsmanship and the Liberal Arts: An Epistemological Inquiry." In *The Norton Reader,* edited by Arthur M. Eastman. New York: Norton, 1965.

Forms of Intellectual and Ethical Development in the College Years: A Scheme. New York: Holt, Rinehart and Winston, 1970.

Petrosky, Anthony R. "The Effects of Reality Perception and Fantasy on Response to Literature: Two Case Studies." *Research in the Teaching of English* 10 (1976): 239–58.

"Genetic Epistemology and Psychoanalytic Ego Psychology: Clinical Support for the Study of Response to Literature." *Research in the Teaching of English* 11, 1 (1977): 28–38.

"Reading Achievement." In *Secondary School Reading: What Research Reveals for Classroom Practice,* edited by Allen Berger and H. Alan Robinson. Urbana, Ill.: ERIC Clearinghouse on Reading and Communication Skills, 1982.

"Response: A Way of Knowing." In *Researching Response to Literature and the Teaching of Literature: Points of Departure,* edited by Charles R. Cooper. Norwood, N.J.: Ablex, 1985.

Phillips, John L., Jr. *The Origins of Intellect: Piaget's Theory.* 2nd ed. San Francisco: Freeman, 1969.

Piaget, Jean. "Intellectual Evolution from Adolescence to Adulthood." *Human Development* 15 (1972): 1–12.

The Language and Thought of the Child. Translated by Marjorie Gabain. New York: World-Meridian, 1955.

Play, Dreams and Imitation in Childhood. Translated by C. Gattegno and F. M. Hodgson. New York: Norton, 1951.

and Barbel Inhelder. *The Psychology of the Child.* New York: Basic Books, 1969.

Pitcher, E. G., and E. Prelinger. *Children Tell Stories: An Analysis of Fantasy.* New York: International Universities Press, 1963.

Poulet, George. "The Phenomenology of Reading." *New Literary History* 1 (1969–70): 53–68.

Propp, Vladimir. *Morphology of the Folktale.* Austin: University of Texas Press, 1968.

Purves, Alan C., with Delwyn L. Harnisch, Donald L. Quirk, and Barbara

Bauer. "Reading and Literature: American Achievement in International Perspective." NCTE Research Report No. 20. Urbana, Ill.: National Council of Teachers of English, 1981.

Purves, Alan C., and Richard Beach. *Literature and the Reader: Research in Response to Literature, Reading Interests, and the Teaching of Literature*. Urbana, Ill.: National Council of Teachers of English, 1972.

Rabinowitz, Peter J. *Before Reading: Narrative Conventions and the Politics of Interpretation*. Ithaca, N.Y.: Cornell University Press, 1987.

Radway, Janice A. *Reading the Romance: Women, Patriarchy, and Popular Literature*. Chapel Hill: University of North Carolina Press, 1984.

Raglan, FitzRoy R. S. *The Hero: A Study in Tradition, Myth, and Dream*. London: Watts, 1949.

Rank, Otto. *The Myth of the Birth of the Hero, and Other Writings*, edited by Philip Freund. New York: Vintage, 1959.

Rich, Adrienne. "When We Dead Awaken: Writing as Revision." *College English* 34 (1972): 18–30.

Richards, I. A. *Practical Criticism: A Study of Literary Judgment*. New York: Harcourt Brace, 1929.

Ricoeur, Paul. *The Conflict of Interpretations: Essays in Hermeneutics*, edited by Don Ihde. Evanston, Ill.: Northwestern University Press, 1974.

"Narrative Time." In *On Narrative*, edited by W. J. T. Mitchell. Chicago: University of Chicago Press, 1981.

The Symbolism of Evil. Translated by Emerson Buchanan. Religious Perspectives, 17. New York: Harper & Row, 1967.

Time and Narrative. 3 vols. Translated by Kathleen McLaughlin and David Pellauer. Chicago: University of Chicago Press, 1984–1988.

Riegel, Klaus F. "Adult Life Crises: A Dialectic Interpretation of Development." In *Life-Span Developmental Psychology: Normative Life Crises*, edited by Nancy Datan and Leon H. Gindberg. New York: Academic Press, 1975.

"Dialectic Operations: The Final Period of Cognitive Development." *Human Development* 16 (1973): 346–70.

"The Dialectics of Human Development." *American Psychologist* 31, 10 (1976): 689–700.

Riffaterre, Michael. *Semiotics of Poetry*. Bloomington: Indiana University Press, 1978.

Rimmon-Kenan, Shlomith. *Narrative Fiction: Contemporary Poetics*. New York: Methuen, 1983.

Robinson, Lillian S. *Sex, Class, and Culture*. Bloomington: Indiana University Press, 1978.

Rosenblatt, Louise M. *The Reader, the Text, the Poem: The Transactional Theory of the Literary Work*. Carbondale, Ill.: Southern Illionis University Press, 1978.

"The Transactional Theory of the Literary Work: Implications for Research." In *Researching Response to Literature and the Teaching of Literature: Points of Departure*, edited by Charles R. Cooper. Norwood, N.J.: Ablex, 1985.

Rubin, Kenneth H. "Fantasy Play: Its Role in the Development of Social Skills and Social Cognition." In *Children's Play*, edited Kenneth H. Rubin. New Directions for Child Development, 9. San Francisco: Jossey-Bass, 1980.

Rumelhart, D. E. "Understanding and Summarizing Brief Stories." In *Basic Processes in Reading: Perception and Comprehension*, edited by D. LaBerge and S. J. Samuels. Hillsdale, N.J.: Erlbaum, 1977.

Salinger, J. D. *The Catcher in the Rye*. Boston: Little Brown, 1951.

Salomon, Gavriel. "Television Watching and Mental Effort: A Social Psychological View." In *Children's Understanding of Television: Research on Attention and Comprehension*, edited by Jennings Bryant and Daniel R. Anderson. New York: Academic Press, 1983.

Savater, Fernando. *Childhood Regained: The Art of the Storyteller*. Translated by Frances M. Lopez-Morillas. New York: Columbia University Press, 1982.

Scarlett, W. George, and Dennie Wolf. "When It's Only Make-Believe: The Construction of a Boundary between Fantasy and Reality in Storytelling." In *Fact, Fiction, and Fantasy in Childhood*, edited by Ellen Winner and Howard Gardner. New Directions for Child Development, 6. San Francisco: Jossey-Bass, 1979.

Schlager, Norma. "Predicting Children's Choices in Literature: A Developmental Approach." *Children's Literature in Education* 9 (1978): 136–42.

Scholes, Robert. *Protocols of Reading*. New Haven, Conn.: Yale University Press, 1989.

Structuralism in Literature: An Introduction. New Haven, Conn.: Yale University Press, 1974.

Textual Power: Literary Theory and the Teaching of English. New Haven, Conn.: Yale University Press, 1985.

and Robert Kellogg. *The Nature of Narrative*. London: Oxford University Press, 1966.

Schweickart, Patrocinio P. "Reading Ourselves: Toward a Feminist Theory of Reading." In *Gender and Reading: Essays on Readers, Texts, and Contexts*, edited by Elizabeth A. Flynn and Patrocinio P. Schweickart. Baltimore: Johns Hopkins University Press, 1986.

Scollon, Ron. "Language, Literacy, and Learning: An Annotated Bibliography." In *Literacy, Language, and Learning: The Nature and Consequences of Reading and Writing*, edited by David R. Olson, Nancy Torrance, and Angela Hildyard. Cambridge University Press, 1985.

and Suzanne Scollon. *Narrative, Literacy, and Face in Interethnic Communication*. Norwood, N.J.: Ablex, 1981.

Segel, Elizabeth. "'As the Twig is Bent . . .': Gender and Childhood Reading." In *Gender and Reading: Essays on Readers, Texts, and Contexts*, edited by Elizabeth A. Flynn and Patrocinio P. Schweickart. Baltimore: Johns Hopkins University Press, 1986.

Shores, J. Harlan. "Reading Interests and Informational Needs of High School Students." *Reading Teacher* 17 (1964): 536–44.

Showalter, Elaine, editor. *The New Feminist Criticism: Essays on Women, Literature, and Theory*. New York: Pantheon, 1985.

Singer, Jerome L. *The Child's World of Make-Believe*. New York: Academic Press, 1973.

and Dorothy G. Singer. "Implications of Childhood Television Viewing for Cognition, Imagination, and Emotion." In *Children's Understanding of Television: Research on Attention and Comprehension*, edited by Jennings Bryant and Daniel R. Anderson. New York: Academic Press, 1983.

Smith, Barbara Herrnstein. *On the Margins of Discourse: The Relation of Literature to Language*. Chicago: University of Chicago Press, 1978.

Smith, Frank. *Understanding Reading: A Psycholinguistic Analysis of Reading and Learning to Read*. New York: Holt, Rinehart and Winston, 1971.

Soderbergh, Peter A. "The Stratemeyer Strain: Educators and the Juvenile Series Book, 1900–1980." In *Only Connect: Readings on Children's Literature*, edited by Sheila Egoff, G. T. Stubbs, and L. F. Ashley. 2nd ed. Toronto: Oxford University Press, 1980.

Sontag, Susan. *Against Interpretation*. New York: Farrar, Strauss and Giroux, 1966.

Spacks, Patricia Meyer. *The Adolescent Idea: Myths of Youth and the Adult Imagination*. New York: Basic Books, 1981.

Squire, James R., editor. *Response to Literature*. Champaign, Ill.: National Council of Teachers of English, 1968.

The Responses of Adolescents while Reading Four Short Stories. Urbana, Ill.: National Council of Teachers of English, 1964.

Steig, Michael. *Stories of Reading: Subjectivity and Literary Understanding*. Baltimore: Johns Hopkins University Press, 1989.

Stein, N. L., and C. G. Glenn. "An Analysis of Story Comprehension in Elementary School Children." In *New Directions in Discourse Processing*, edited by R. O. Freedle. Hillsdale, N.J.: Ablex, 1979.

Sugarman, Susan. *Piaget's Construction of the Child's Reality*. Cambridge University Press, 1987.

Suleiman, Susan R., and Inge Crosman, editors. *The Reader in the Text: Essays on Audience and Interpretation*. Princeton, N.J.: Princeton University Press, 1980.

Sutton-Smith, Brian. *The Folkstories of Children*. Philadelphia: University of Pennsylvania Press, 1981.

editor. *Play and Learning*. New York: Gardner, 1979a.

"Presentation and Representation in Children's Fictional Narrative." In *Fact, Fiction, and Fantasy in Childhood*, edited by Ellen Winner and Howard Gardner. New Directions for Child Development, 6. San Francisco: Jossey-Bass, 1979b.

Sypher, Wylie. *Comedy*. New York: Doubleday, 1956.

Taylor, Denny, and Catherine Dorsey-Gaines. *Growing up Literate: Learning from Inner-City Families*. Portsmouth, N. H.: Heinemann, 1988.

Thorndyke, P. "Cognitive Structures in Comprehension and Memory of Narrative Discourse." *Cognitive Psychology* 9 (1977): 77–110.

Tobin, Joseph J., David Y. H. Wu, and Dana H. Davidson. *Preschool in Three Cultures: Japan, China and the United States*. New Haven, Conn.: Yale University Press, 1989.

Todorov, Tzvetan. *The Poetics of Prose*. Ithaca, N.Y.: Cornell University Press, 1977. "The Two Principles of Narrative." *Diacritics* 1, Fall (1971): 37–44.

Tolkien, J. R. R. "On Fairy-Stories." In J. R. R. Tolkien *Tree and Leaf*. London: Unwin, 1964.

Tompkins, Jane P., editor. *Reader-Response Criticism: From Formalism to Post-Structuralism*. Baltimore: Johns Hopkins University Press, 1980.

Tucker, Nicholas. *The Child and the Book: A Psychological and Literary Exploration*. Cambridge University Press, 1981.

Vaillant, George E. *Adaptation to Life*. Boston: Little, Brown, 1977.

Vandergrift, Kay E. *Child and Story: The Literary Connection*. New York: Neal-Schuman, 1980.

Vygotsky, L. S. *Thought and Language*. Cambridge, Mass.: MIT Press, 1962.

Watt, Ian. *The Rise of the Novel: Studies in Defoe, Richardson, and Fielding*. Berkeley: University of California Press, 1957.

Wells, Gordon. "Preschool Literacy-Related Activities and Success in School." In *Literacy, Language, and Learning: The Nature and Consequences of Reading and Writing*, edited by David R. Olson, Nancy Torrance, and Angela Hildyard. Cambridge University Press, 1985.

Whalen-Levitt, Peggy. "The Critical Theory of Children's Literature: A Conceptual Analysis." Ph.D. thesis, University of Pennsylvania, 1983.

White, Dorothy. *Books before Five*. New York: Oxford University Press, 1956.

Whitehead, F., A. C. Capey, Wendy Maddren, and Allan Wellings. *Children and Their Books*. Schools Council Research Studies. London: Macmillan Education, 1977.

Williams, Raymond. *Marxism and Literature*. New York: Oxford University Press, 1977.

Wimsatt, W. K., Jr., and Monroe C. Beardsley. "The Affective Fallacy." In W. K. Wimsatt, Jr., *The Verbal Icon: Studies in the Meaning of Poetry*. New York: Noonday, 1954.

Winn, Marie. *The Plug-In Drug*. rev. ed. New York: Viking, 1985.

Winner, Ellen. *Invented Worlds: The Psychology of the Arts*. Cambridge, Mass.: Harvard University Press, 1982.

The Point of Words: Children's Understanding of Metaphor and Irony. Cambridge, Mass.: Harvard University Press, 1988.

and Howard Gardner, editors. *Fact, Fiction, and Fantasy in Childhood*. New Directions for Child Development, 6. San Francisco: Jossey-Bass, 1979.

A. Rosensteil, and H. Gardner. "The Development of Metaphoric Understanding." *Developmental Psychology* 12 (1976): 289–97.

Winnicott, D. W. *Playing and Reality*. New York: Basic Books, 1971.

Wolf, Denise Palmer. *Reading Reconsidered: Literature and Literacy in High School*. New York: College Entrance Examination Board, 1988.

Wolf, Katherine M., and Marjorie Fiske. "The Children Talk about Comics." In *Communications Research 1948–1949*, edited by Paul F. Lazarsfeld and Frank N. Stanton. New York: Harper & Row, 1949.

Yeats, W. B. "Anima Hominis." In *Mythologies*. New York: Macmillan, 1959. "Ego Dominus Tuus." In *The Poems of W. B. Yeats*, edited by Richard J. Finneran, pp. 160–62. New York: Macmillan, 1983.

The Letters of W. B. Yeats, edited by Allan Wade. London: Rupert-Hart-Davis, 1954.

Zipes, Jack. *Breaking the Magic Spell: Radical Theories of Folk and Fairy Tales.* New York: Methuen, 1984.

Zuckerman, Diana M., Dorothy G. Singer, and Jerome L. Singer. "Television Viewing, Children's Reading, and Related Classroom Behavior." *Journal of Communication* 30 (1980): 166–74.

Index

Abrams, M. H., 4–5, 147–8
accommodation, 42
adolescent readers: reading habits, 99; reading preferences, 99–100 (differences according to sex), 99; (tragedy), 109–10; reading responses, *see* involvement; identification; realism; thinking about stories
adolescent readers, psychological development: characteristic features, 96–7; Erikson's psychosocial account, 97–9; myth of adolescence, 96; Piaget's cognitive account, 97
adult readers: reading habits, 155–6; uses adults make of reading, 163–4 (*see also* escaping; searching for truth; discovering usable images)
adult readers, psychological development: controversy about the predictability of, 161; Erikson on, 160; Jung on, 160; overall picture, 162–3; Riegel's four dimensions of change, distinctive adult thinking, 162
Adventures of Huckleberry Finn, The (Twain), 105
Adventures of Tom Sawyer, The (Twain), 60
Alcott, Louisa May, 100
"Altar of the Dead, The" (James), 175
Althuser, Louis, 151
Altick, R. D., 196n11
Altieri, Charles, 104–5
Ambassadors, The (James), 175
Ames, Louise, 33, 36
Anderson, Daniel R., 199n9
Animal Farm (Orwell), 153
Applebee, Arthur N., 9, 27, 28, 30–1, 33, 71, 81, 82, 106–7, 199–200n9
"Araby" (Joyce), 112
Aristotle, 18, 71, 152, 177

Arlin, P. K., 162
assimilation, 35, 42
atmosphere vs. excitement, 86
Austen, Jane, 142, 157
author: author-focused strategies of interpretation, 132; high school students' discovery of the author, 119; in New Critical theory, 119; reader's implicit relationship with author, 119; as source of story's meaning, 111–13

Baillargeon, R., 196n16
Baker, Russell, 158
Baldwin, R. Scott, 92
"Barn Burning" (Faulkner), 126–7
Barthelme, Donald, 157
Barthes, Roland, 70, 174, 192, 195n6
Barton, Griselda, 195n1
Basseches, Michael, 162, 175
Baum, L. Frank, 61, 72–4
Baym, Nina, 151
Beach, Richard, 60, 80, 91, 155, 195n4, 201n1
Beardsley, Monroe C., 6
Bechhofer, Robin, 33
Beckett, Samuel, 154
Bellow, Saul, 165
Belsey, Catherine, 138
Benveniste, Emile, 68
Berg, Leila, 77, 197nn1, 3
Bergman, Ingmar, 184
Best, Raphaela, 91
Bettelheim, Bruno, 11, 36–41, 44
Beyle, Henri [pseud. Stendahl], 172–3, 180
Billman, Carol, 200n1, 200–1n2
Bissex, Glenda, 57–8
Blasi, Augusto, 98
Bleich, David, 92, 140, 196n10
Blinn, William, 108

219